IMAGES
of America

MIDDLETOWN

On the Cover: The cover features a photograph of the Wayside Inn alongside the famed US Route 11. (Middletown Heritage Society.)

IMAGES
of America

MIDDLETOWN

Charles Harbaugh IV
and Jeff Pennington

ARCADIA
PUBLISHING

ISBN 978-1-4671-2242-9

Published by Arcadia Publishing
Charleston, South Carolina

Printed in the United States of America

Library of Congress Control Number: 2014934854

For all general information, please contact Arcadia Publishing:
Telephone 843-853-2070
Fax 843-853-0044
E-mail sales@arcadiapublishing.com
For customer service and orders:
Toll-Free 1-888-313-2665

Visit us on the Internet at www.arcadiapublishing.com

This book is dedicated to the people of Middletown, Virginia, with many thanks for their stories, pictures, and generosity in helping with this project.

Contents

Acknowledgments

The authors would like to thank the staff at the Stewart Bell Jr. Archives at Handley Regional Library for their patience and eagerness to help with the research. Archivist Rebecca Ebert is a true gem and champion of the area, along with the assistance of Helen Lee Fletcher, a great Middletown resource who provided so many images for this project. Special thanks to Mildred Brumback for her stories and information on the town. Additional thanks go to Joyce D. Tucker, Tess Klimm, John Owings, Sharon Daily, Harold Gardenhour Jr., Providence LoPresti, Nancy Keaton, Ray Steele, and the Middletown Heritage Society for their use of images in this book.

Charles H. Harbaugh IV would like to thank Kate Brenner, author of Images of America: *Middleburg*, for giving him the idea to write about Middletown. Most of all, he would like to thank Mark D'Arezzo for instilling in him a passion of history and encouragement at a young age. Lastly, he would like to extend gratitude to the residents of Middletown for having the confidence to elect him as mayor and to his family (Charles Jr., Faith, Darrell, and Kelsey) for their love and support.

Jeff Pennington would like to thank his wife, Laura Pennington, for her love and patience while completing this project.

INTRODUCTION

The story of Middletown is one of a developing transportation corridor established along a migratory animal path, which became the Warrior's Trail, the Great Wagon Road, and the Valley Turnpike, known today as US Route 11. So important is this corridor that Interstate 81 was built parallel to Route 11 for much of the length of the old turnpike. It was natural for native peoples to utilize animal trails, and when European settlers crossed the mountains and moved south from Pennsylvania, they too followed the path as a line of settlement. Led by pioneers like Daniel Boone, settlements progressed south along the Great Wagon Road, then diverged from the road and went west into Kentucky and Tennessee.

Just prior to 1800, the Valley Turnpike Company was founded as a means to maintain the road through an established toll system. In 1796, Dr. Peter Senseney plotted the town of Middleton (later Middletown) in expectation of a tollhouse halfway between Newtown (Stephens City) and Strasburg. His plans showed great insight, as the streets were designed to be wider than those of other towns in anticipation of commerce and traffic on the pike. His speculation was on target, resulting in the tollhouse, along with an inn and horse-changing station, currently known as the Wayside Inn. Eventually, blacksmiths, coopers and wheelwrights, shopkeepers, and other taverns moved into the new turnpike town, while several types of milling developed along Meadow Brook. By 1834, the Turnpike Company had completed paving the road with a crushed-stone surface, a method called macadamization. Thereby, the Valley Turnpike became America's first paved road.

By the time of the Civil War in 1861, the turnpike that passed through Middletown had fully developed as a commercial and private transportation route, with livestock herds kept mainly on the parallel back and middle roads west of the pike. The rich grain-producing farms along the pike, along with their livestock herds, quickly became important to the survival of the Confederacy, as well as an objective for the Federals. Middletown had a bird's-eye view as the armies ebbed and flowed up the pike toward Harrisonburg and down the pike toward Winchester (as the river flows north). From this vantage point, the town and its citizens witnessed the early Virginia volunteer companies marching to Harpers Ferry (now West Virginia), where Col. Thomas J. Jackson organized companies into regiments, and Jackson dragging at least parts of rolling stock up the pike to the railhead at Strasburg.

In 1862, this same Jackson returned as a general known as Stonewall Jackson and waged a raging war up and down the old turnpike as his foot cavalry marched amazing distances daily. After defeating the Federals at Front Royal on May 23, 1862, Jackson's forces pursued the remnant and caught Gen. Nathaniel P. Banks's rear guard where Front Royal Road connected with the Valley Pike (present-day First Street) in Middletown, now the site of the Wayside Inn. A sharp fight ensued and ended near Newtown (Stephens City), resulting in the first Battle of Winchester the next day. As the Federals fled their camps in Strasburg and near Belle Grove Plantation, they left a wake of supplies behind for the Confederates, which gave "Commissary" Banks his moniker.

Subsequent troop movements through Middletown included those traveling down the Valley Pike to Antietam and Gettysburg, then back up the pike with wounded Confederates. In 1864, Franz Sigel's Federals moved south to New Market, where a smaller, hastily assembled army defeated them on May 15, 1864. The next Yankee general to pass through Middletown was "Black" David Hunter, so named because of his tendency to burn homes, barns, and mills, including property owned by his Virginia relatives. He burned, sacked, and looted his way through Staunton and Lexington on his raid to Lynchburg in June, crossing the Peaks of Otter and marching out of the mountains in double columns so as to trample corn on both sides of the road. Jubal Early's Confederates finally stopped him at Lynchburg, where he and his troops retreated west into the mountains.

With the Shenandoah Valley free of Federals, Early marched north along the turnpike through Middletown and crossed the Potomac on a quest to raid the Federal capital at Washington City. Two veteran Federal corps that had arrived by ship and marched to the battle area near the old Walter Reed Army Hospital site stopped him at Fort Stevens. Under the command of Horatio Wright and later Phillip Sheridan, the 6th and 19th Corps veterans chased Early's Confederates back to the Shenandoah Valley, fighting multiple battles, the most notable of which were Second Kernstown, Third Winchester, Fisher's Hill, Tom's Brook, and Cedar Creek (fought in and around Middletown). After a major Confederate defeat at Fisher's Hill on September 21, 1864, Sheridan pursued Early's army close to Waynesboro and began a systematic, destructive withdrawal down the valley to the banks of Cedar Creek, burning mills, destroying crops, killing and procuring livestock, and depriving the Confederacy of the supplies needed to wage war. The "Burning," as it is still referred to locally, ruined the area's economy for many years.

The Federal army then established what they expected to be their winter camp along Cedar Creek, with headquarters at Belle Grove Plantation. Sheridan no longer considered Early's Confederates much of a threat in the northern valley, thinking that Cedar Creek offered his forces adequate protection. The long-standing Confederate objective was to keep the Shenandoah Valley free of the dreaded Yankees. Early's subordinates, Gen. John B. Gordon and the famous mapmaker Jed Hotchkiss, devised a plan to surprise Sheridan's Federals by crossing the Shenandoah River and Cedar Creek at several points while under the cover of darkness. In the predawn of October 19, 1864, Confederate forces attacked the Federal 8th Corps (fragmented remains of Hunter's old army) in their partially entrenched camp, located approximately where Interstate 66 and Interstate 81 intersect. Heavy fog allowed Gordon's men to nearly enter the camp before unleashing their first volley of musketry. Upon hearing the opening volleys, other Confederate units crossed and began engaging the Federals, while Confederate artillery moved forward from Hupp's Hill, where Early had held them for fear their wheels would be heard on the macadamized turnpike. Union reaction was mixed at best. Some units immediately prepared to fight; others remained at rest or continued their normal morning routines. Custer's Federal Cavalry Division rode from their camp (near the Middletown Park) to the high ground at the south edge of town, deploying artillery and dismounting troopers in a brief effort to stem the tide. The 8th Corps was routed completely from their camp, and their refugees alerted the 19th Corps camped at Belle Grove Plantation, near the turnpike. Eventually, they were pushed back while trying to resist. The Federal 6th Corps moved forward from their camps behind Belle Grove, also offering resistance. The Federals were having trouble establishing defensive positions in the foggy darkness of predawn and had no idea what they faced.

All Federal corps were eventually driven from their camps and the fields surrounding Belle Grove and the Heater farm. Fleeing Federals swarmed across the fields west of town and down the turnpike through Middletown. So loud was the fighting that Sheridan heard it from Winchester and immediately began his 12-mile ride to the battlefield. Most Middletown residents took shelter in their cellars as the battle flowed north. The 2nd Division of the Federal 6th Corps took position on high ground of the town cemetery (Mount Carmel) and fought a delaying action, which allowed much of the Federal army to move north of town and begin regrouping under the direction of General Wright. General Early became preoccupied with the 6th Corps position and ordered repeated attacks, which began from the south side of town, with artillery deployed on the high ground between town and the late-1800s mansion known as Monte Vista.

The Confederate attacks began to lose steam as their troops plundered the Union camps. The Confederates established surgeries in St. Thomas Chapel Episcopal Church on Church Street and at the Methodist Episcopal Church, which stood across the street from today's Grace United Methodist Church. Confederate lines were set at the north edge of town in the area of today's Reliance Road, and the Union troops began reorganizing on the high ground north and west of what is now Middletown Elementary School. A skirmisher's no-man's-land existed between these positions as a lull settled over the battlefield. Union commander Gen. Phil Sheridan arrived on the scene, locating his staff and changing horses, then rode the length of his lines to rousing cheers. After ordering two cavalry charges against a Confederate artillery position and losing 200 horses, Sheridan determined that only Early's small army faced him and no reinforcements, as it had been rumored. In the late afternoon, Sheridan ordered an advance of his entire army up the pike. The battle again flowed in and around the town. Heavy fighting occurred at Miller's Mill. There, Confederate general Stephen Dodson Ramseur was mortally wounded and sent to the rear by wagon. A brigade of Custer's Cavalry, under command of his West Point classmate Alexander C.M. Pennington, found the left flank and rear of Early's line, creating panic and thereby the collapse of the line. Panic soon gripped the Confederates as they fled toward the pike and safety beyond Cedar Creek. The pursuit was carried to Strasburg. Darkness, which had brought victory to Early, now allowed what was left of his army to escape.

Throughout the fight, Middletown became a place for the wounded from both armies to seek shelter from zipping minié balls and shrieking, exploding artillery rounds. This safety proved relative, however, as the town found itself in the unenviable position of catching both undershot and overshot rounds as the battle waged in and around it. There is ample evidence that structures in the town were severely damaged by artillery as well as musket fire. A house on Main Street still has the cannonball that entered the house and lodged in the wall. St. Thomas Church was hit several times and may still contain a shell in the bell tower. According to the *James E. Taylor Sketchbook*, a shell also hit the Wayside Inn, exploding in a woman's dresser and filling the room with undergarments. Taylor is a good source, as he describes several burned-out wagons in front of the inn, a Union soldier decapitated by artillery next to the tollhouse, and another stripped of everything but his birthday suit lying in the street in front of the inn. Nearly every home sheltered the wounded. Bloodstains remain on some floors, including the former Civil Cricket restaurant. It is said that relic hunters removed a large number of both exploded and unexploded artillery rounds from town yards in the 1970s.

As the war wound down, it moved from the valley to the lines at Petersburg. Middletown and the valley were left to marauding partisan rangers and occasional Yankee patrols as the citizens tried to repair damages and survive in an economy destroyed by war, sometimes through reparation payments from the federal government. The burnings of farms, crops, homes, and mills wrecked the grain-based agriculture of the region and impacted commerce in towns like Middletown, as well as traffic on the old turnpike. Late in the war, citizens and even local jurisdictions were heavily invested in Confederate bonds, which were nearly worthless then and completely worthless by the end. There was a lack of hard cash, and it is surmised that, for a while after the war, cash remained very tight and a barter-based economy existed to some degree.

Slowly, some businesses reemerged, but many households in Middletown functioned on a level of self-sufficiency that is almost unheard of today. The Willeys were but one such enterprising family in the post–Civil War era. Most of the men were stonemasons, and being a large family, a number of homes were built in town. It seems that one family had hogs, another had cattle, some had chickens, many had fruit trees (one of which had eight fruit-producing pear trees), and all had gardens. It seems reasonable to assume that they were close and shared within the family. Fruit trees and gardens meant canning for winter survival and perhaps extra to sell or trade. People survived.

Donating much of their time and materials, the town's stonemasons built the Grace United Methodist Church, which replaced the Methodist Episcopal Church in 1897. Around 1900, a bank was established, becoming one of the few that would remain open during the Great Depression. The Middletown Bank evolved and became part of the Farmers and Merchants Bank and continues today as the BB&T bank. The original bank building now houses the Irish Isle Restaurant & Pub. Education became important with the establishment of Middletown's elementary school (the current town hall building) and Virginia's first agricultural high school. Farms came back to life, and a thriving orchard business developed in the region. A woolen mill opened near the old Miller's Mill area northwest of town, and homes were built north of First Street for factory workers. As the early automobile era began, wealthy folks began motoring through the area, often stopping at the Wayside Inn. In 1915, the Army again came to Cedar Creek, but this time to conduct maneuvers on the old battlefield in preparation for World War I. During World War II, Middletown participated in scrap drives and civil defense programs, including blackouts and aircraft identification and observation.

The postwar era saw the town expand with the addition of subdivisions and strip malls as well as the construction of Interstate 81 to carry truck traffic on a parallel path to Route 11, the old Valley Turnpike. Education remains important with the establishment and growth of Lord Fairfax Community College just north of town, easily accessed from Interstate 81 and Route 11. Today's Middletown is largely a residential community that blends the old with the new, but as always, it reflects hardworking small-town America.

One

The Early Years

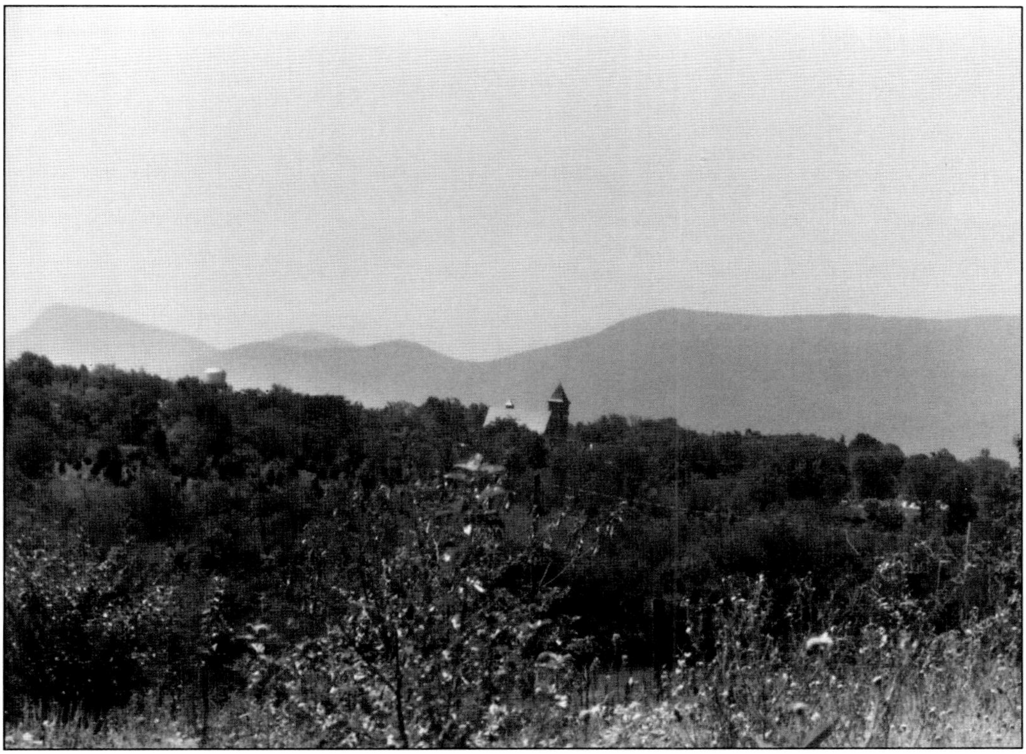

The story of Middletown cannot be told without making note of its natural beauty. When the Native Americans settled here long before the Europeans arrived, they could not have chosen a more picturesque spot. Middletown is located in the Shenandoah Valley, near the Shenandoah River and the confluence of several mountains. Although foliage obscures the view of the town in this image, the bell tower of Middletown's Grace United Methodist Church is visible in the center of Massanutten Mountain. (Middletown Heritage Society.)

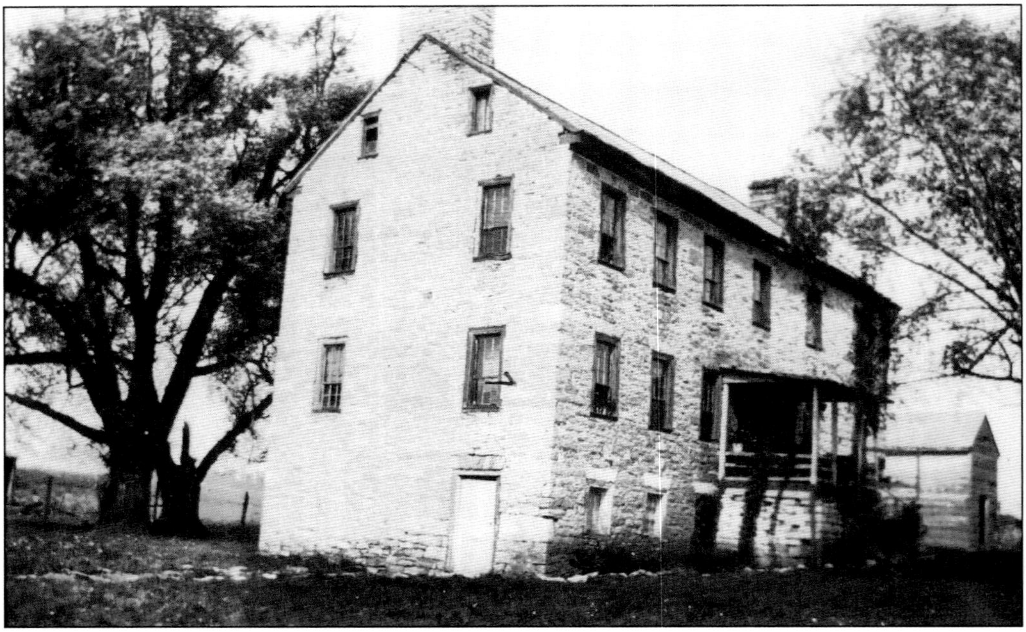

One mile west of town stood the Nieswander Homstead, or Old Stone Fort, built around 1755. Houses like this were considered safe places where neighbors could seek shelter and fight off Indian raids. The northern end is loopholed for defense against such attacks. Ruins are all that remain of the structure. (Joyce D. Tucker.)

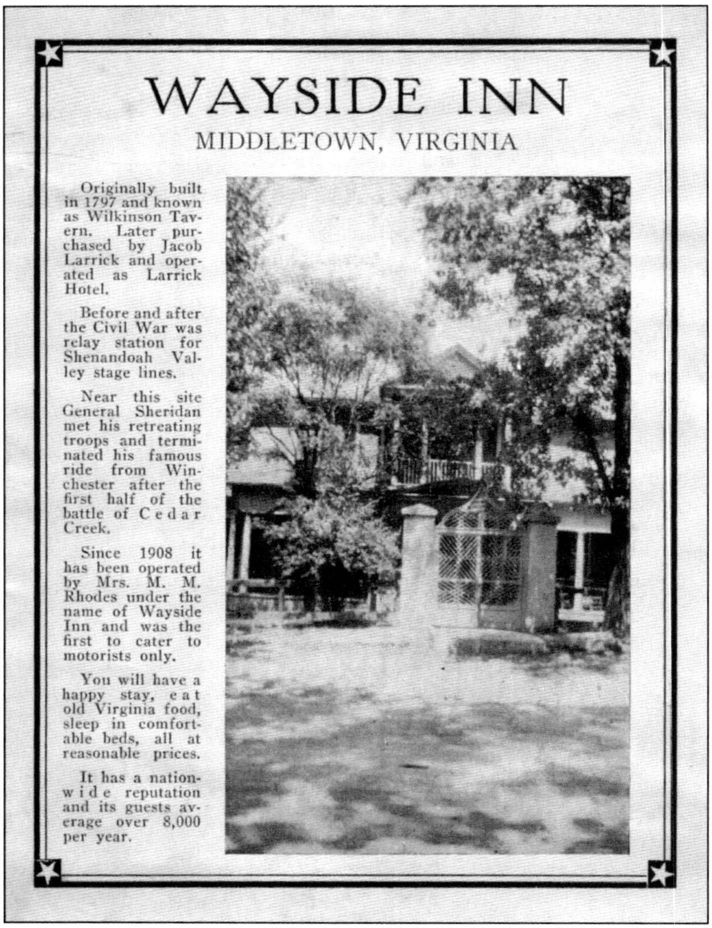

WAYSIDE INN

MIDDLETOWN, VIRGINIA

Originally built in 1797 and known as Wilkinson Tavern. Later purchased by Jacob Larrick and operated as Larrick Hotel.

Before and after the Civil War was relay station for Shenandoah Valley stage lines.

Near this site General Sheridan met his retreating troops and terminated his famous ride from Winchester after the first half of the battle of Cedar Creek.

Since 1908 it has been operated by Mrs. M. M. Rhodes under the name of Wayside Inn and was the first to cater to motorists only.

You will have a happy stay, eat old Virginia food, sleep in comfortable beds, all at reasonable prices.

It has a nation-wide reputation and its guests average over 8,000 per year.

With several travelers came the need for an inn as a stagecoach stop and horse-changing station. In 1797, the inn started serving guests and became influential to the town's future. (Joyce D. Tucker.)

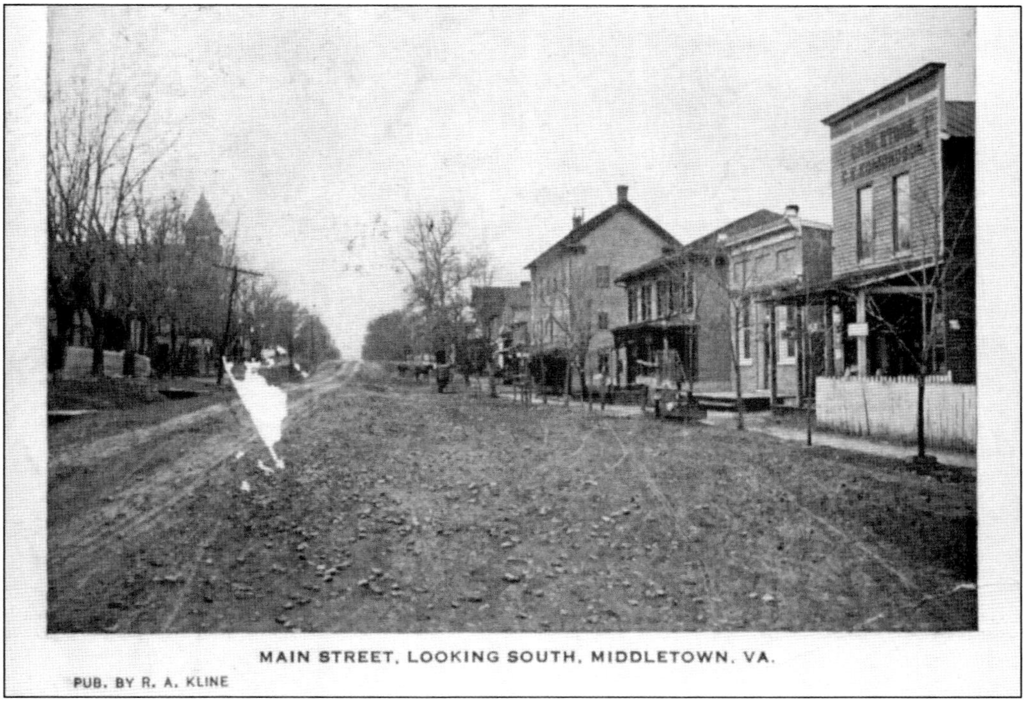

Middletown sprang up along the Valley Pike, which was an Indian trail and migratory route between Georgia and Canada. In the 1730s, Europeans used it to move south from Pennsylvania to North Carolina and west to Kentucky to establish settlements. Now it encompasses the famed Route 11 that cuts through the heart of town. (Joyce D. Tucker.)

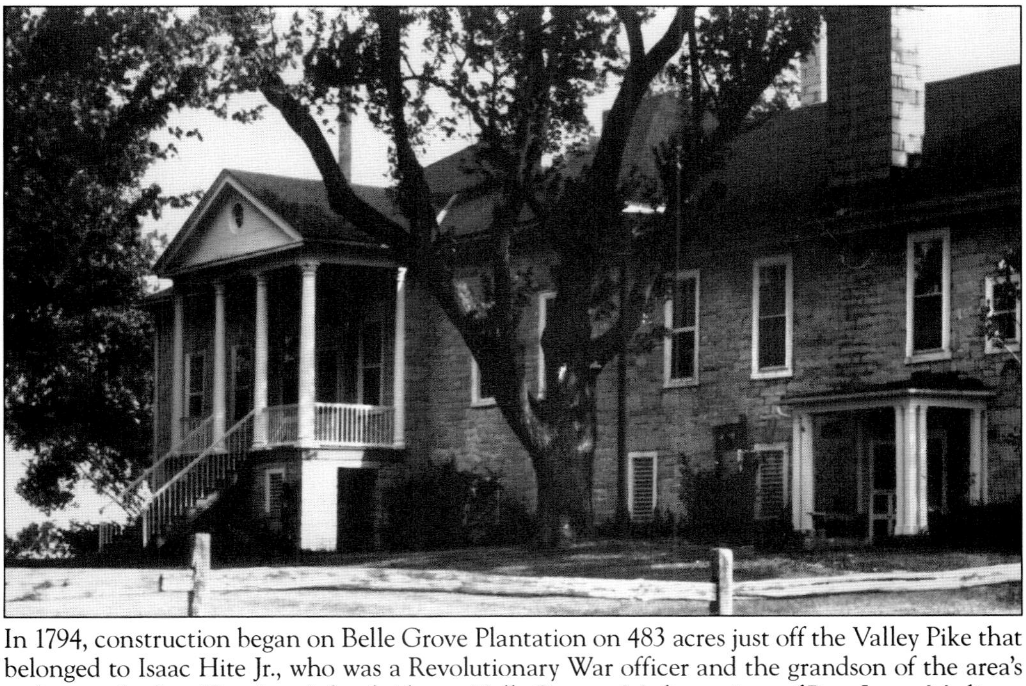

In 1794, construction began on Belle Grove Plantation on 483 acres just off the Valley Pike that belonged to Isaac Hite Jr., who was a Revolutionary War officer and the grandson of the area's earliest settler, Jost Hite. Isaac's first bride was Nelly Conway Madison, sister of Pres. James Madison. The manor house was completed in 1797. (Middletown Heritage Society.)

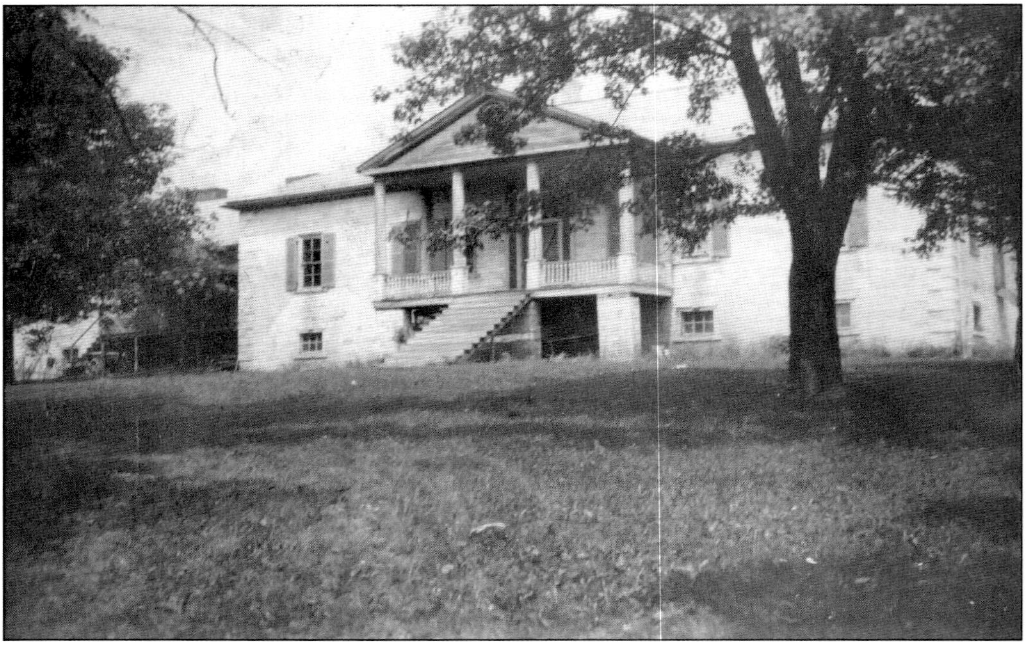

This early-20th-century photograph of Belle Grove shows the home when it was a working farm. Belle Grove was a Jeffersonian pavilion-style limestone mansion. Today, it is open to the public as a National Trust historic site. (Stewart Bell Jr. Archives.)

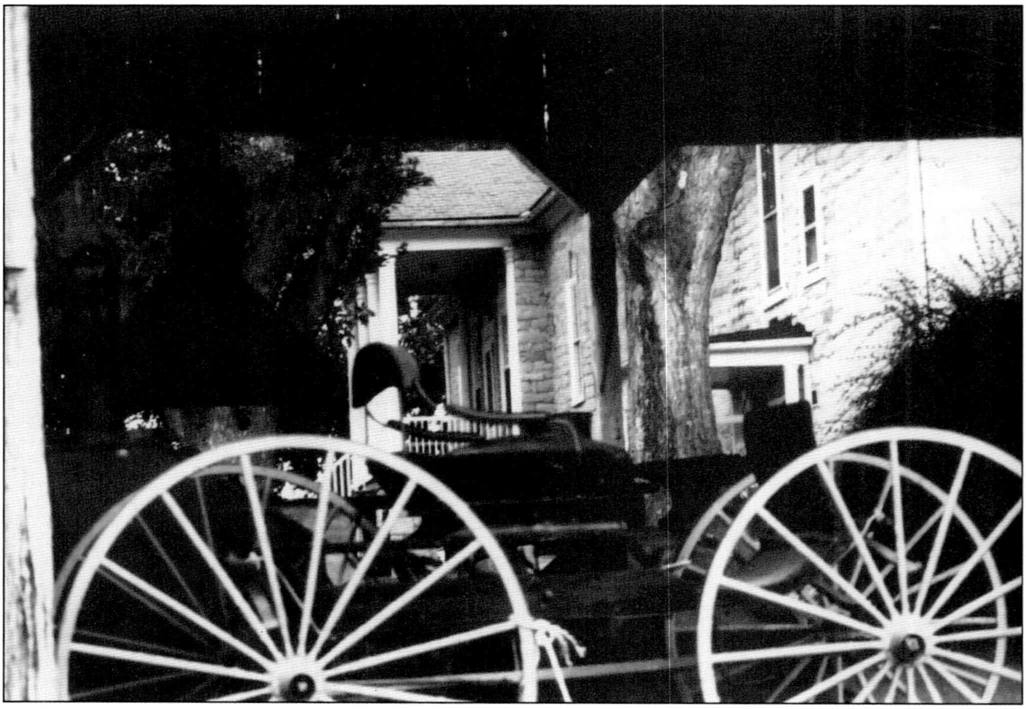

In 1815, as the family and plantation grew to 7,500 acres and 103 slaves, an addition was built to accommodate Isaac Hite Jr.'s 13 children from two wives, Nelly Conway Madison and Ann Tunstall Maury. (Middletown Heritage Society.)

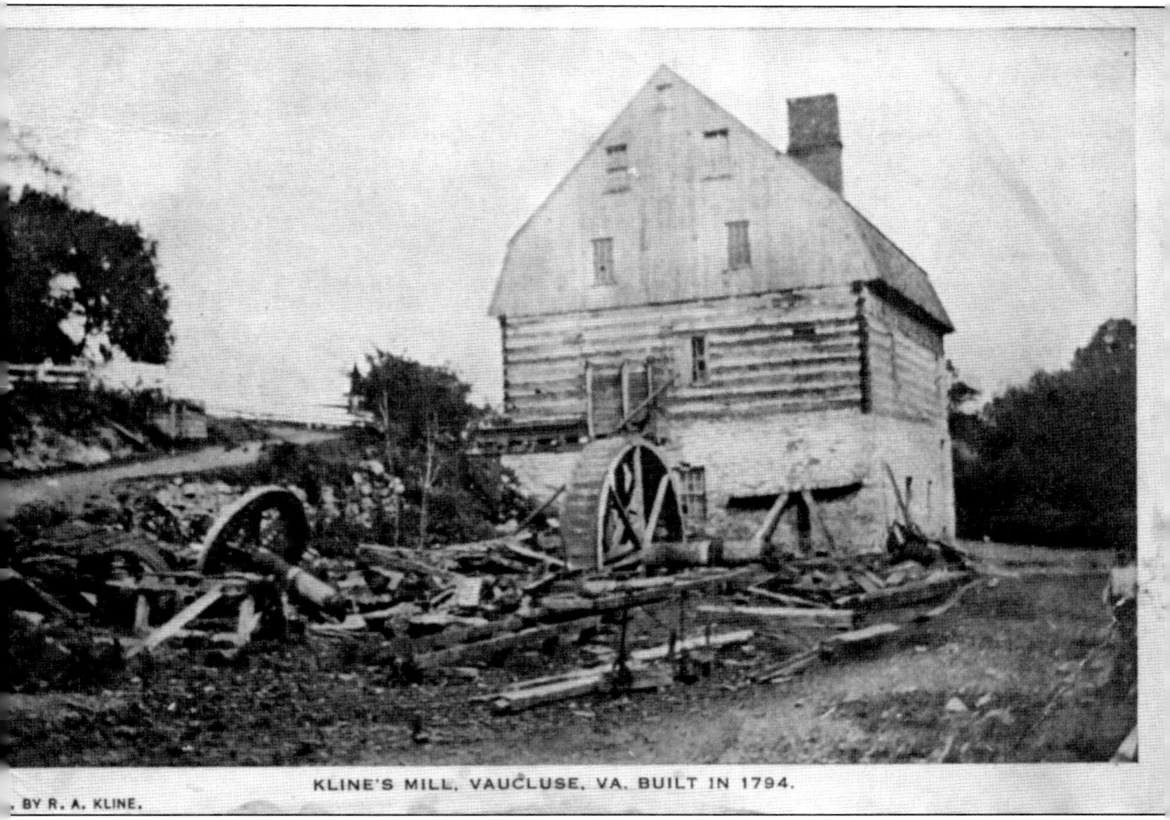

With the local economy roaring from numerous wheat-, rye-, corn-, and barley-producing farms and plantations along the busy Valley Pike, mills like this sprouted up to support the grain industry in the Shenandoah Valley. During the Civil War, the valley was known as "the breadbasket of the Confederacy." Seeking an end to the war, Union troops left mills like this in ruin, wrecking civilian support and starving the Confederate army. (Joyce D. Tucker.)

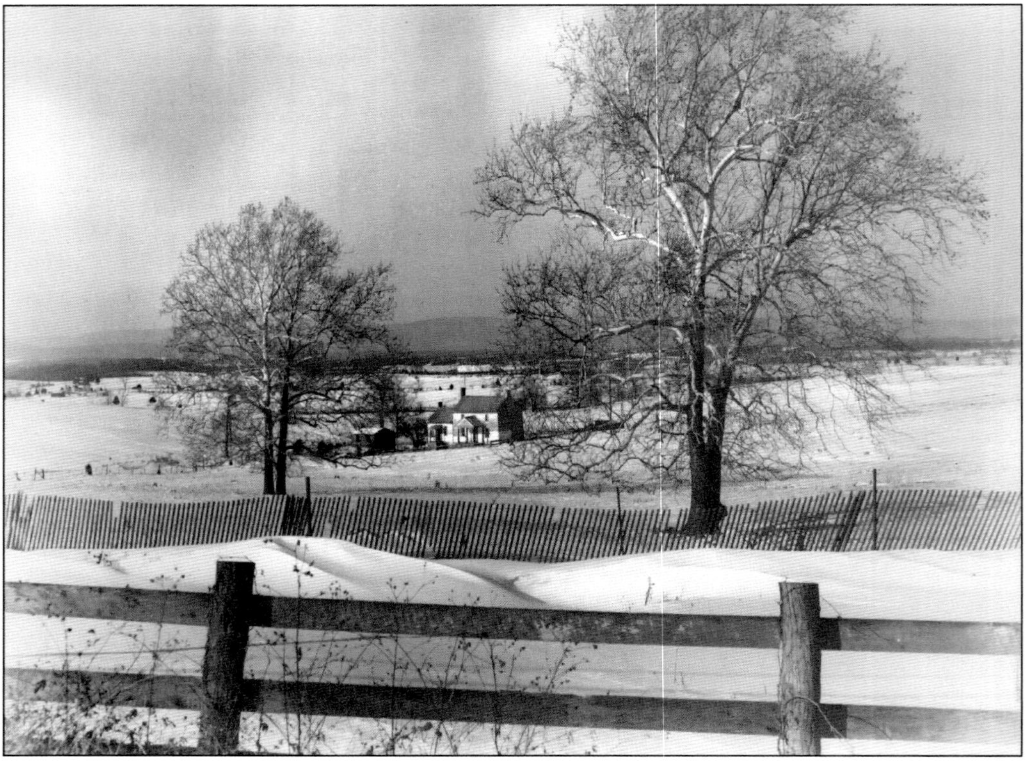

Solomon Heater established his home and farm around 1797, building a barn, kitchen, cider mill, and springhouse. With 600 acres on both sides of the turnpike, the Heater farm became the principle burial ground for Union soldiers at the Battle of Cedar Creek. (Harold Gardenhour Jr.)

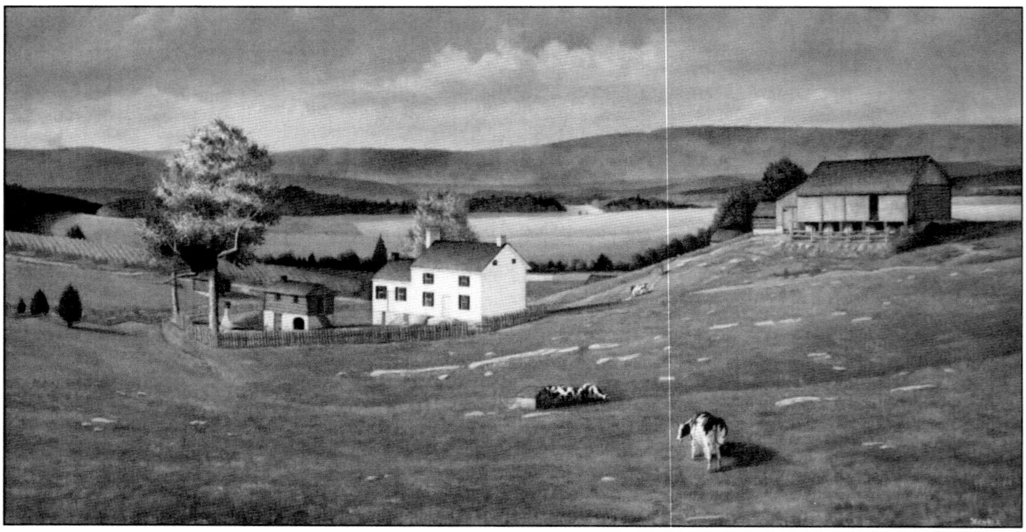

This image depicts the Heater house during tranquil times just before the Battle of Cedar Creek on October 19, 1864. The painting by Dorothy Henkle is appropriately titled *The Gathering Storm*. Solomon and Caroline Heater lost two sons who died fighting for the Confederacy. Caroline, however, was a Union sympathizer who frequently aided the troops. In 1901, her loyalty was repaid with a federal grant for wartime damages. The house is all that is left standing today. (Joyce D. Tucker.)

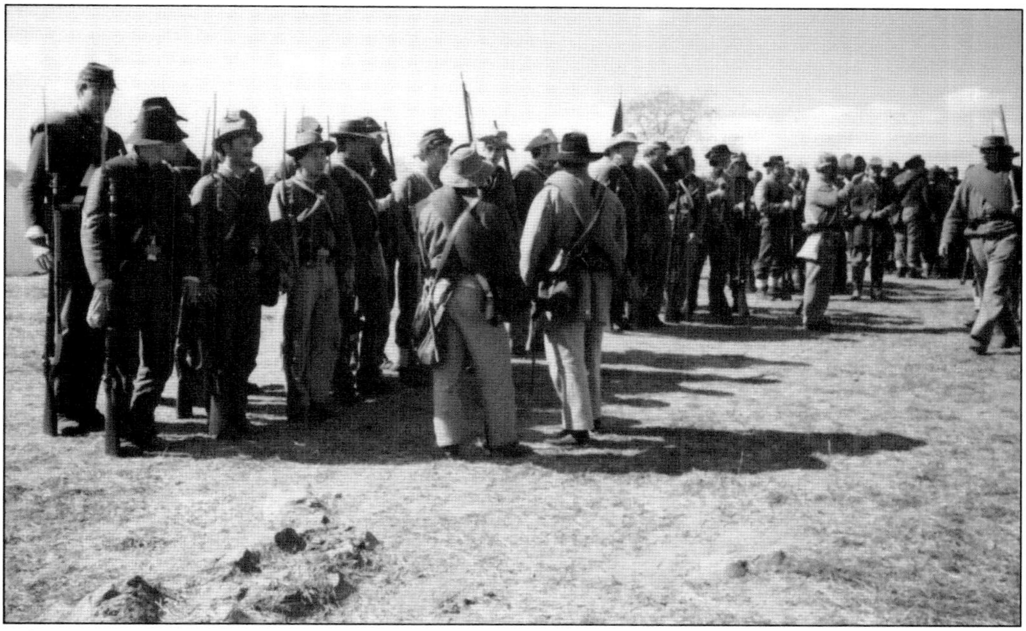

When the War Between the States ignited, Middletown saw more than its fair share of fighting. The first taste of action took place during Stonewall Jackson's famed Valley Campaign in 1862. Middletown was key to the Confederacy for several reasons: the fertile farmland provided food and shelter to fight the conflict and the mountains above the area, particularly the Signal Knob on Massanutten Mountain, provided observation points to keep tabs on the Union army. (Sharon Daily.)

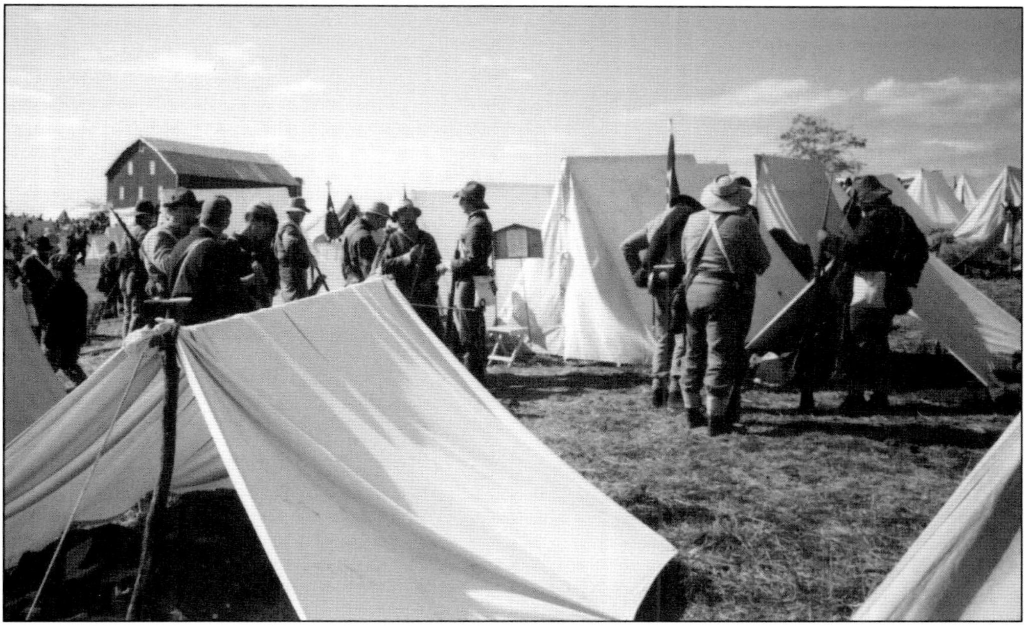

The town once again became center stage during the Civil War when Confederate general Jubal Early led a surprise raid on the morning of October 19, 1864, crossing Cedar Creek to attack the Federals camped near Belle Grove Plantation. The ambush was such a shock that it drove the Federals through the town and would have been a crushing defeat if not for the Confederates' "fatal halt" to search for food and supplies, which allowed the North to regroup its forces. (Sharon Daily.)

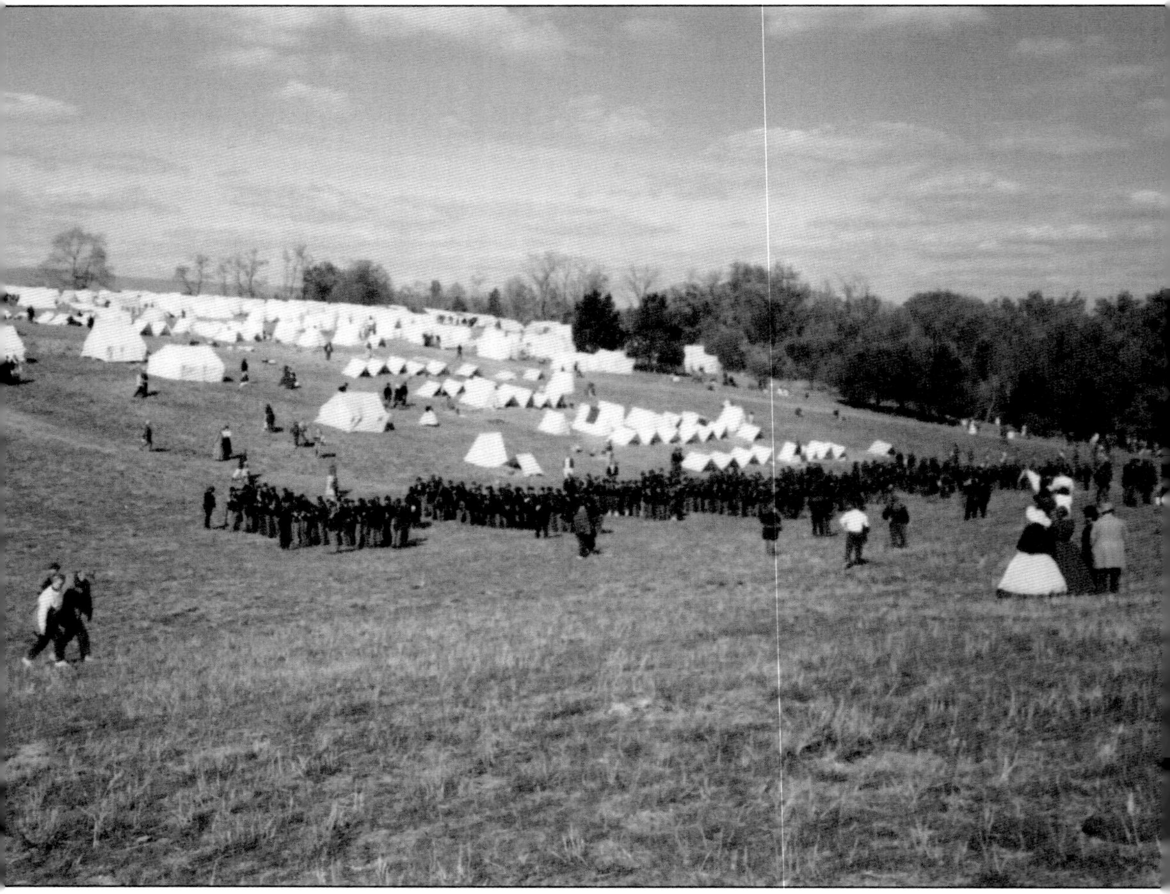

The delay of the Confederate forces allowed the Federal army to gather itself and prepare for a counterattack led by Union general Phillip Sheridan, who dramatically rode the 12 miles from Winchester when he heard the first shots of the opening sequence. Sheridan rallied his troops and led them through town, pushing the Confederates back and taking the day. The Union victory helped ensure President Lincoln's reelection in November 1864 and drove the Confederates from the valley for the remainder of the war. (Sharon Daily.)

This church was the primary field hospital for the Confederates in Middletown, but when Union troops retook the town, surgeons of both armies worked together on blue and gray soldiers alike. The building's tower was hit and damaged by several artillery rounds during the conflict. Afterward, many makeshift graves were dug behind the chapel until they were reinterred to nearby Winchester, Virginia. (Joyce D. Tucker.)

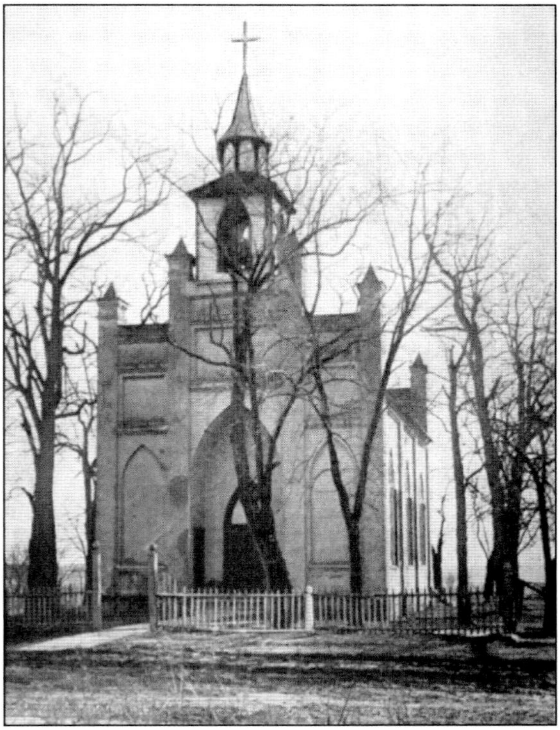

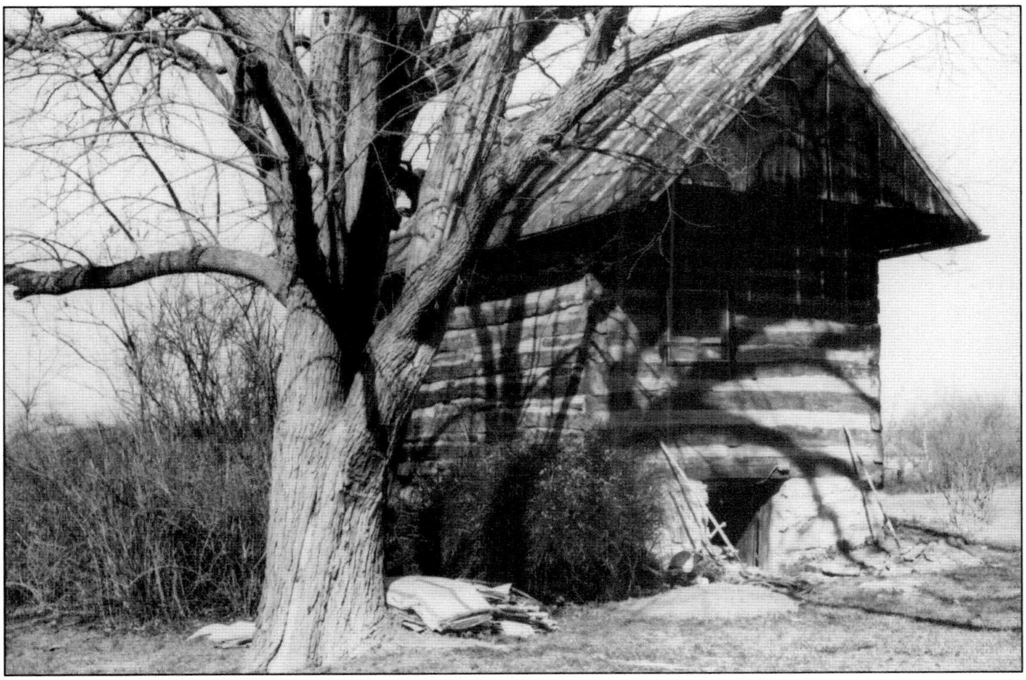

This springhouse served as a Confederate field aid station behind the Rhodes house on the south end of town. It supported wounded soldiers of Jubal Early's command in the aftermath of repeated failed assaults against Union troops on Mount Carmel Cemetery. The attacks were launched from here, and many of the town's buildings essentially became makeshift hospitals. During the battle, 964 men from both sides lost their lives, and over 5,000 were wounded. (Helen Lee Fletcher.)

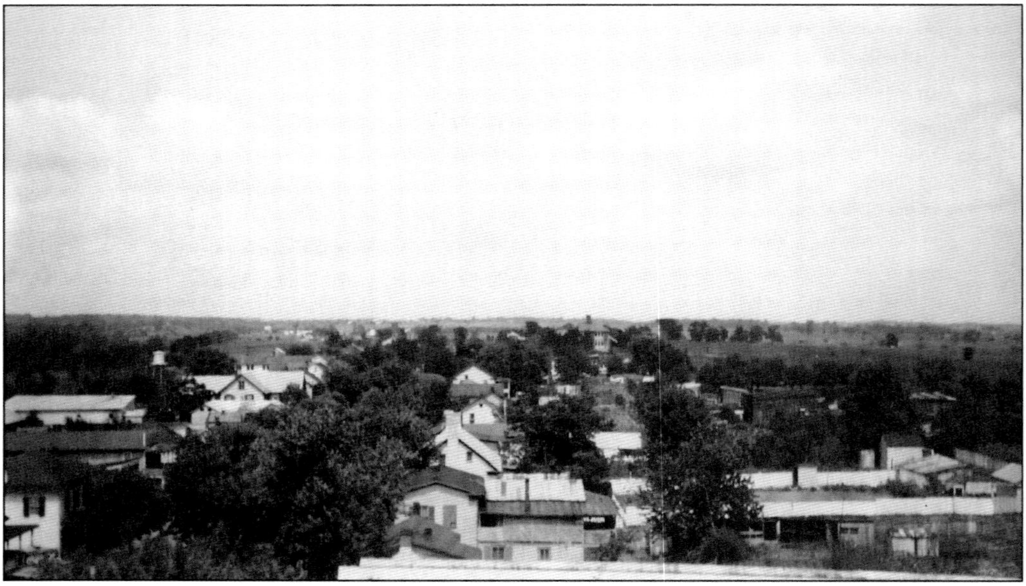

After the Civil War, a slow rebuilding process occurred throughout the valley. This 1938 view of Main Street was taken from the bell tower of Grace United Methodist Church. (Middletown Heritage Society.)

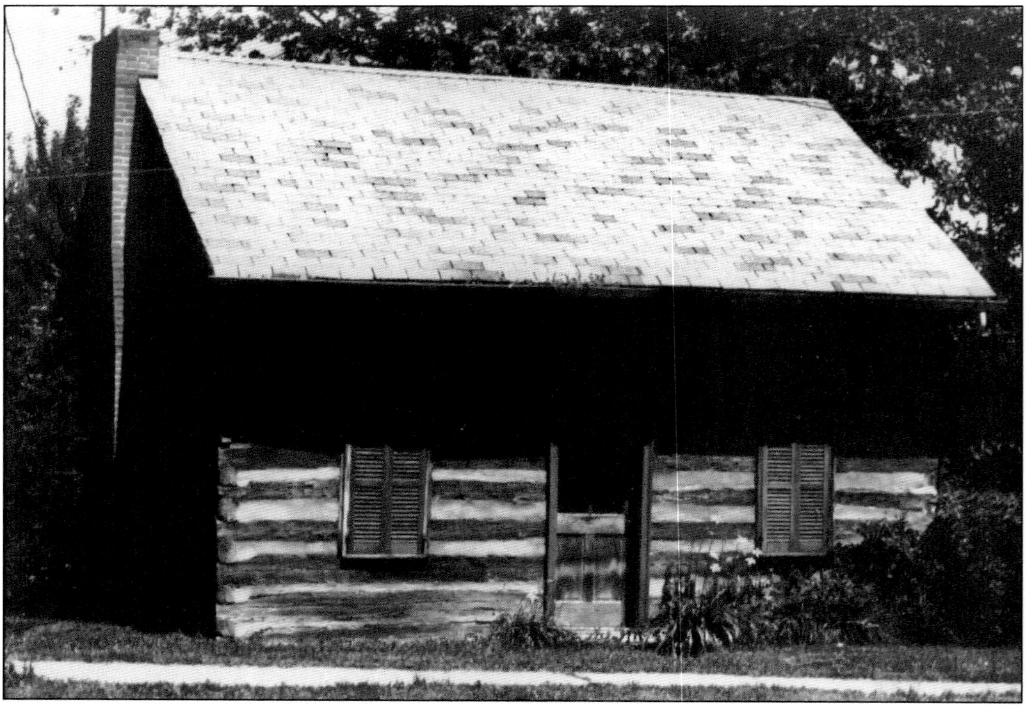

This humble cabin was the home of an African American woman known only as "Aunt Caroline Jenkins." Local lore says she was born into slavery in the Carolinas and walked hundreds of miles to Middletown after her purchase by a local master. Despite very few available details about her life, Aunt Caroline maintained a reputation as an excellent midwife, assisting in many Middletown births before and after the Civil War. (Helen Lee Fletcher.)

This is perhaps the only surviving image of Aunt Caroline Jenkins. She is said to have worked for John Wright until her death in 1907, after the Civil War. (Helen Lee Fletcher.)

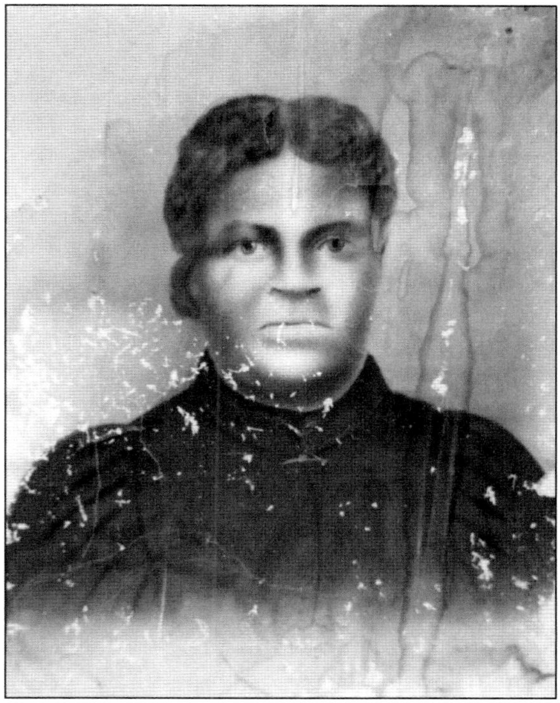

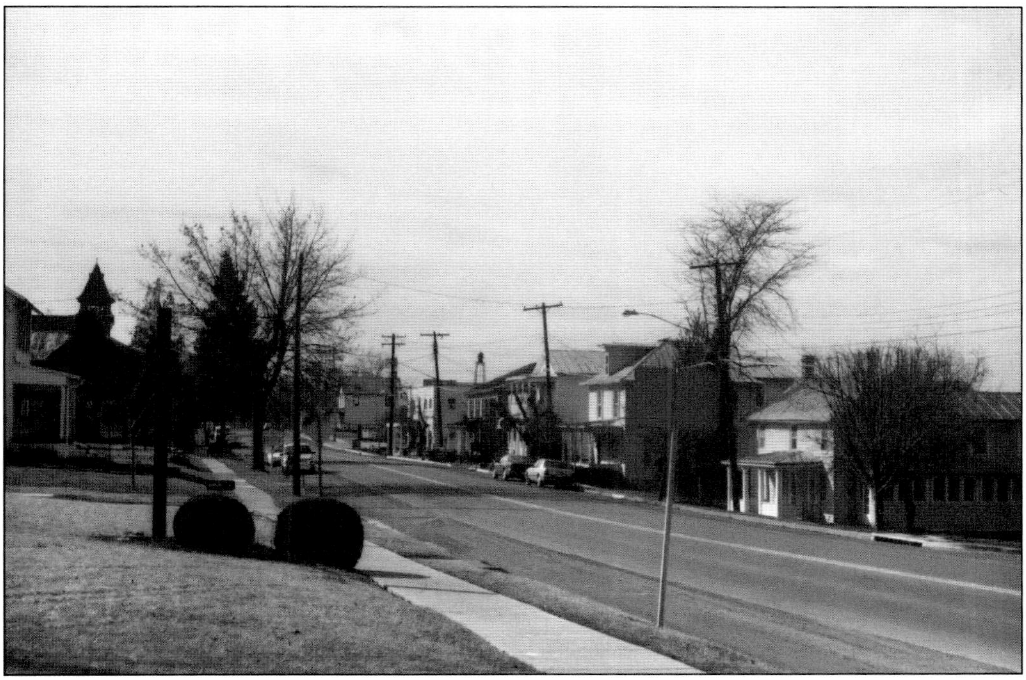

This picture shows a more modern-day view of Main Street. Dr. Peter Senseney, the town's founder, had the forethought to lay out the lots so houses were farther from the street. As a medical doctor, Dr. Senseney understood there was a correlation between the filthy roads of the 1700s and 1800s and people's health. The action proved worthwhile, because in the 1930s, when Valley Pike was widened, it was the only town in the valley that did not have to move houses. (Helen Lee Fletcher.)

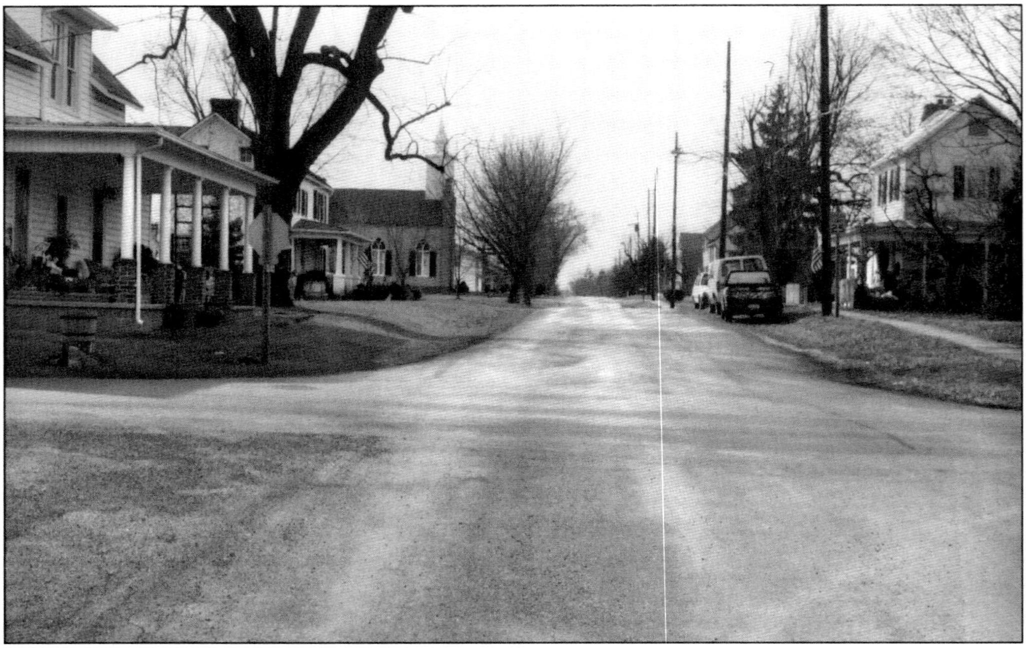

Church Street is notable for several reasons, including its many prominent buildings and wide array of architecture, such as Vernacular, Queen Anne, Victorian, and Colonial Revival. (Helen Lee Fletcher.)

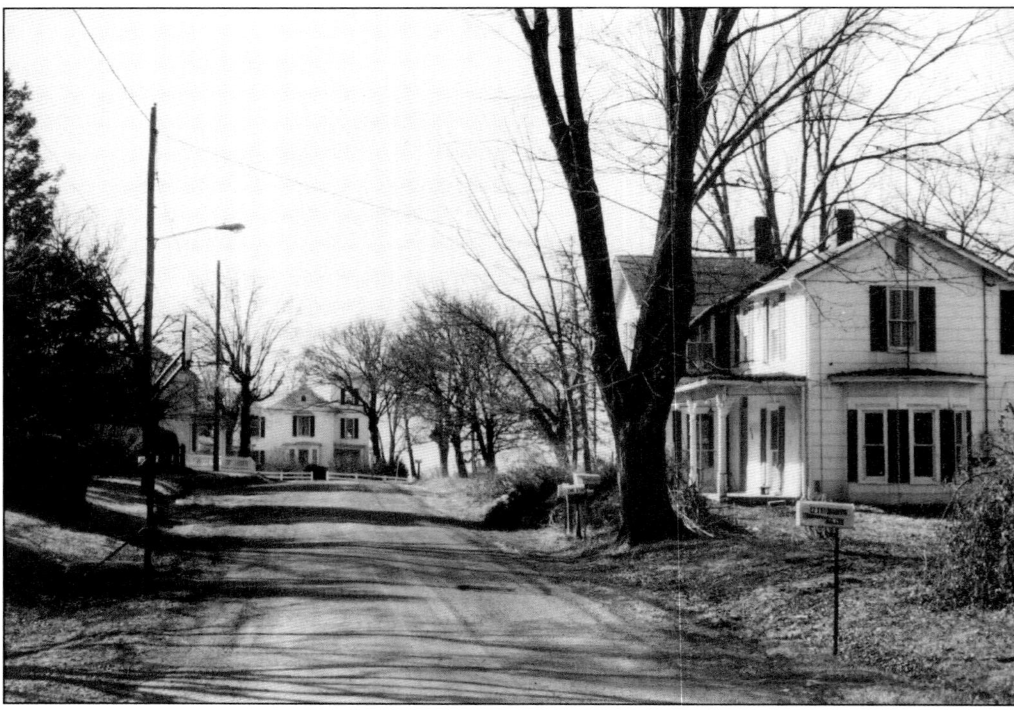

Church Street, seen here looking south to Sixth Street, was originally called Slate Street because the underlying rock changes from limestone to slate along the path of the street. On the right is the c. 1879 home of Catherine Kitts Willey, and at the end of the street is Arthur N. Bragg's c. 1871 farmhouse, with its unique tower. The farm was later called Maplewood. (Helen Lee Fletcher.)

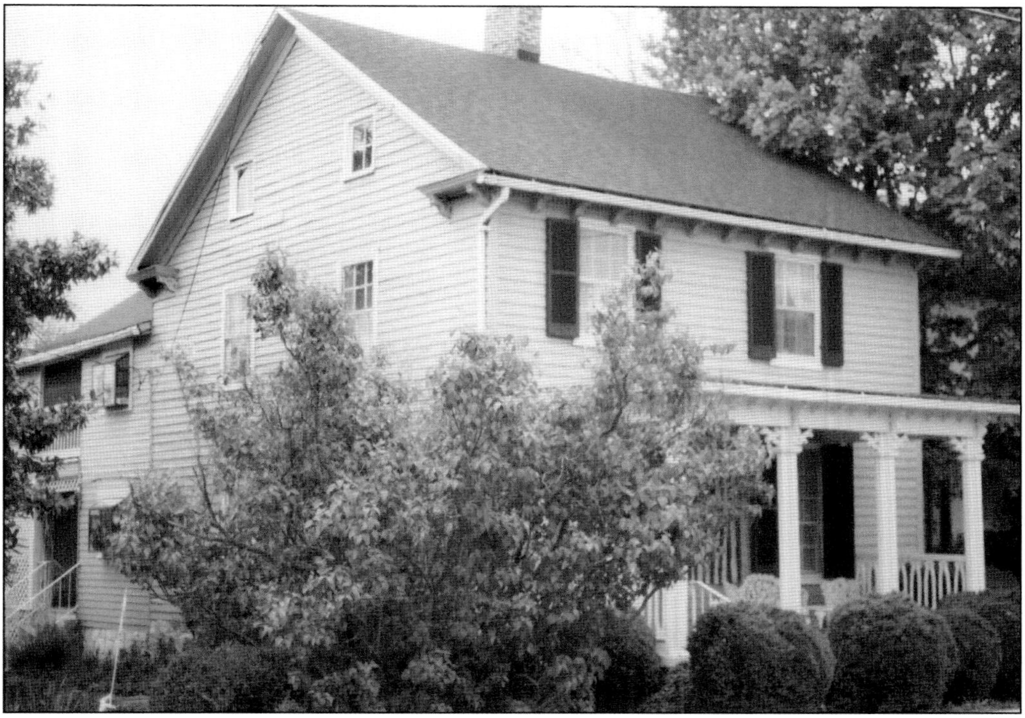

In 1797, Joseph Danner constructed this house, now one of the oldest buildings in town. The log structure is original to the property, but the home's subsequent 11 owners have made many alterations since then. (Helen Lee Fletcher.)

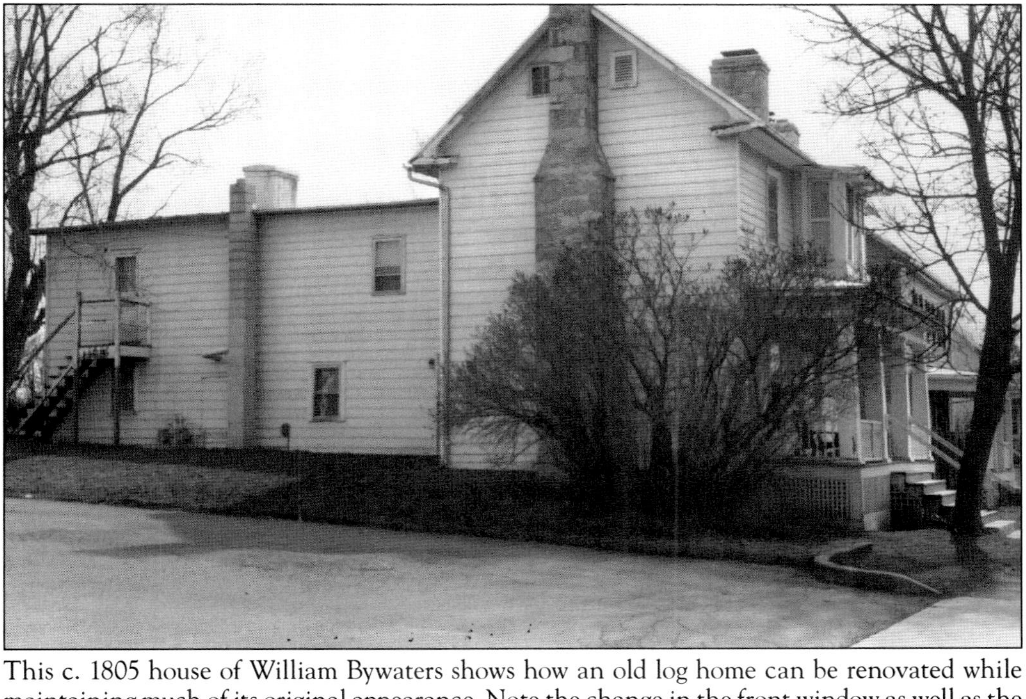

This c. 1805 house of William Bywaters shows how an old log home can be renovated while maintaining much of its original appearance. Note the change in the front window as well as the enclosed back porch, connecting to what was likely a detached kitchen. (Helen Lee Fletcher.)

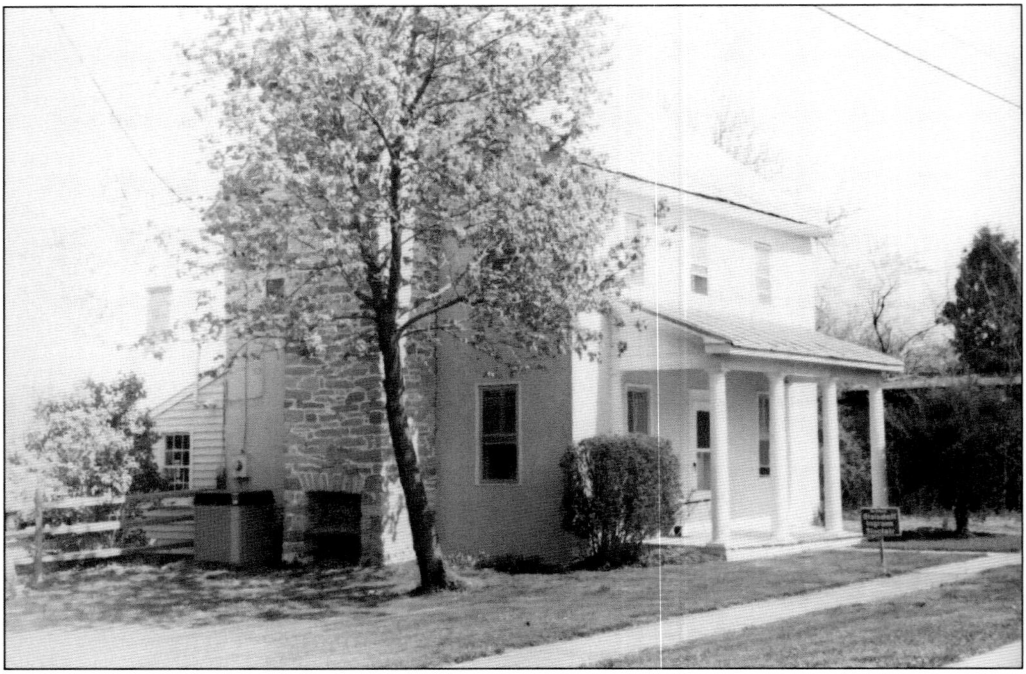

Depicted in the *James E. Taylor Sketchbook*, this house, with its unique outdoor fireplace, was built by Isaac Overacre in 1800. It is now the current home of two businesses: Valley Needleworks and Joe Can Fix It All. (Helen Lee Fletcher.)

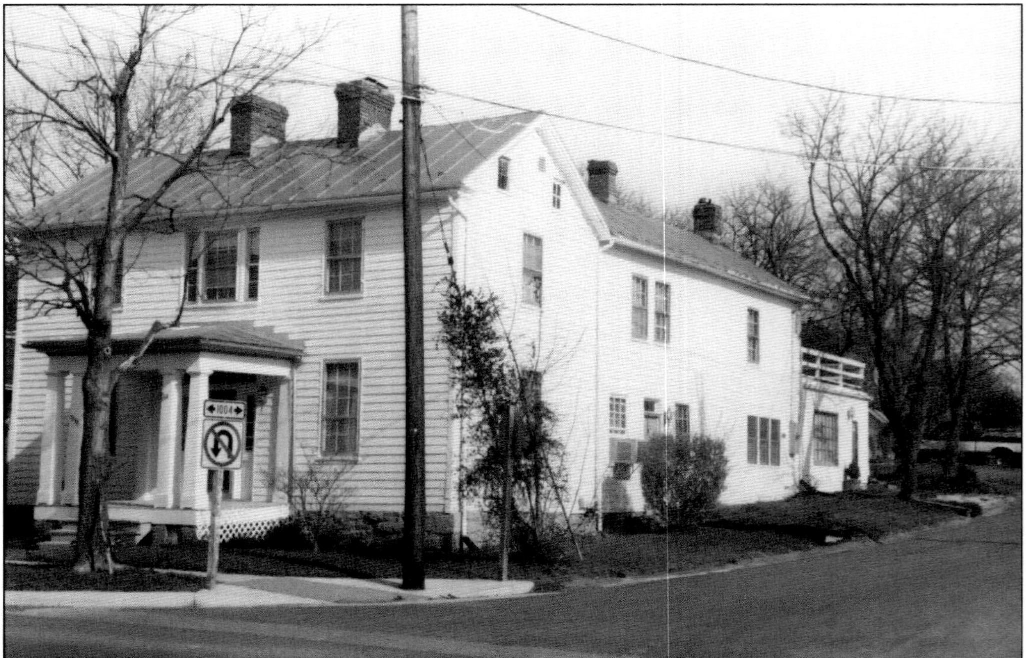

David Stickley built this house on Main Street around 1820. Its architecture resembles earlier period construction. (Helen Lee Fletcher.)

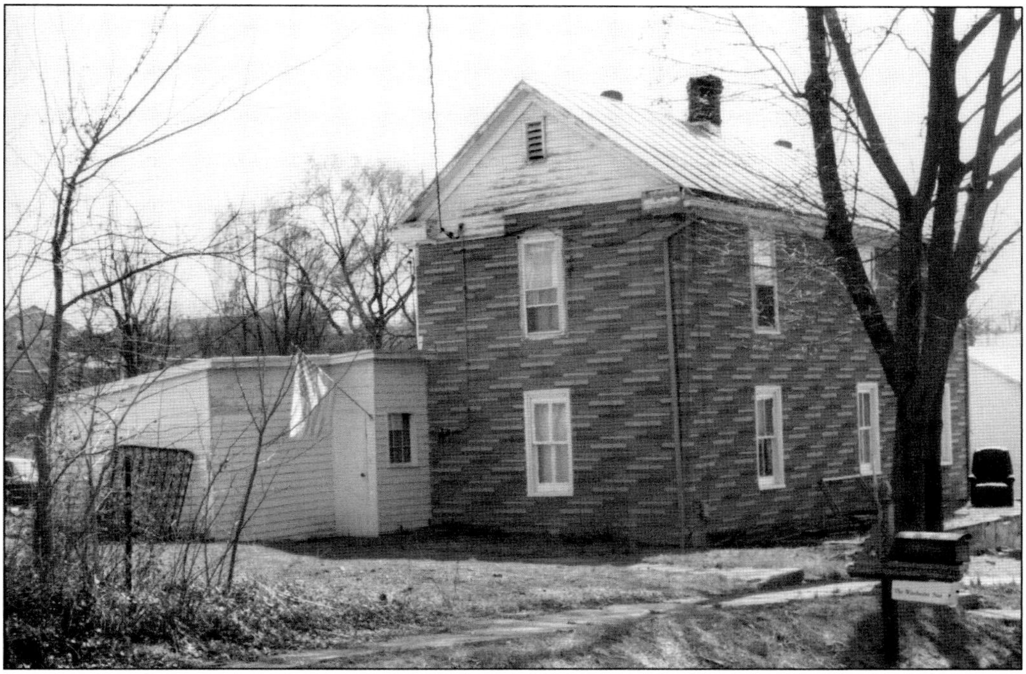

The William Steward house was built in 1801. The front log portion was constructed first, followed by many changes over the years. According to an anecdote about Elsie Grim and her husband, William was a horseshoe-throwing champion who accumulated so many trophies that Elsie told him to keep them in the many outbuildings on the half-acre lot. (Helen Lee Fletcher.)

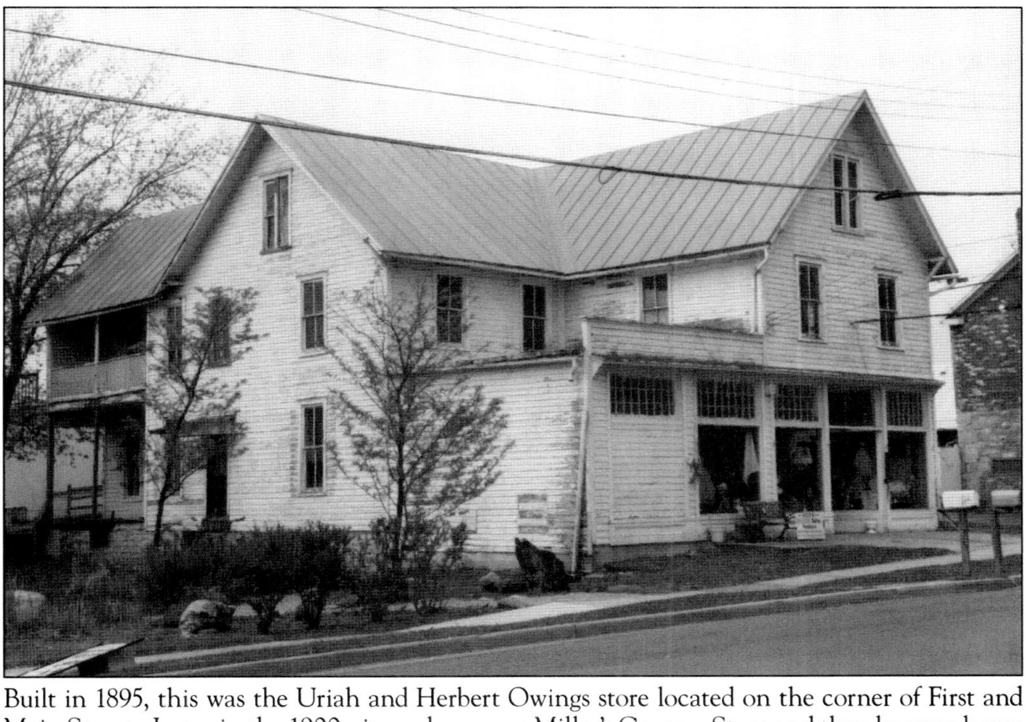

Built in 1895, this was the Uriah and Herbert Owings store located on the corner of First and Main Streets. Later, in the 1900s, it was known as Miller's Grocery Store and then became home to the Carpetbagger, a sutler of the Civil War era. (Helen Lee Fletcher.)

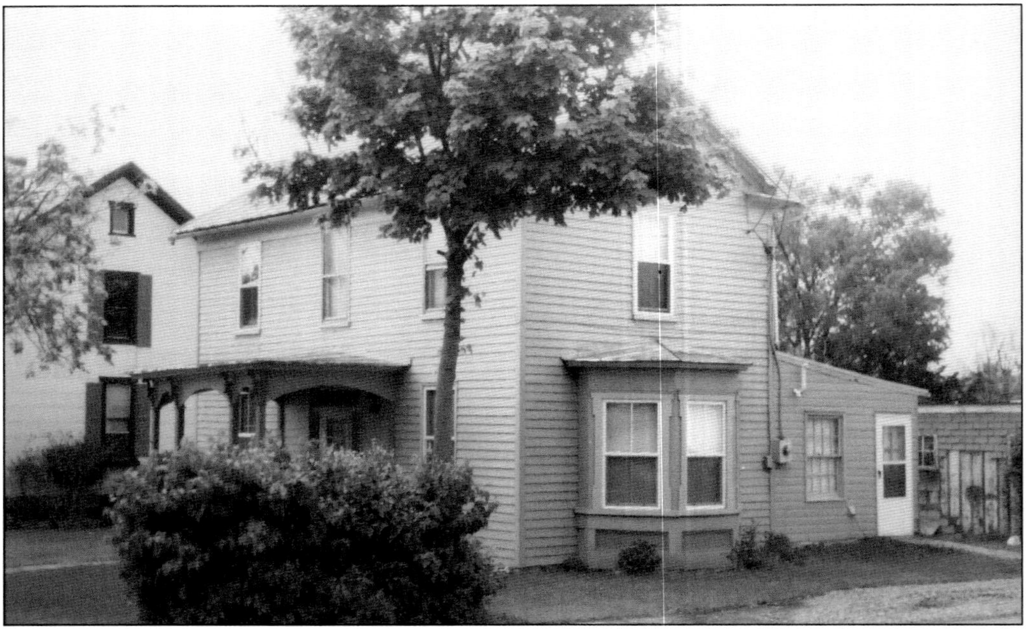

This is a mid-19th-century dwelling built on the west corner of Third and Main Streets by Benjamin S. Gilmore. During a recent renovation, the unique porch was completely changed. A similar house is depicted in the *James E. Taylor Sketchbook* as the location where Union colonel Joseph Thoburn was carried away after he was mortally wounded at the Battle of Cedar Creek. (Helen Lee Fletcher.)

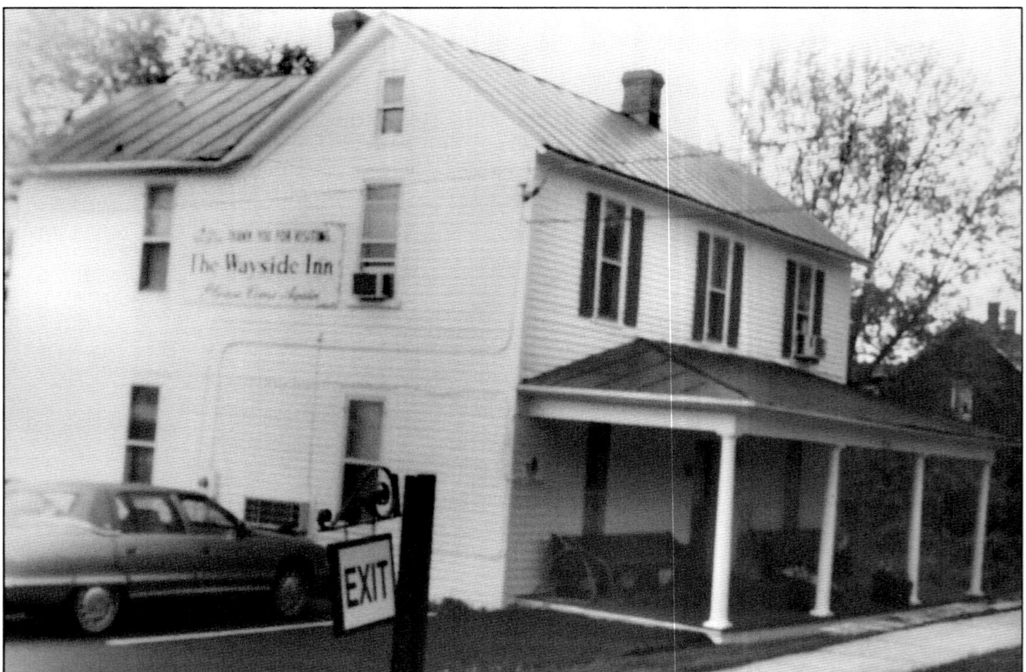

The c. 1890 home of Peck Wright is now owned by the Wayside Inn, which formerly used it as office space and lodging for the managers. It is built on the approximate location of the old tollhouse, where heavy fighting took place during the battle on October 19, 1864. (Helen Lee Fletcher.)

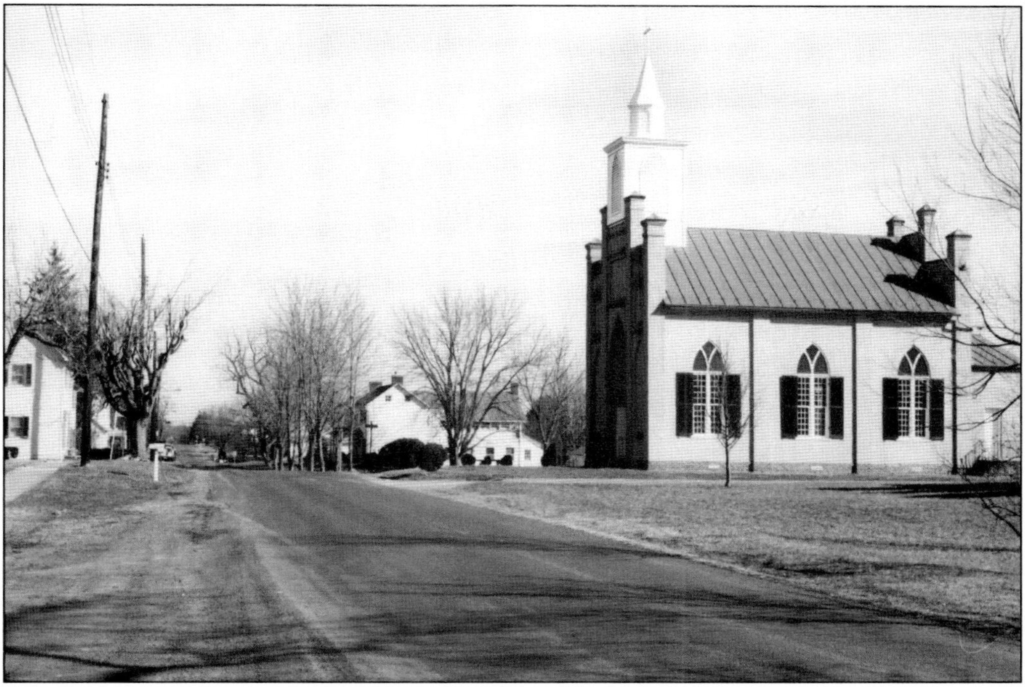

In 1835, Dr. Walker Hite built the white house at right in the distance. Coincidentally, Dr. John S. Guyer bought the home in 1858, then served in the Civil War as a physician. (Helen Lee Fletcher.)

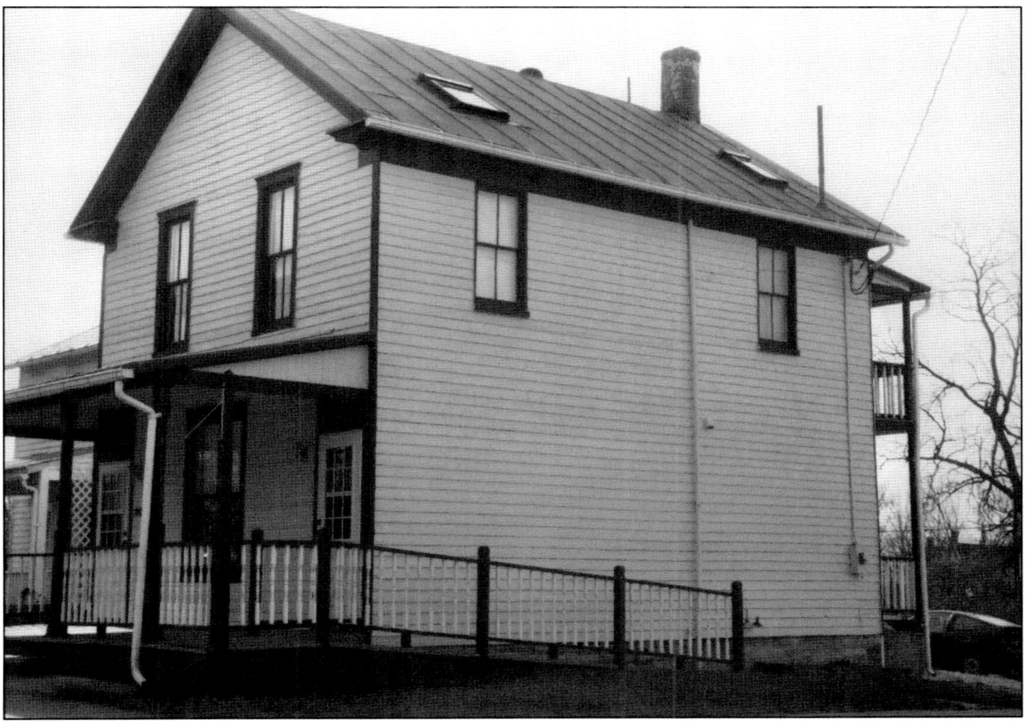

This Main Street house was built in 1915 and served as the Democratic post office. Today, the building is used as apartments. (Helen Lee Fletcher.)

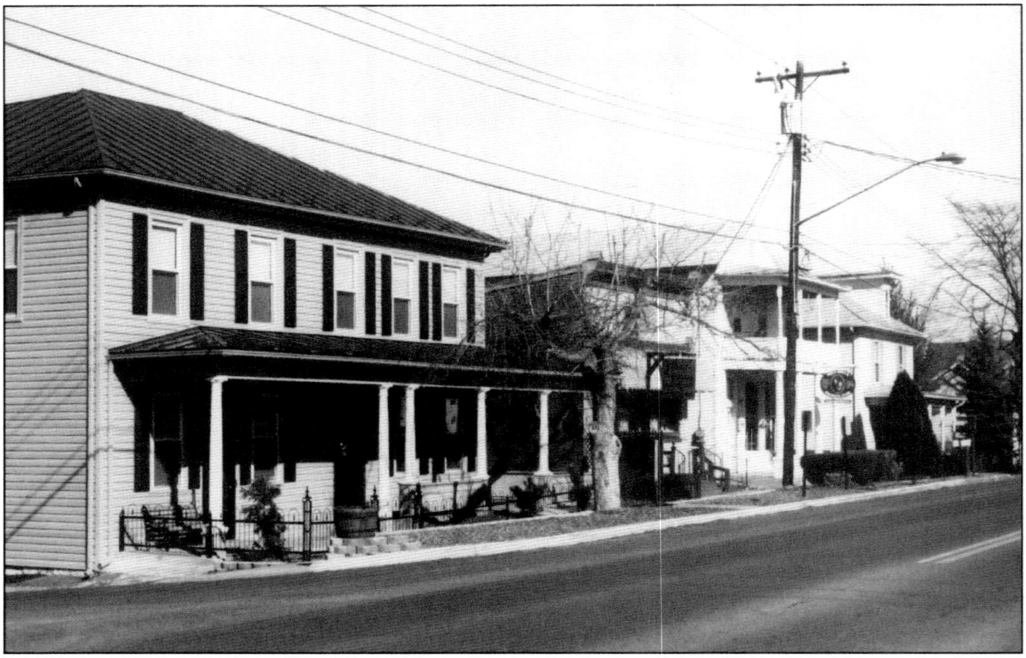

This Main Street view shows the 1902 site of M. Herber Rhodes's store and post office at left. This site was also known as the Republican post office. Today, the building on the corner is utilized as an apartment complex. To the right is the c. 1908 Middletown State Bank, currently the Irish Isle Restaurant & Pub. To the right of that is the former location of Dudley Edmonston's store, built in 1902. (Helen Lee Fletcher.)

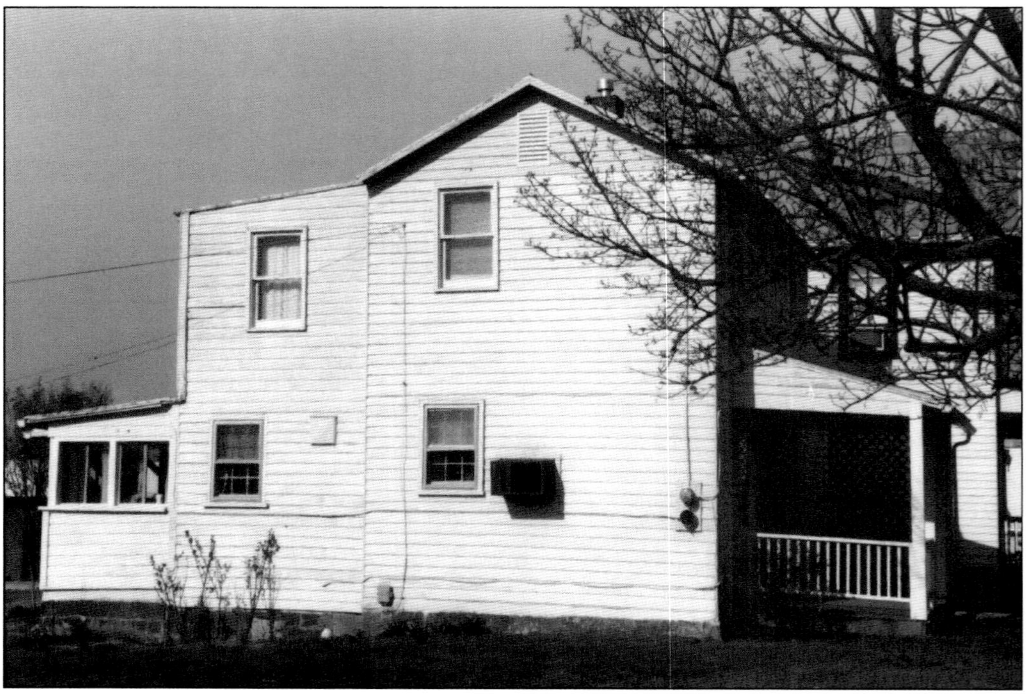

Here is a side view of the Wilber Mowery home on Main Street. This house is just south of the Middletown Volunteer Fire Department. (Helen Lee Fletcher.)

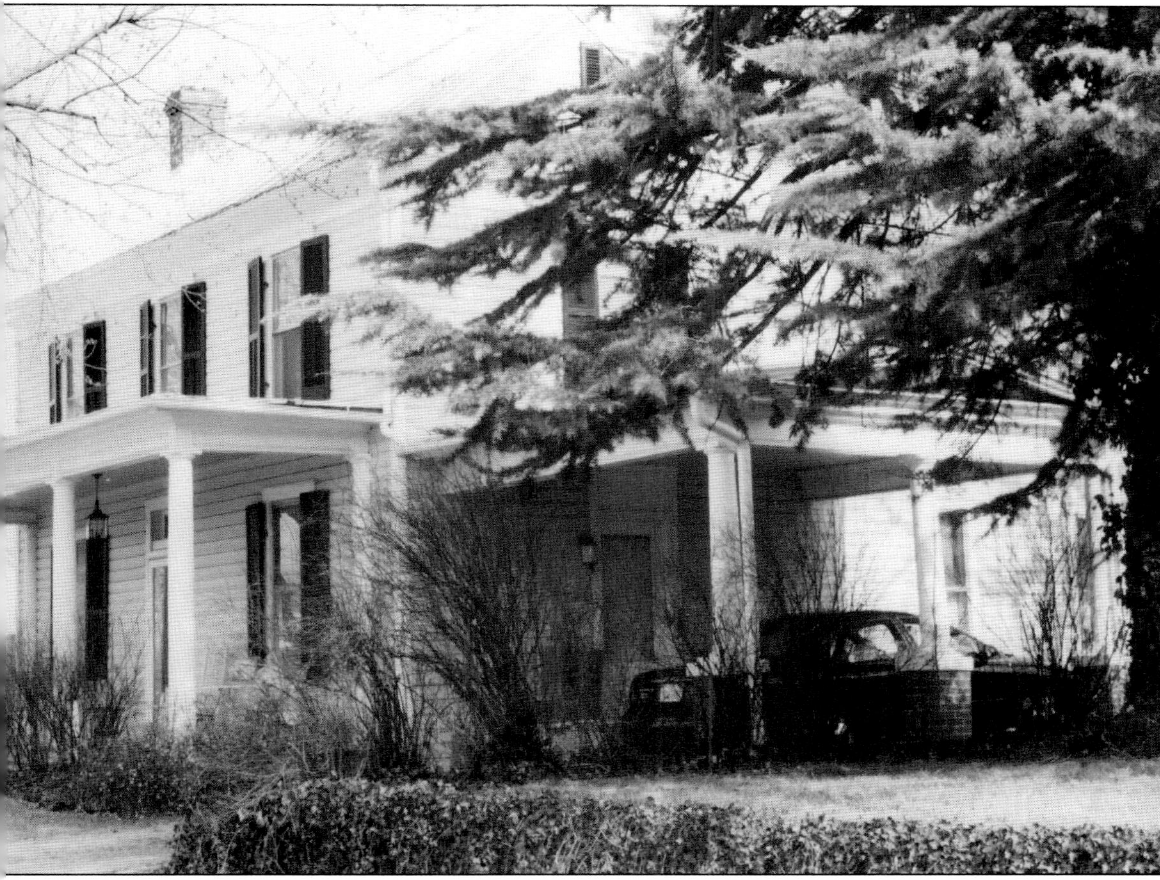

Located on Main Street, between Fourth and Fifth Streets, is the Lillah W. Willey home. It was constructed in 1916 and retains the single hanging lamp on the front porch, which was common among Shenandoah Valley houses. The modern-day carport is interesting in that it was designed to retain the home's original character. (Helen Lee Fletcher.)

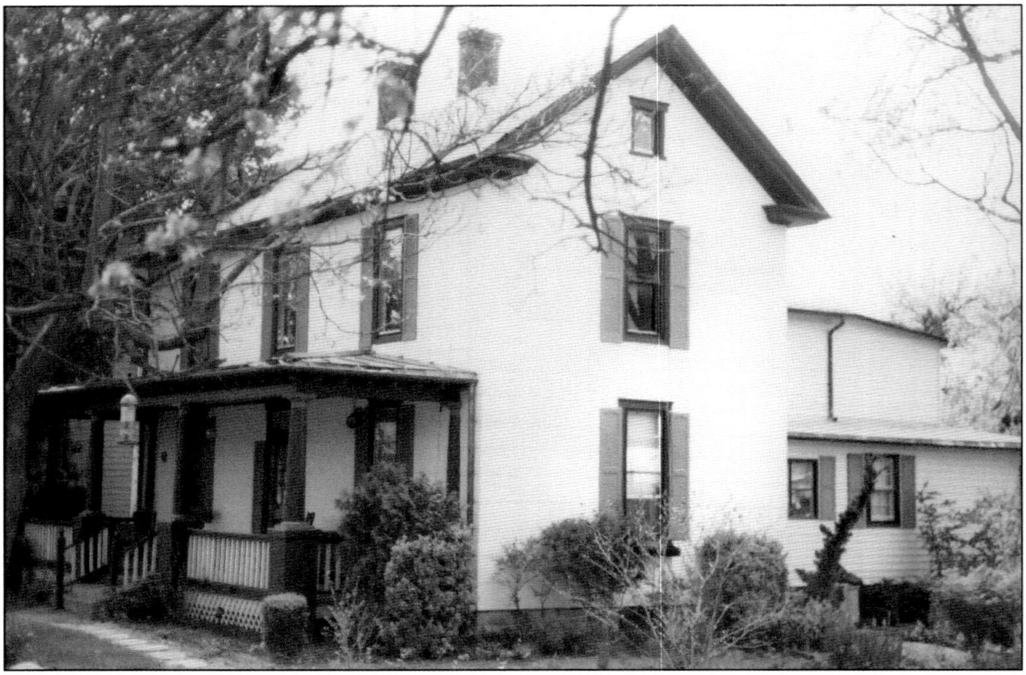

Located on Main Street, this is the 1910 home of Herschel C. Border, who was a merchant in the town for years and had his shop within the town as well. (Helen Lee Fletcher.)

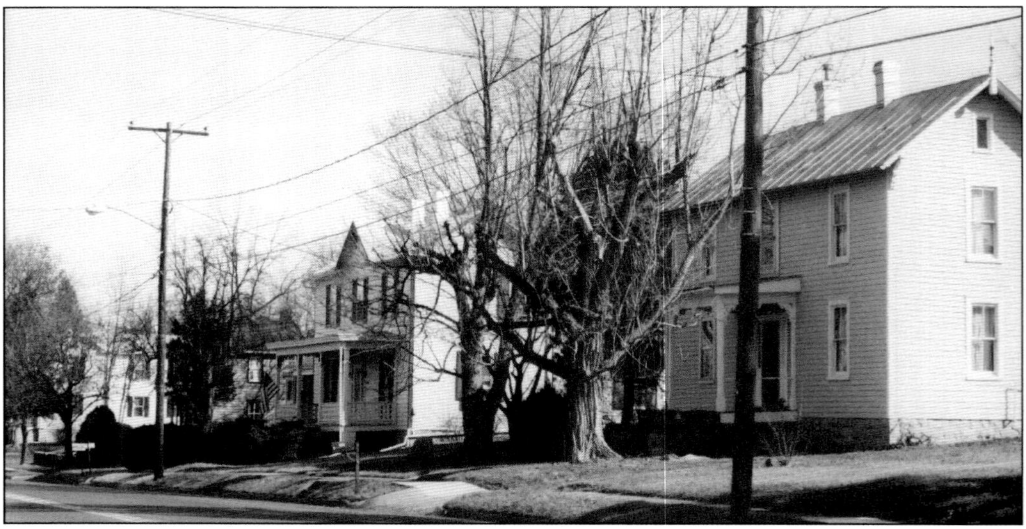

These are two of the Willey family homes. Both were built in 1888 on Main Street, between Fifth and Sixth Streets. They have the same basic floor plan, with variations according to the needs and tastes of each family. The house on the left was George William Willey's home. It has arched windows from the 1852 Methodist Episcopal Church in the north and south gables, along with a gable on the front. The house on the right was the home of James Lawson Willey. Instead of a front gable, the house has a door in the center above the porch. The scrolled woodwork is very different on each home, as are the windows. G.W. Willey's home has coffin windows that reach to the porch so coffins could be brought in and out of the front parlors. Both had separate summer kitchens and many outbuildings. Like most homes, they were electrified after the Rural Electrification Act of 1936. Both houses were modified for indoor plumbing around 1970. (Helen Lee Fletcher.)

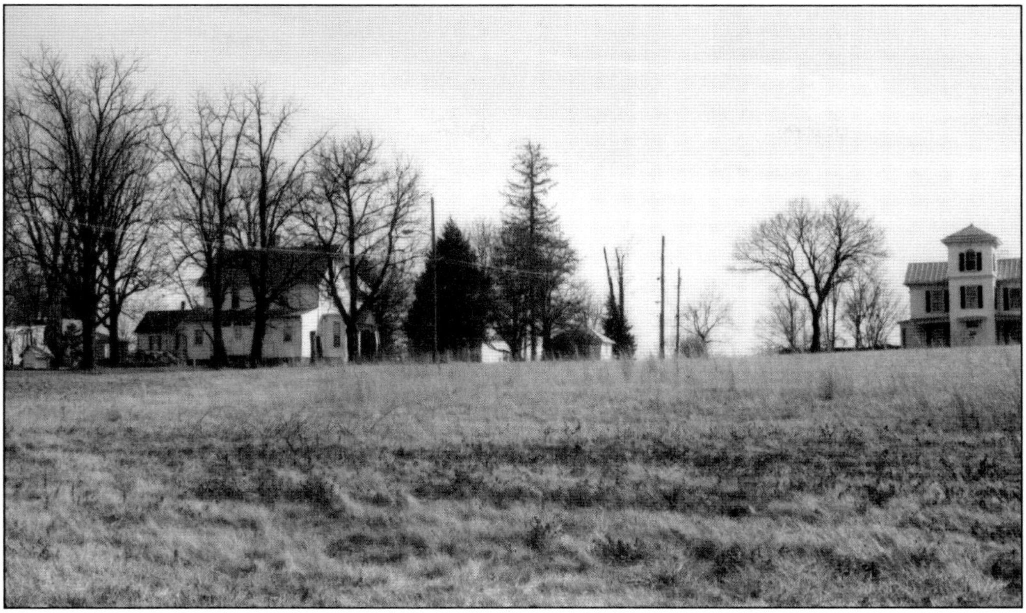

On the right is Maplewood Farm, as seen from the Valley Pike (Route 11). On the left is a rear view of the c. 1890 home of George William Bragg. From this vantage point, Sixth Street runs roughly from left to right. Originally connected to Buck's Ford (or Buckton Ford) Road, Sixth Street was a well-traveled route across the Shenandoah River in earlier times. Interstate 81 now splits the roads. (Helen Lee Fletcher.)

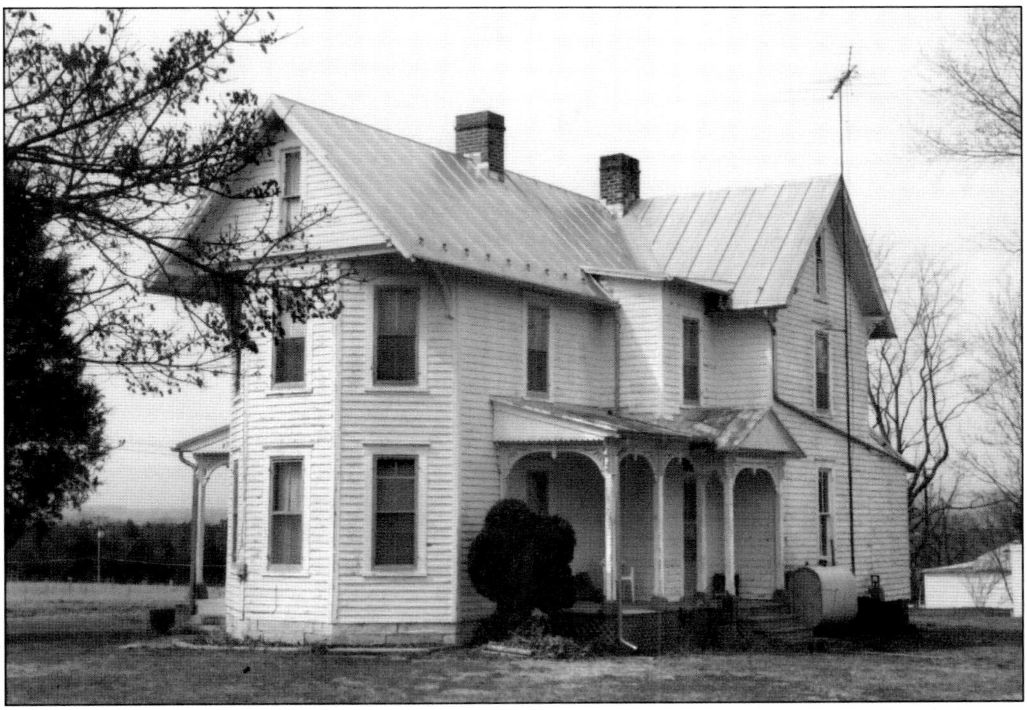

Here is a front view of the c. 1890 home of George William Bragg, as seen from Church Street. The interesting style and shape of the home, as well as the small but ornate porches, are a good example of the variety of architecture in Middletown. (Helen Lee Fletcher.)

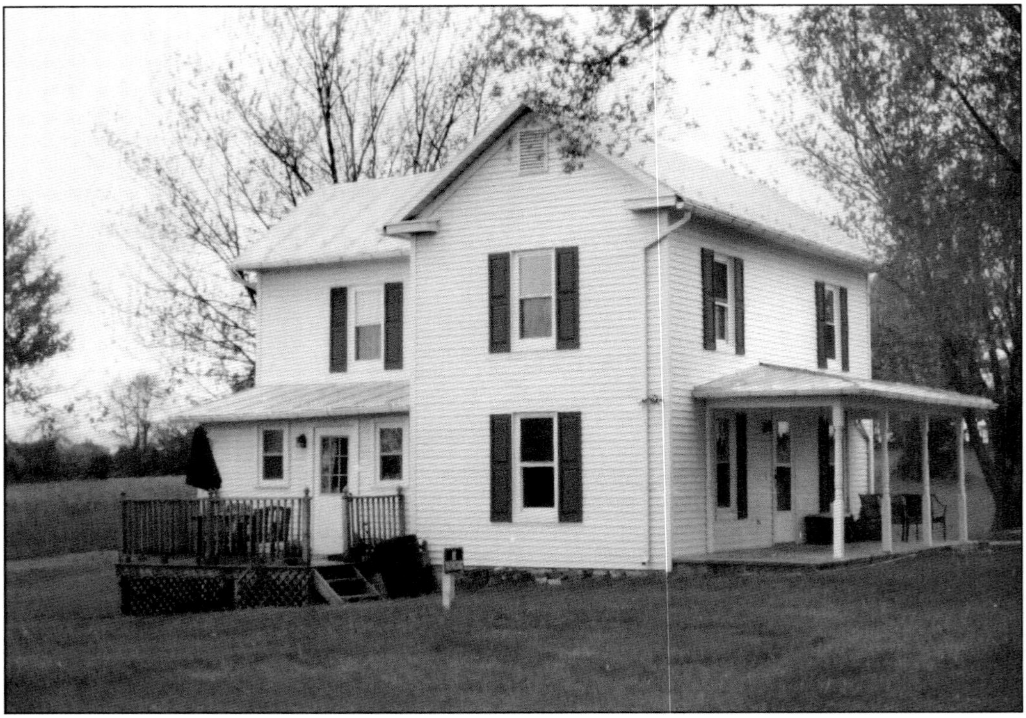

Constructed in the early 1900s, this rather plain but symmetrical frame structure was the tenant house for the Maplewood Farm. (Helen Lee Fletcher.)

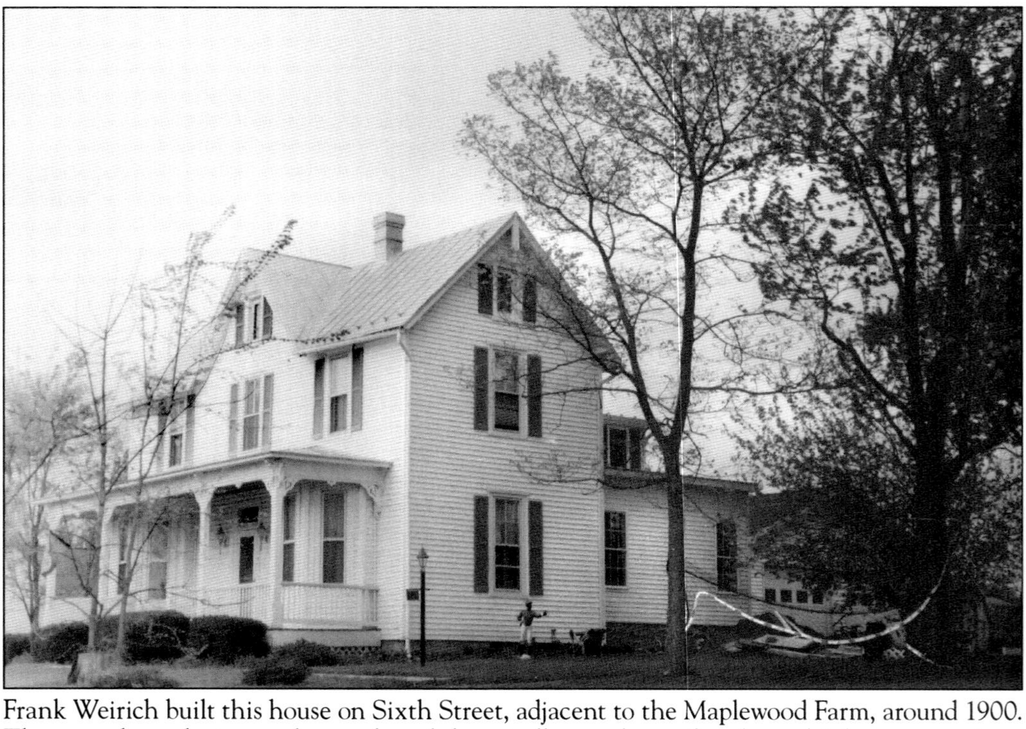

Frank Weirich built this house on Sixth Street, adjacent to the Maplewood Farm, around 1900. The carved wood trim on the porch and the spindles on the roof peak set this home apart from those around it. (Helen Lee Fletcher.)

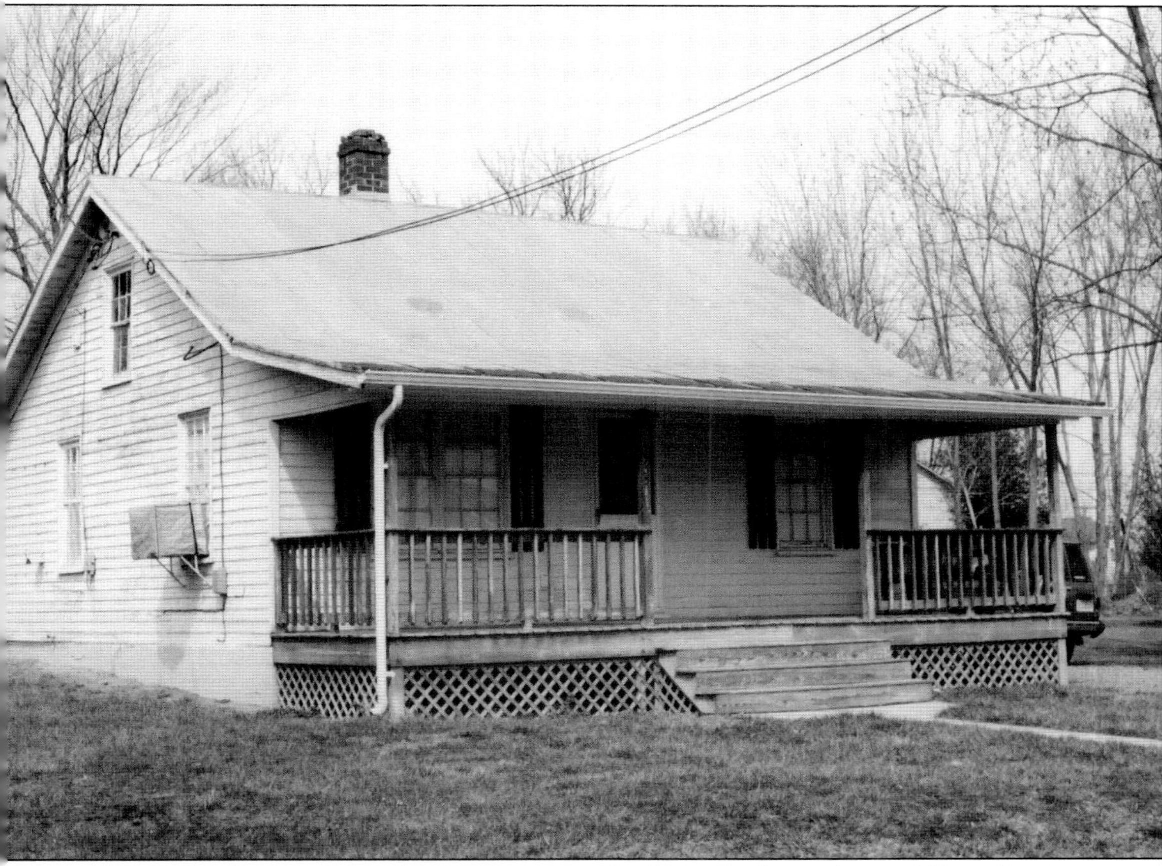

A small bungalow house on Church Street is an example of a catalog home that could be ordered and assembled on-site. (Helen Lee Fletcher.)

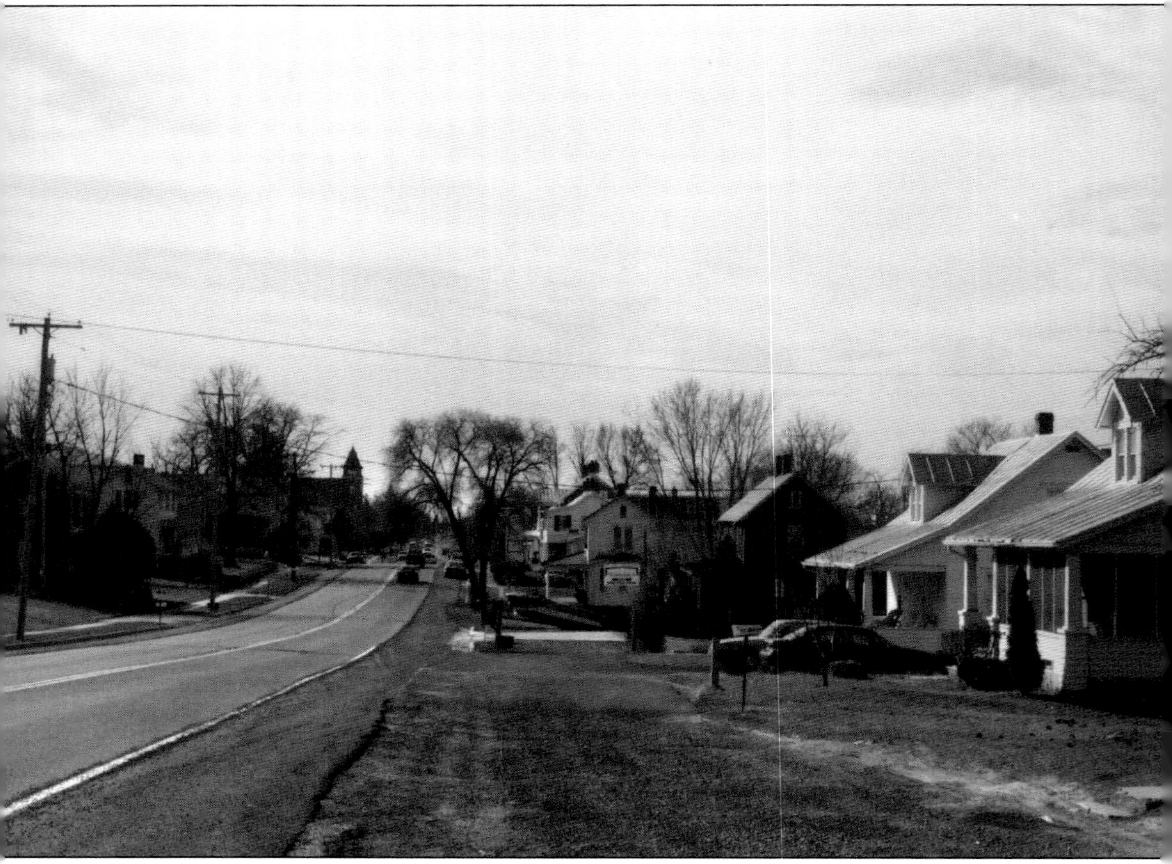

In this Main Street scene on the north end of town, the outline of Grace United Methodist Church and its bell tower are visible in the distance on the left side of the Valley Pike. The Wayside Inn is seen on the crest of the small hill at right. In the foreground at right are two houses that were built for mill workers in the early 1900s. (Helen Lee Fletcher.)

Two

Education, Industry, and Government

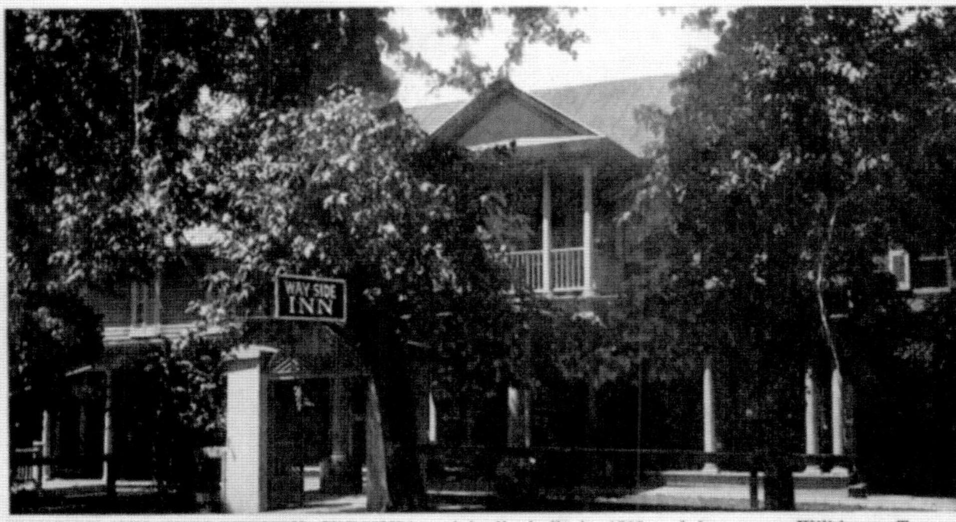

WAYSIDE INN, MIDDLETOWN, VIRGINIA, originally built in 1797 and known as Wilkinson Tavern. Later purchased by Jacob Larrick and operated as Larrick Hotel. Before and after Civil War was relay station for Shenandoah Valley stage lines. Near this site General Sheridan met his retreating troops and terminated his famous ride from Winchester after the first half of the battle of Cedar Creek. Since 1908 operated by Mrs. M. M. Rhodes under name of Wayside Inn, and was the first American hostelry to cater to the automobile tourists only. It has a nation-wide reputation and its guests average over 8,000 yearly.

The Wayside Inn had its beginning in the 1740s with the construction of the brick blockhouse along the Warrior Trail. In 1797, Wilkinson's Tavern was constructed and established in conjunction with a tollhouse and horse-changing station for stagecoaches. A town took shape around this establishment, including blacksmith shops, dry goods stores, and other businesses that supported the growing commerce on the new turnpike road. This view from the early 1900s shows little change from that featured in the *James E. Taylor Sketchbook*. Jacob Larrick ran the inn for the Wilkersons during the war, at which time heavy fighting took place around the inn and tollhouse. After the war, Larrick purchased the inn and renamed it Larrick's Hotel. In 1905, Samuel Rhodes bought it and added a third floor and both wings. He renamed it Wayside Inn. (Joyce D. Tucker.)

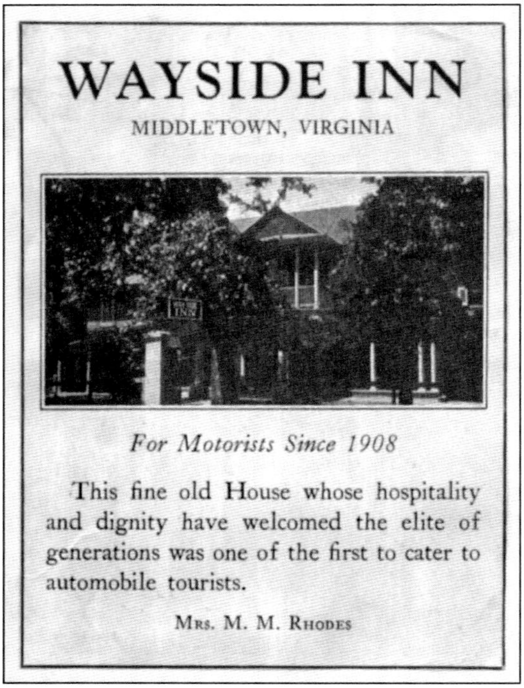

A postcard image from early 1900 touts the Wayside Inn as a primary destination for automobile tourists. Samuel Rhodes referred to the Wayside Inn as "America's first motor inn," though horses were still very much in vogue. (Joyce D. Tucker.)

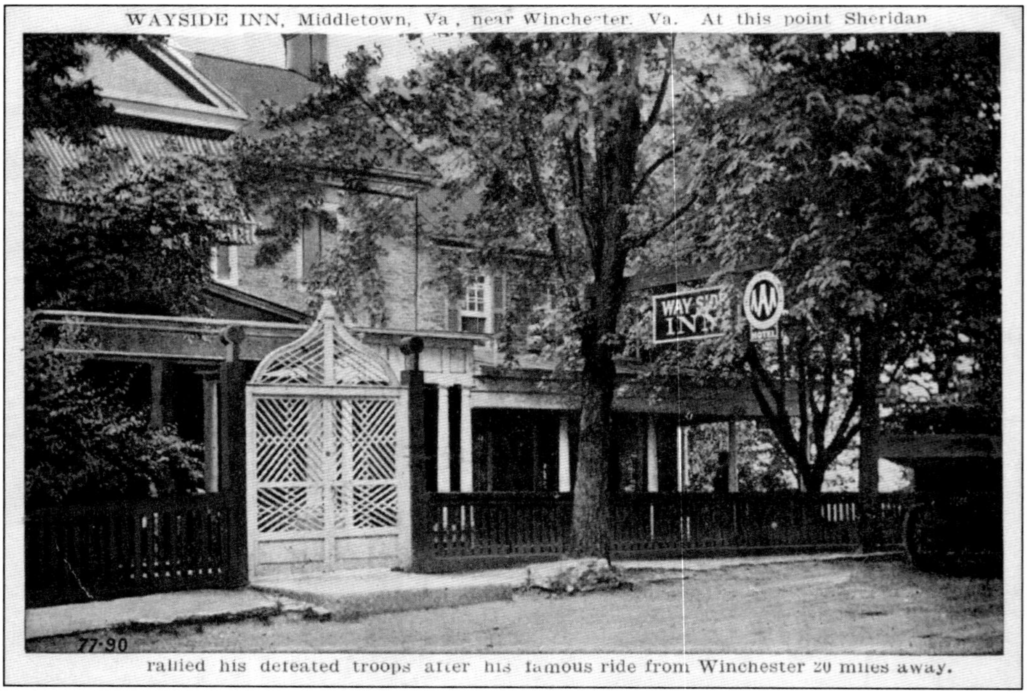

Also from the early 1900s, this is a great Main Street view of the Wayside Inn. The original center portion is seen behind the original gate through which Confederate generals the likes of Stonewall Jackson, Richard Ewell, John B. Gordon, and Jubal Early as well as Union generals Nathaniel P. Banks, John C. Fremont, Franz Sigel, David Hunter, and George Crook had passed a mere 50 years earlier. In the 1900s, the inn catered to the wealthy motoring class, with such guests as Henry Ford, Harvey Firestone, and the Rockefellers. (Joyce D. Tucker.)

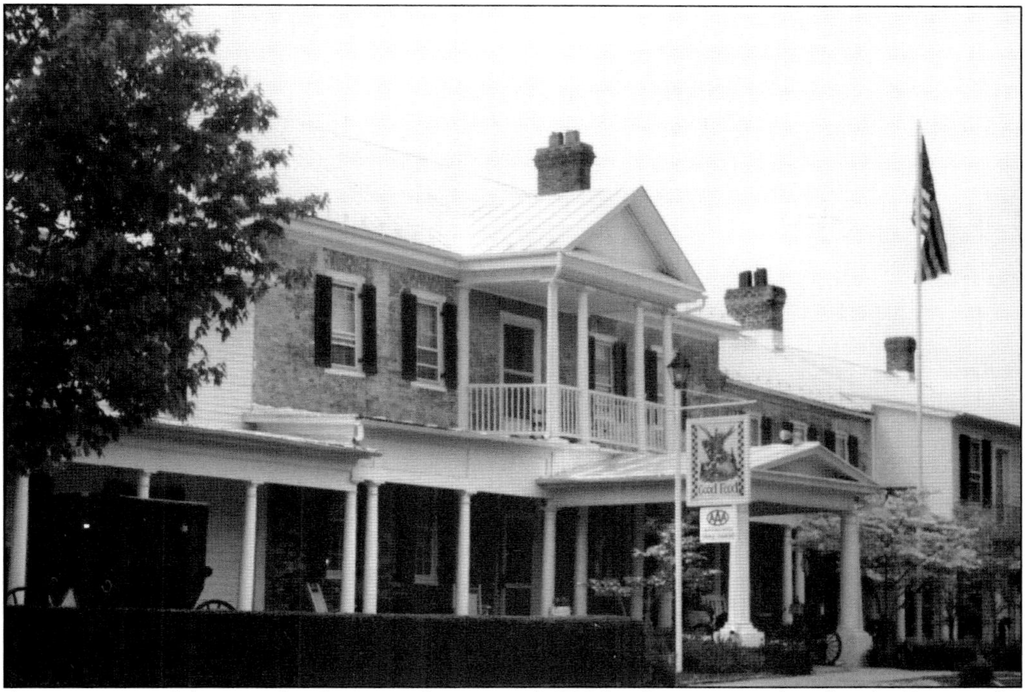

A street view of the inn clearly shows the original 1797 brick portions of its facade. During the 1960s, the inn was purchased by Leo Bernstein, who owned it until his death at 93 in 2008. In 2013, George and Becky Reeves bought the property, which has experienced a renaissance under their ownership. (Helen Lee Fletcher.)

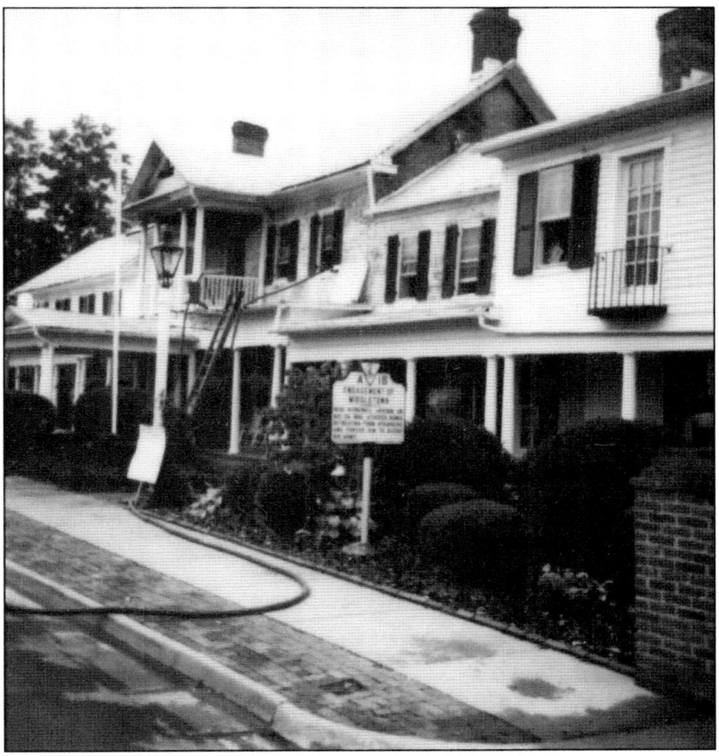

In 1985, a kitchen fire devastated the original portion of the inn, gutting it to only a shell. Leo Bernstein lovingly restored the ambiance of the old tavern by incorporating hand-hewn beams from other historic structures into the renovation. (Middletown Heritage Society.)

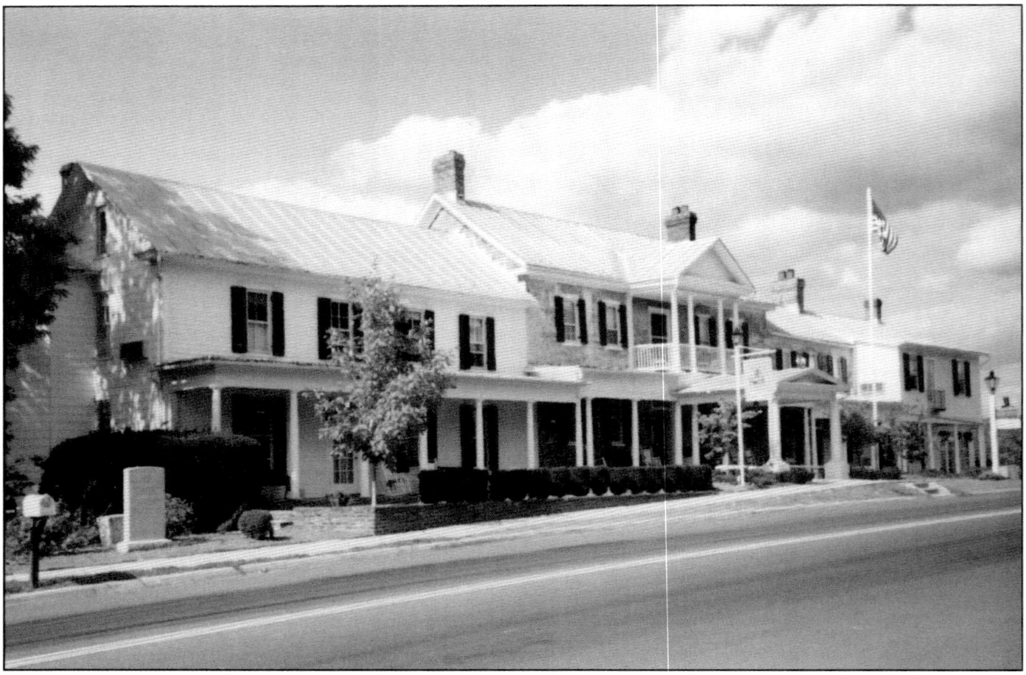

This picture was taken right after the fire restoration in the mid-1980s. At left is a historical marker in memory of Massachusetts colonel Charles Russell Lowell, who was killed leading a cavalry charge north of the inn during the Battle of Cedar Creek. It is possible that he was carried to the inn after his demise. (Helen Lee Fletcher.)

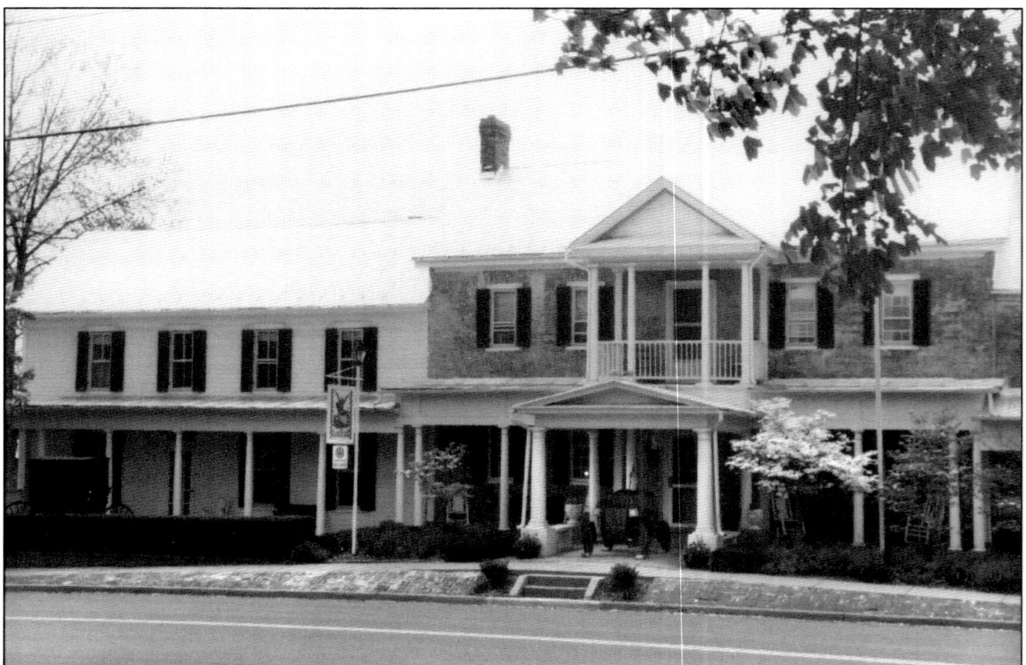

This is another street view of the Wayside Inn in which the buggy at left and a small car in front of the entrance honor its history from horses to horsepower. (Helen Lee Fletcher.)

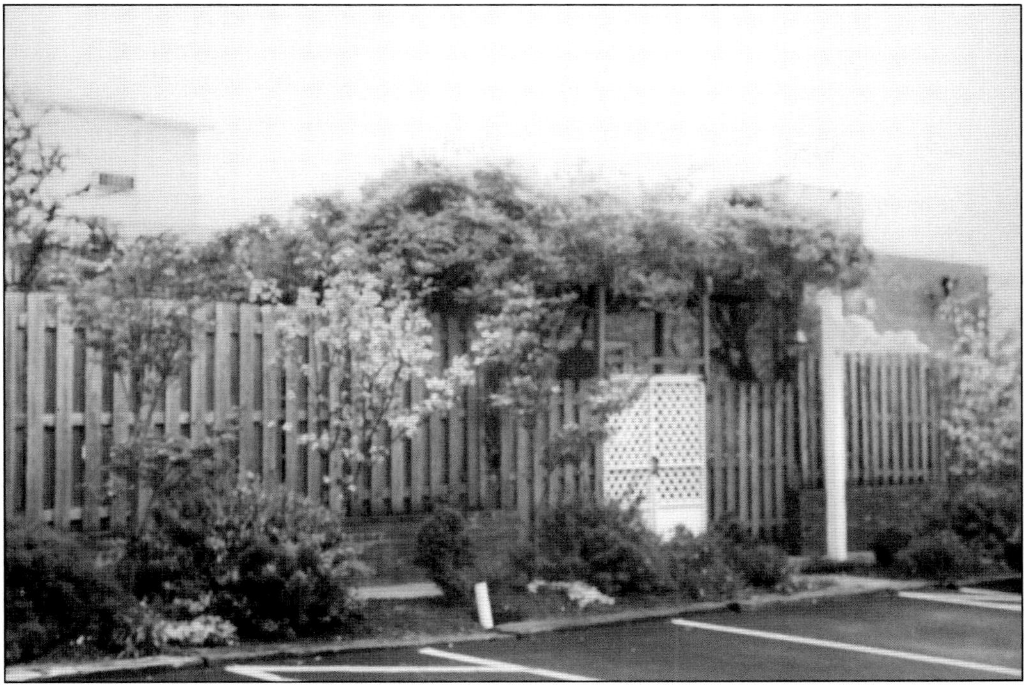

As seen in this view of the Wayside Inn's north side, a portion of the original gate is still in use at the bar entrance to the inn. Another section of the gate can be found inside as a decorative art piece. (Helen Lee Fletcher.)

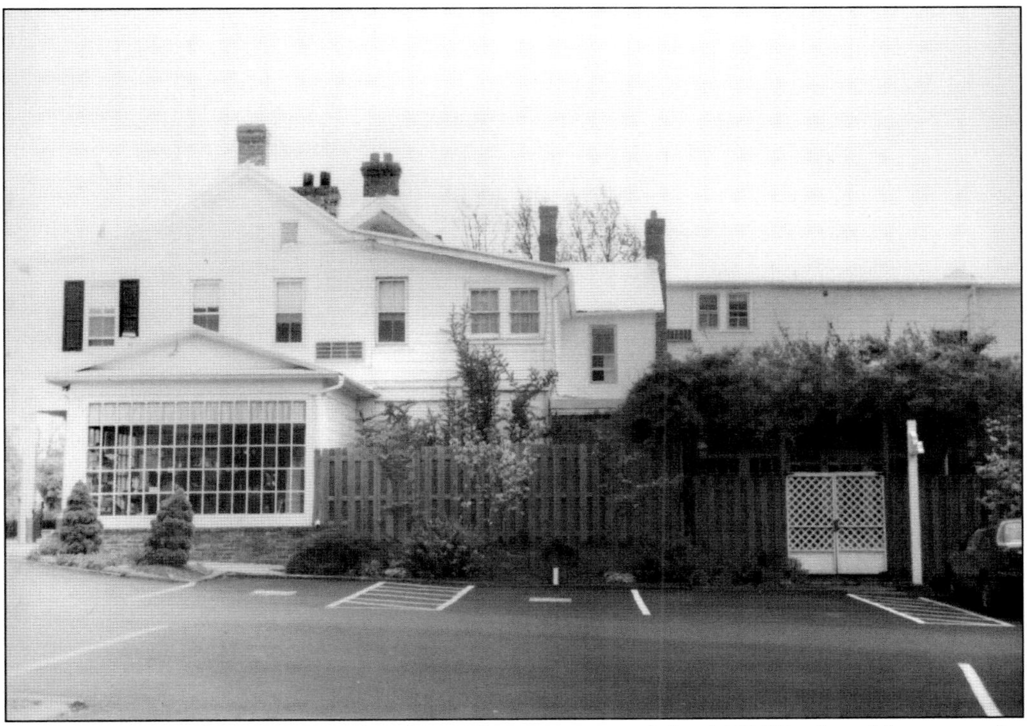

In another view of the inn's north side are the sunroom and the 1905 Rhodes additions to the structure. (Helen Lee Fletcher.)

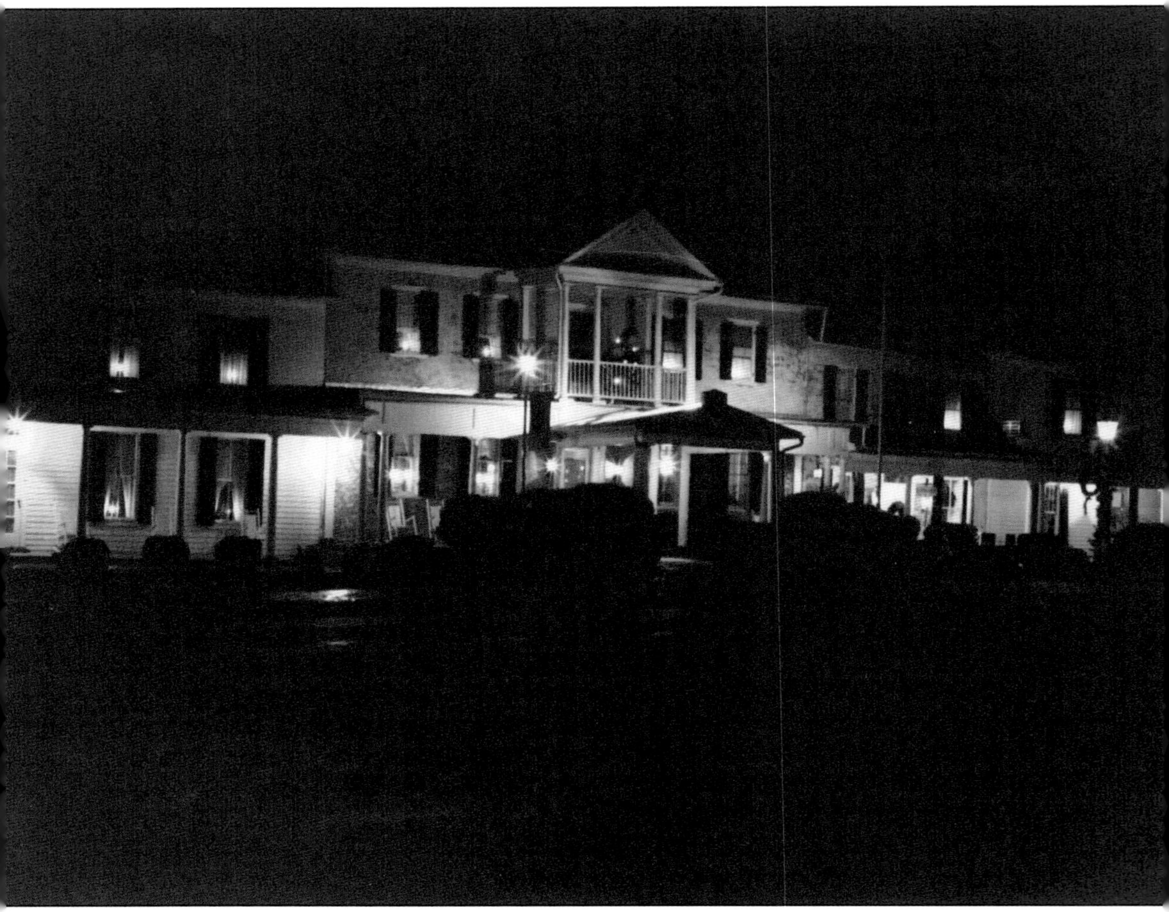

Note the gas lantern at right in this beautiful Christmastime photograph of the Wayside Inn. Middletown was one of the few small towns in the Shenandoah Valley to have gas lanterns. (Harold Gardenhour Jr.)

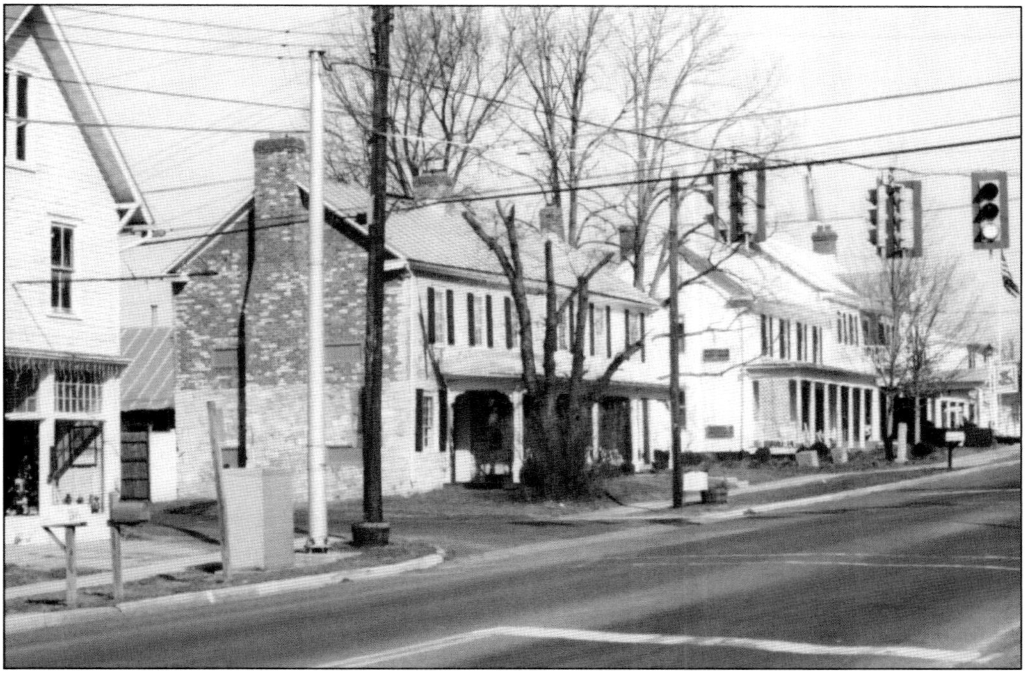

A street view shows the building known as Larrick's Tavern, as named by the Bernstein family. The Larricks, however, did not operate a tavern here, but they did purchase it in 1897. Around 1790, it was actually known as Baileys Retirement and served several purposes, one of which might have included a tavern. One of the reported uses of this building was a dry goods store. (Helen Lee Fletcher.)

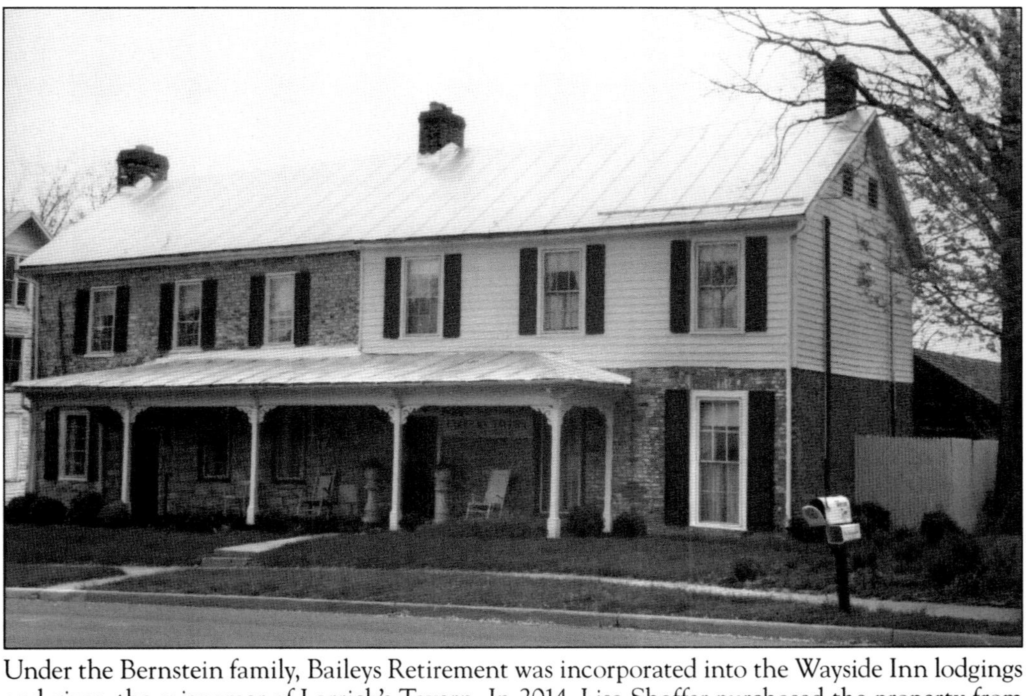

Under the Bernstein family, Baileys Retirement was incorporated into the Wayside Inn lodgings and given the misnomer of Larrick's Tavern. In 2014, Lisa Shaffer purchased the property from the Bernstein Foundation. (Helen Lee Fletcher.)

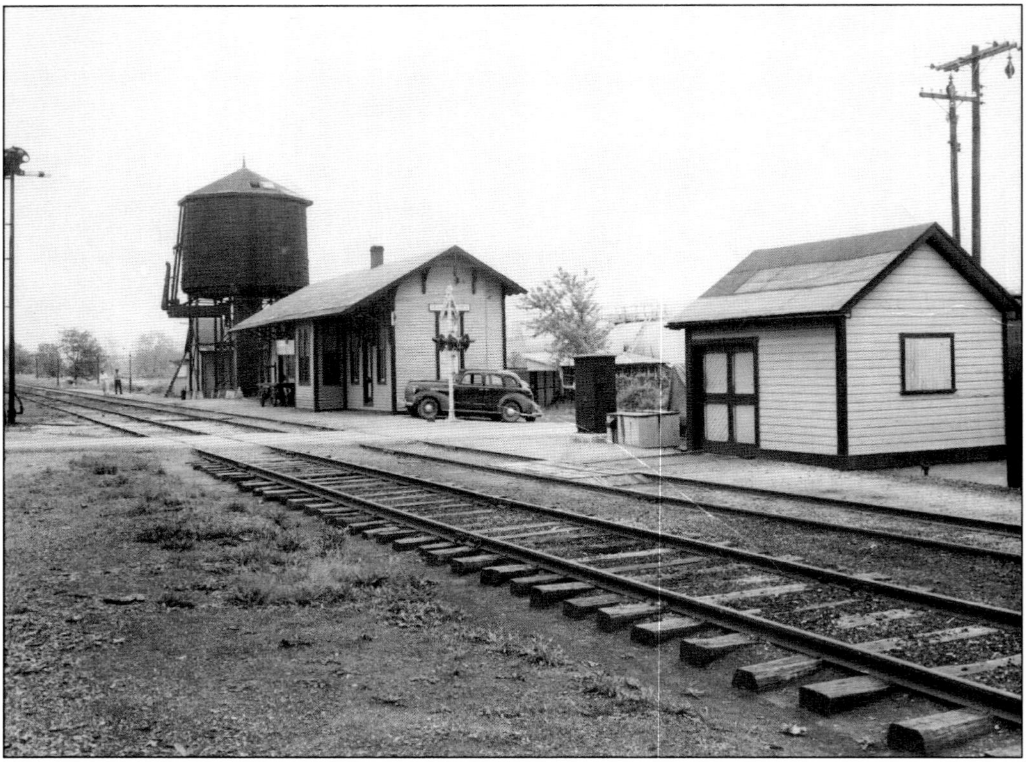

The Middletown train depot is seen here in the 1940s. Rail lines brought passengers from Baltimore and Washington, DC, to country excursions in the 1880s. Today, this freight line is important to local limestone mining industries west of town. (Harold Gardenhour Jr.)

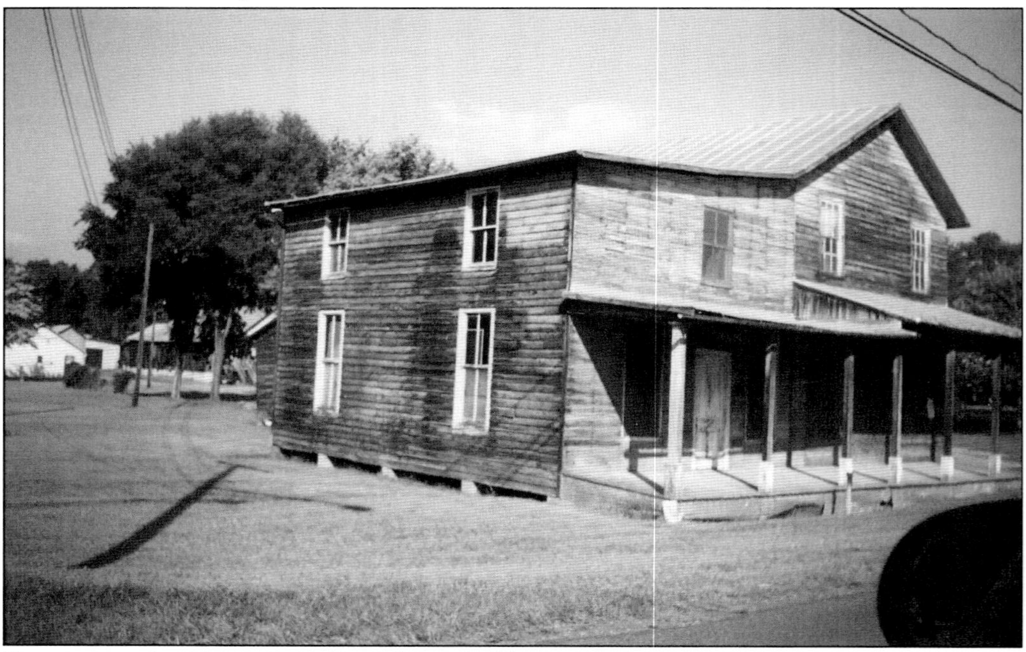

Here is an early-1900s store and warehouse building near the railroad tracks on First Street, west of Senseney Street. (Helen Lee Fletcher.)

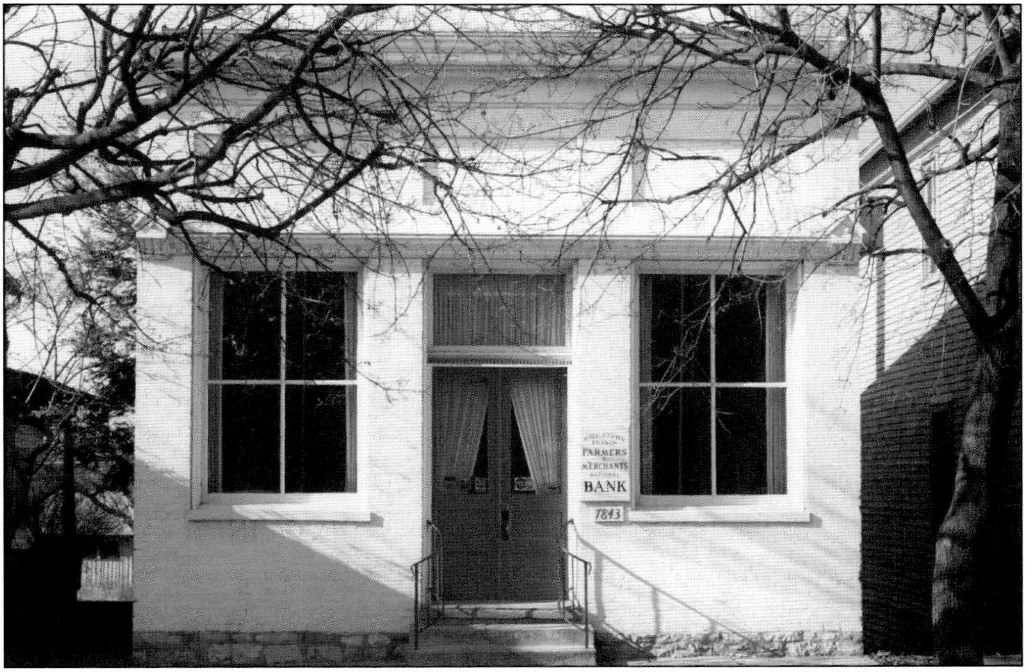

Constructed in 1908, the Middletown State Bank has the distinction of being one of the few institutions to remain open during the Great Depression of the 1930s. Purchased by the Farmers and Merchants Bank in 1967, this building remained an active bank until 1985, when Branch Bank & Trust bought the F&M bank and constructed a new structure on the corner of First and Main Streets. Since 1985, the old bank has been used as a number of restaurants and is now the Irish Isle Restaurant & Pub. (Harold Gardenhour Jr.)

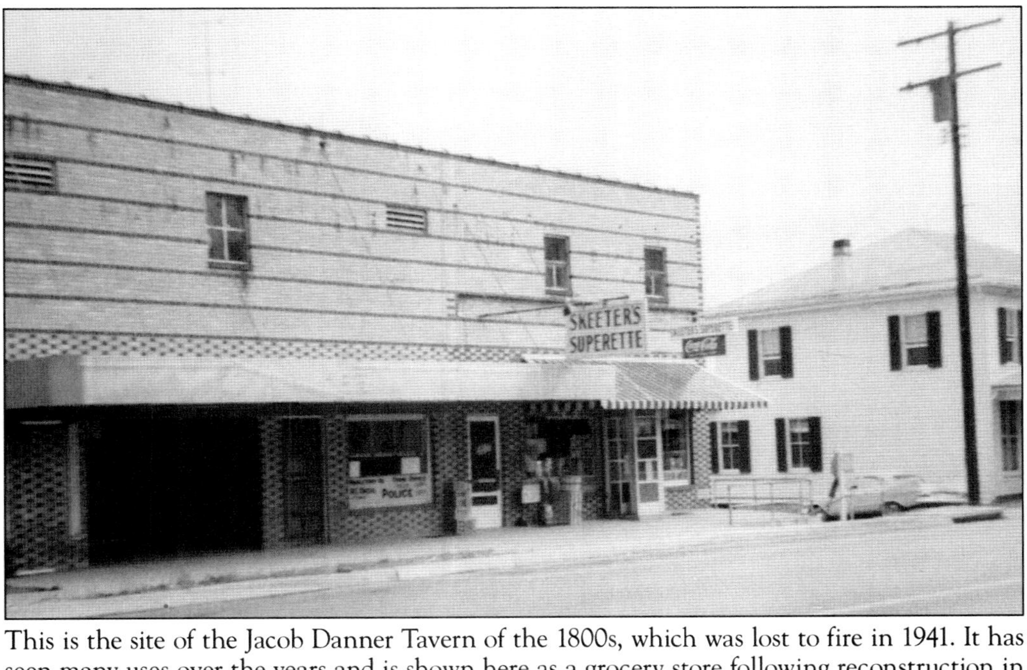

This is the site of the Jacob Danner Tavern of the 1800s, which was lost to fire in 1941. It has seen many uses over the years and is shown here as a grocery store following reconstruction in 1946. (Middletown Heritage Society.)

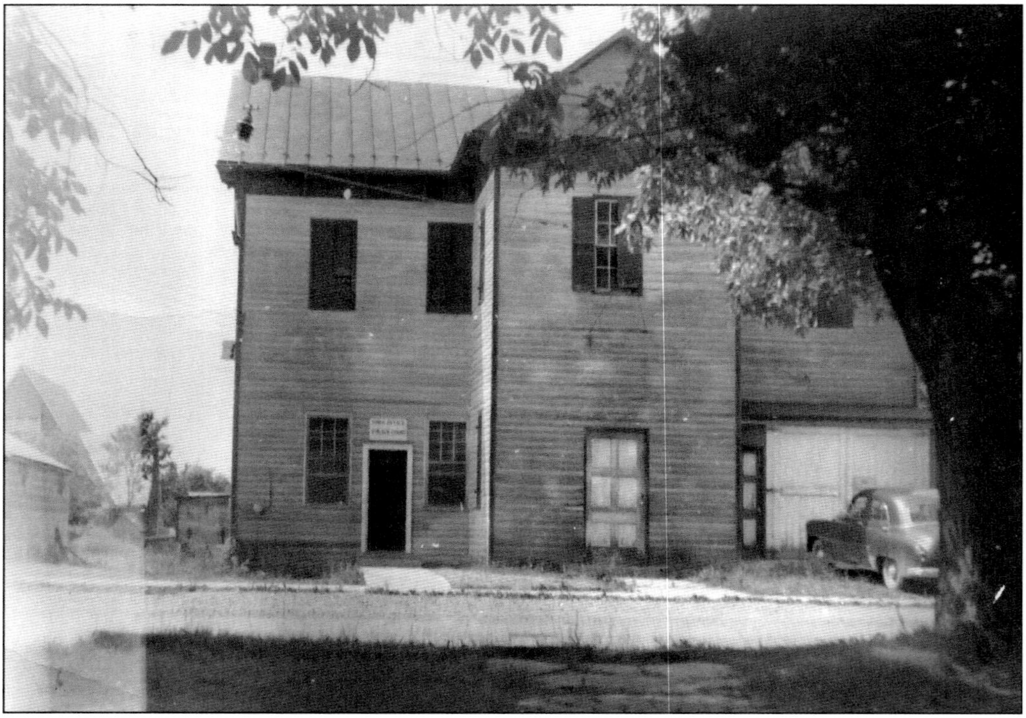

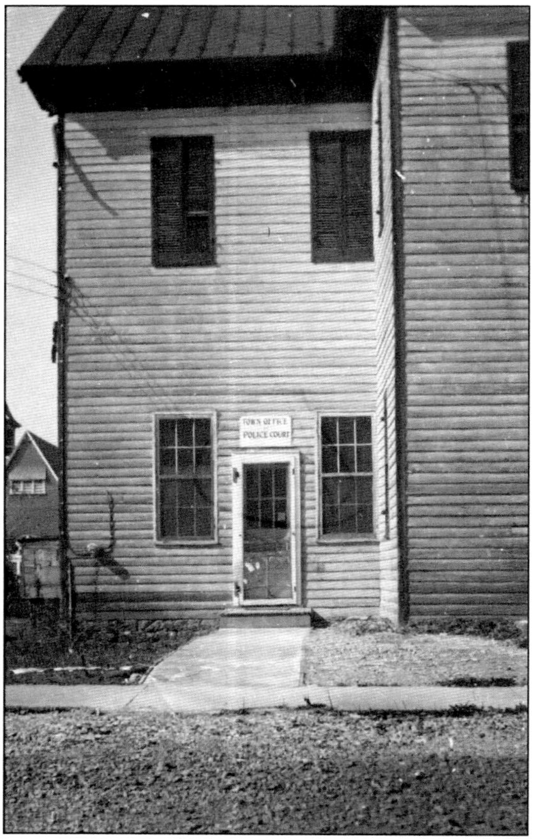

A c. 1800 log school and meetinghouse once stood at this site. This 1880s frame building was Middletown's first public school. Later, it was sold into joint ownership to the town and the Independent Order of Odd Fellows Lodge. This 1950s photograph depicts the building before much modernization occurred. The town offices were located on the first floor, and the lodge was on the second floor. The town assumed complete ownership in 1965. (Middletown Heritage Society.)

Another view of town hall from the mid-1900s shows the humble beginnings of town government. The name of the Independent Order of Odd Fellows, an English secret society that used the second floor, was derived from charitable men of the 1700s who donated money to worthwhile causes. Those who had witnessed these acts deemed these men as "odd fellows." The society grew in the New World, taking hold in many communities in Virginia. (Middletown Heritage Society.)

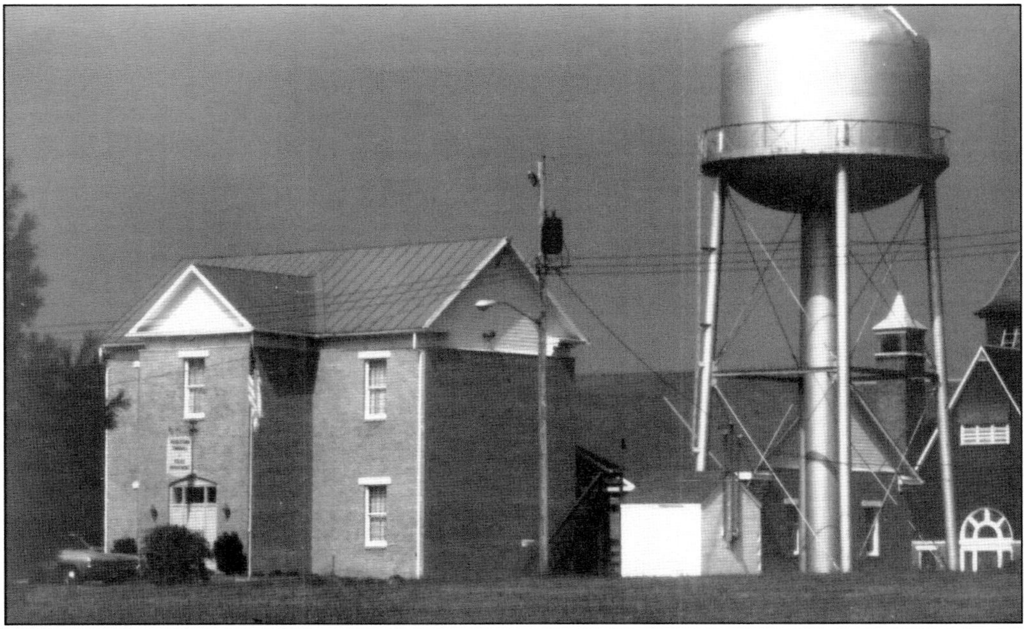

The town office is pictured after the brick veneer was added in 1978. Today, the building looks similar, although the water tower no longer remains. Grace United Methodist Church can be seen at right in this view. (Middletown Heritage Society.)

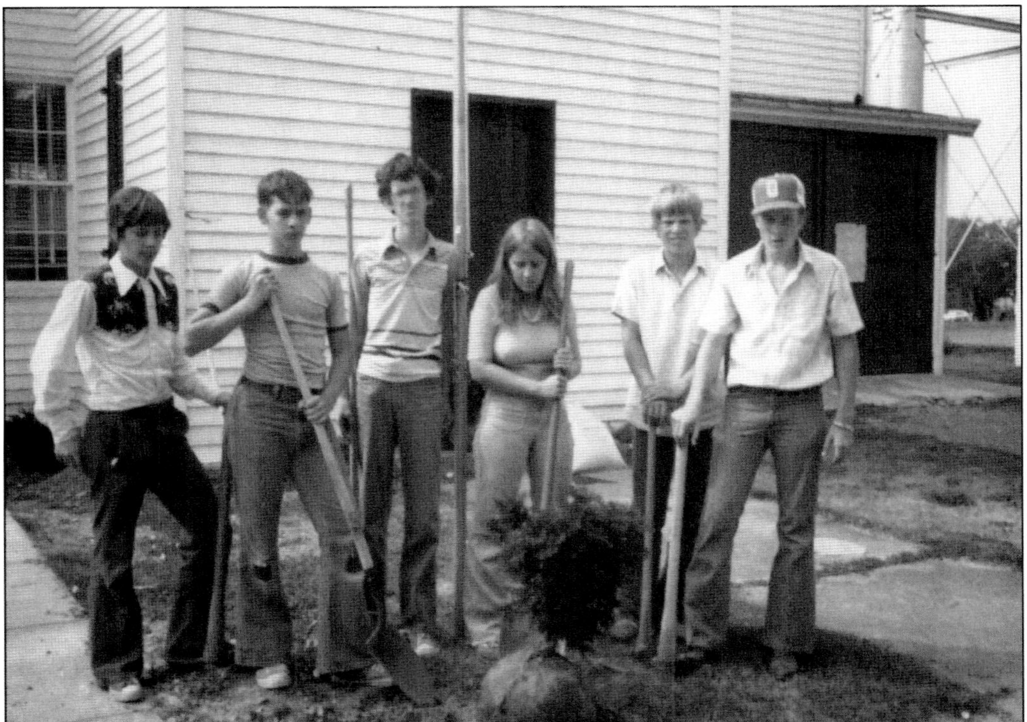

A group of unidentified young people is shown working on the landscaping at town hall in the 1970s. The building in this photograph was improved with the addition of plumbing after 1965. (Middletown Heritage Society.)

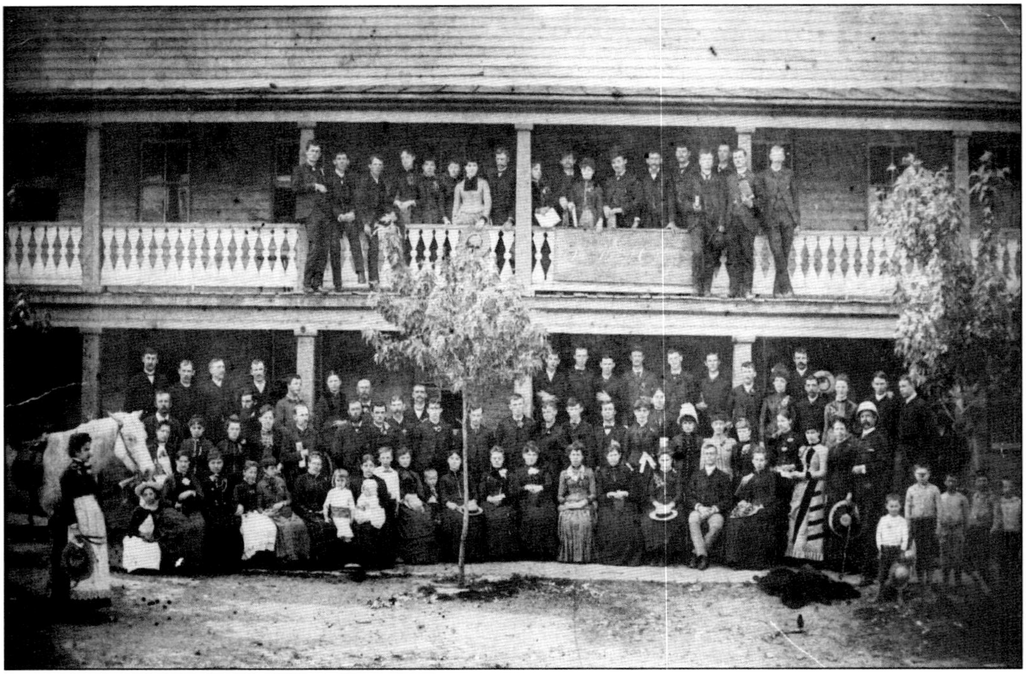

This 1887 photograph of Shenandoah Normal College students was taken at the corner of Main and Second Streets. Later, the school was moved to Reliance, Virginia. Note the picture includes children and animals in addition to the students and instructors of the college. (Stewart Bell Jr. Archives.)

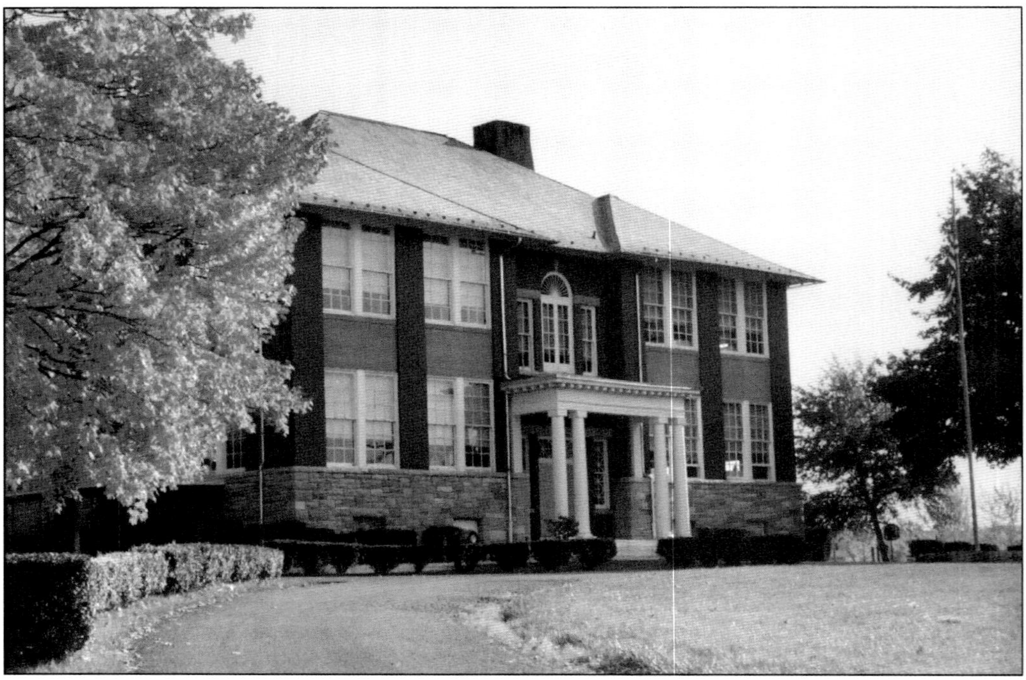

In August 1908, George Wallace sold 12 acres of land on Route 11 for $1,500 for the site of a new school. Work on the school began in the fall of 1908, and the Middletown Agricultural High School was opened on October 4, 1909. This institution was Virginia's first agricultural high school and the first high school in Frederick County. (Harold Gardenhour Jr.)

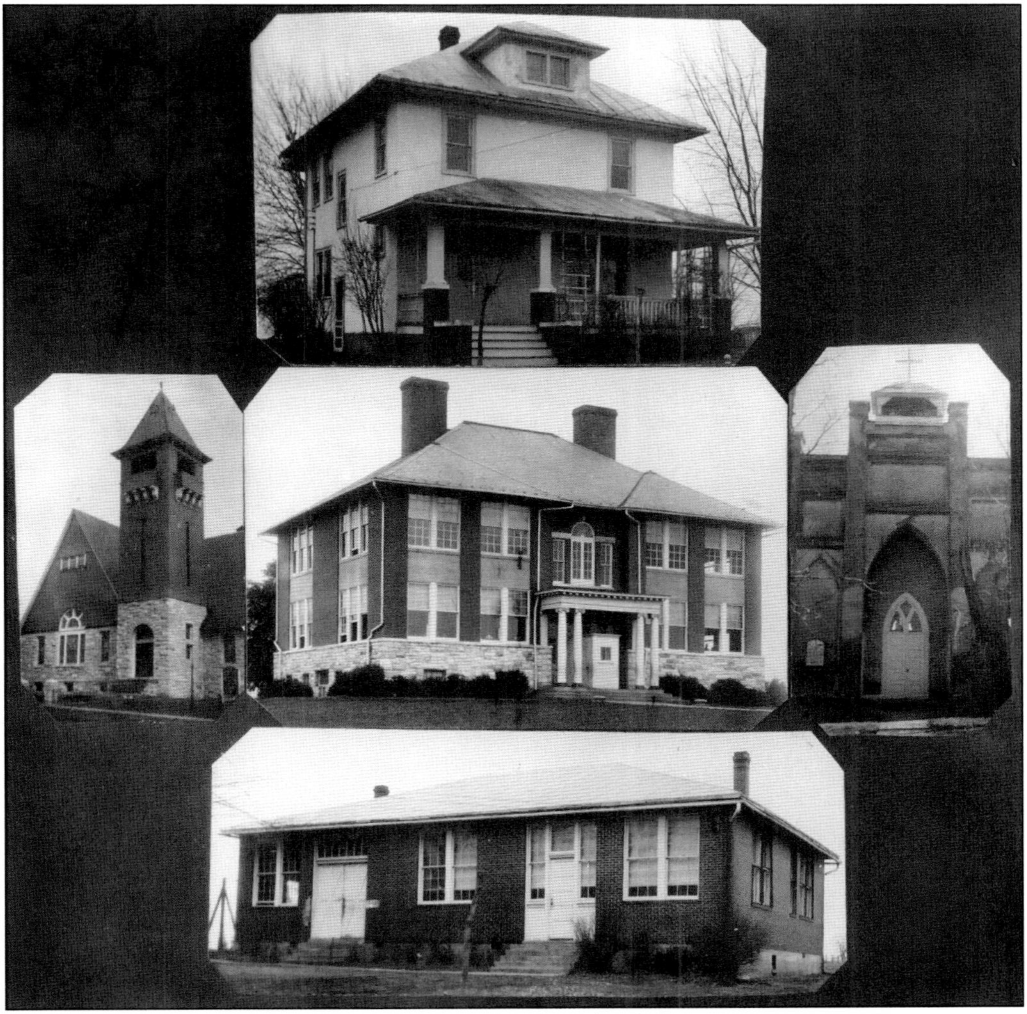

A collage from the 1942 Middletown High School yearbook features prominent places in town: (left to right from top) the principal's house, Grace United Methodist Church, Middletown High School, St. Thomas Chapel, and the home economics and agriculture building of the school. (Middletown Heritage Society.)

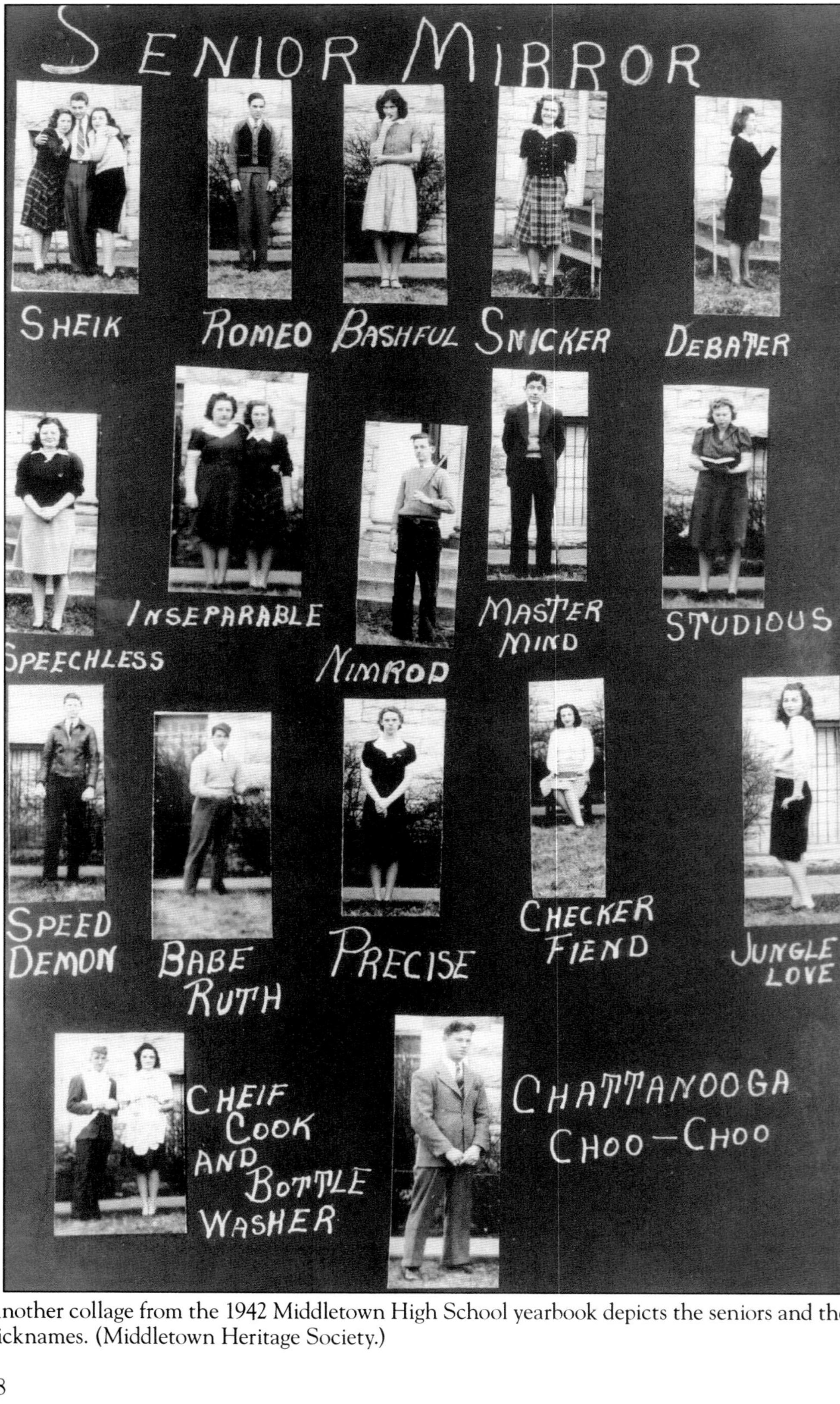

Another collage from the 1942 Middletown High School yearbook depicts the seniors and their nicknames. (Middletown Heritage Society.)

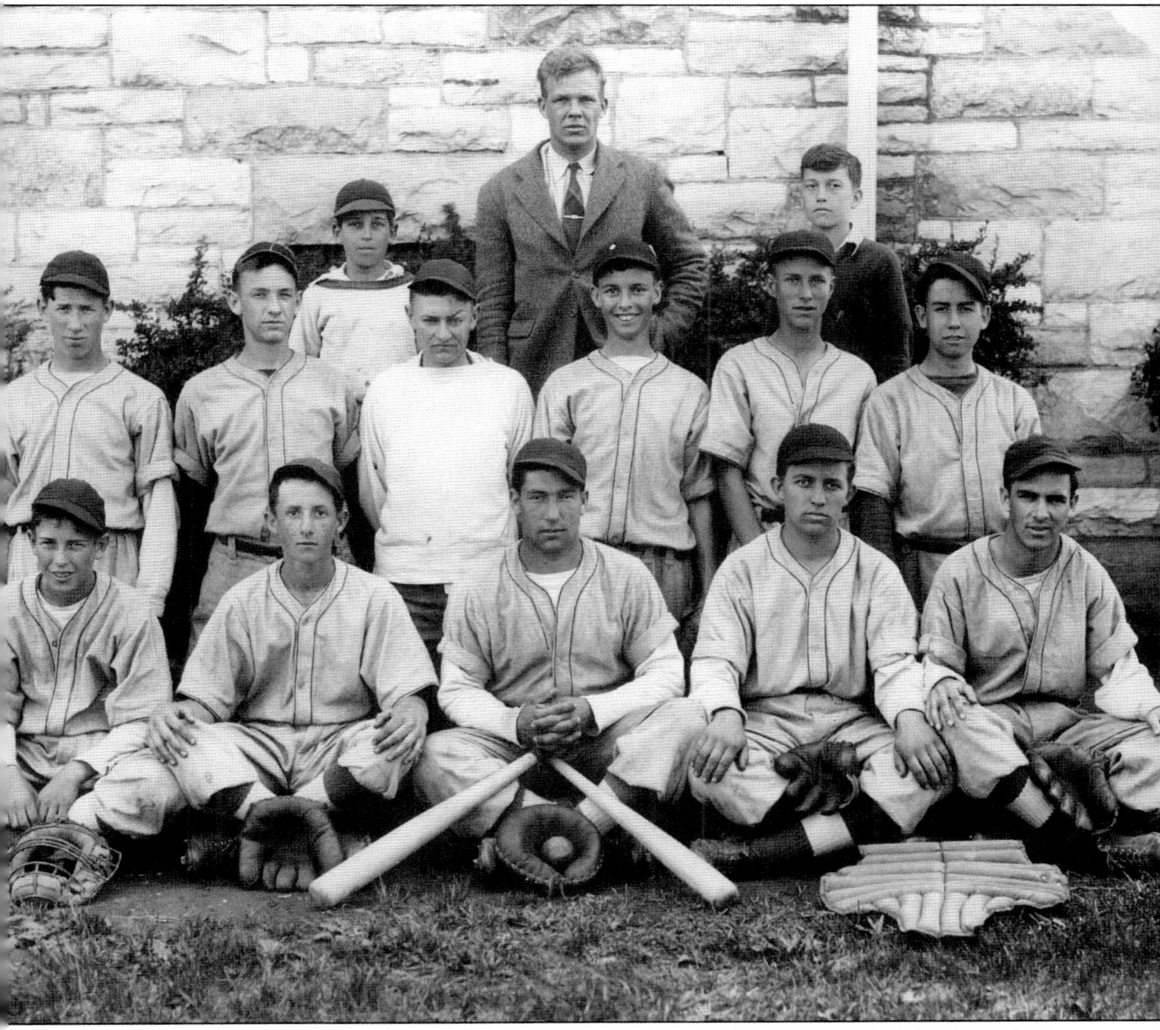

In addition to serving as vice principal, Coach Kurlinski led the Middletown High School baseball team in 1942. The Middletown team was notable for their fighting spirit, good sportsmanship, and most important, their winning record, picking up big wins against the larger towns of Stephens City, Woodstock, Clearbrook, and Berryville. Their hard work paid off with a championship win that year, along with a few more throughout the decade. (Middletown Heritage Society.)

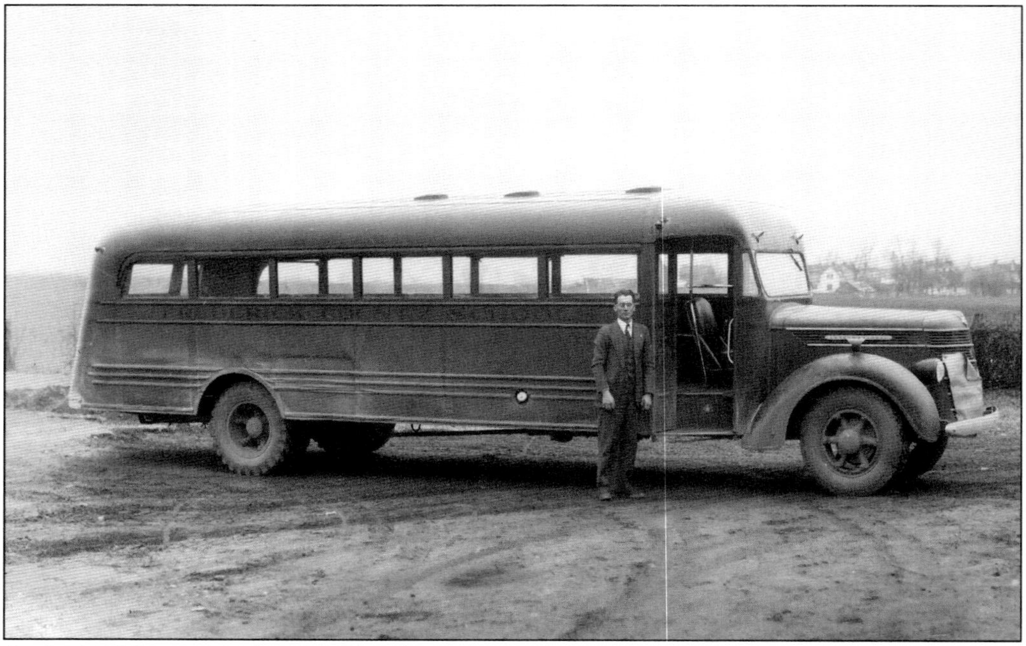

As the Middletown High School bus driver, a Mr. Shiley logged many miles to bring the children from the countryside into town. The school bus was in its third year of service at this time. (Middletown Heritage Society.)

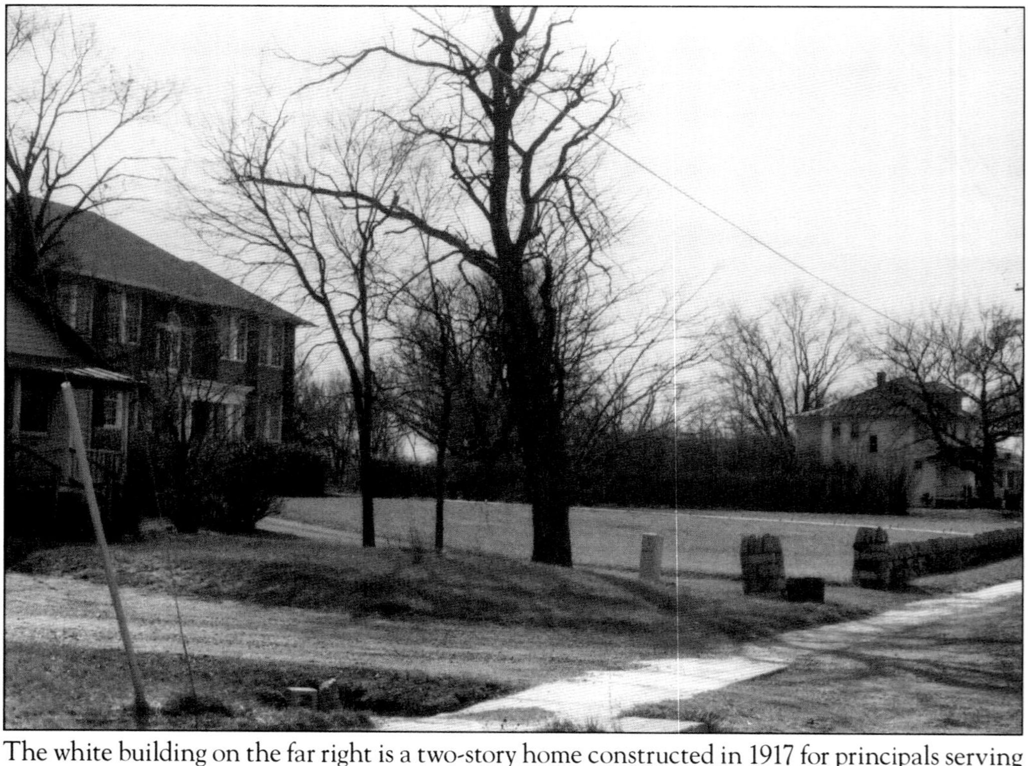

The white building on the far right is a two-story home constructed in 1917 for principals serving the school. Principal Dewayne Raines (1969–1973) credits the principal's house as the first thing he remembered from his tenure at Middletown. (Helen Lee Fletcher.)

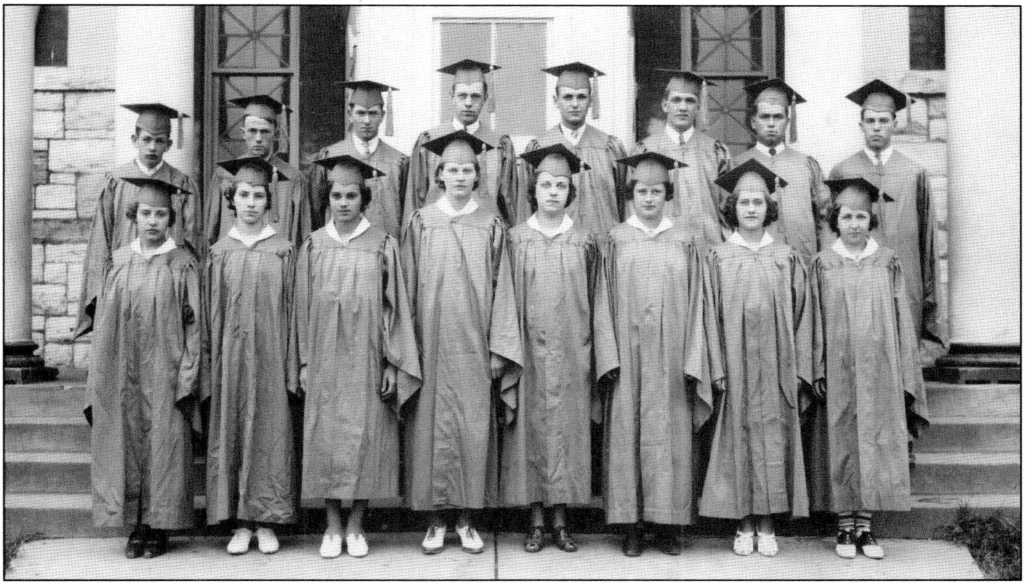

Members of the Middletown High School class of 1938 are, from left to right, (first row) Ellen Brumback, Edna Brumback, Rebecca Keeler, Marie Petty, Elaine Sperry, Anna Virginia Campbell, Janey Willey, and Alice Manuel; (second row) Maurice Boyer, John Weirich, Julian Boyer, Harry Matthews, Donald Borden, Randolph Larrick, Bob Brumback, and John Painter. (Middletown Heritage Society.)

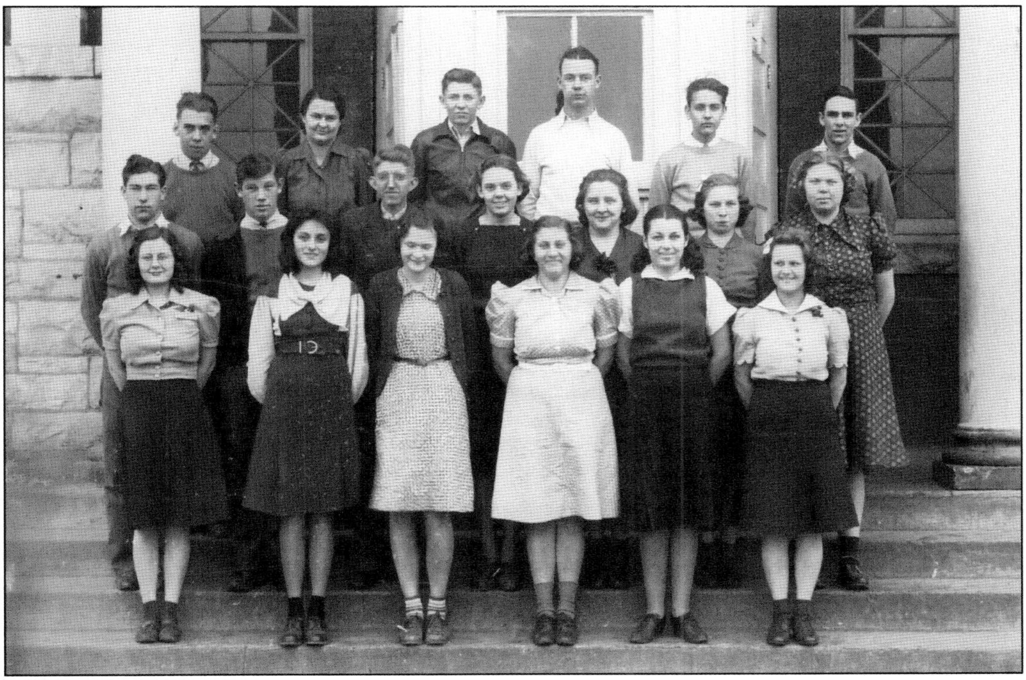

The Middletown High School class of 1942 is pictured here. As stated in an issue of the *Middletown Mirror* on May 26, 1909, "About two thousand people traveled by bicycle, foot, buggy, carriage, rail and automobile to witness the laying of the school's cornerstone." Roland M. Ward, senator, and Willey M. Hayes, assistant secretary of the US Department of Agriculture, addressed the crowd when the cornerstone was laid. (Middletown Heritage Society.)

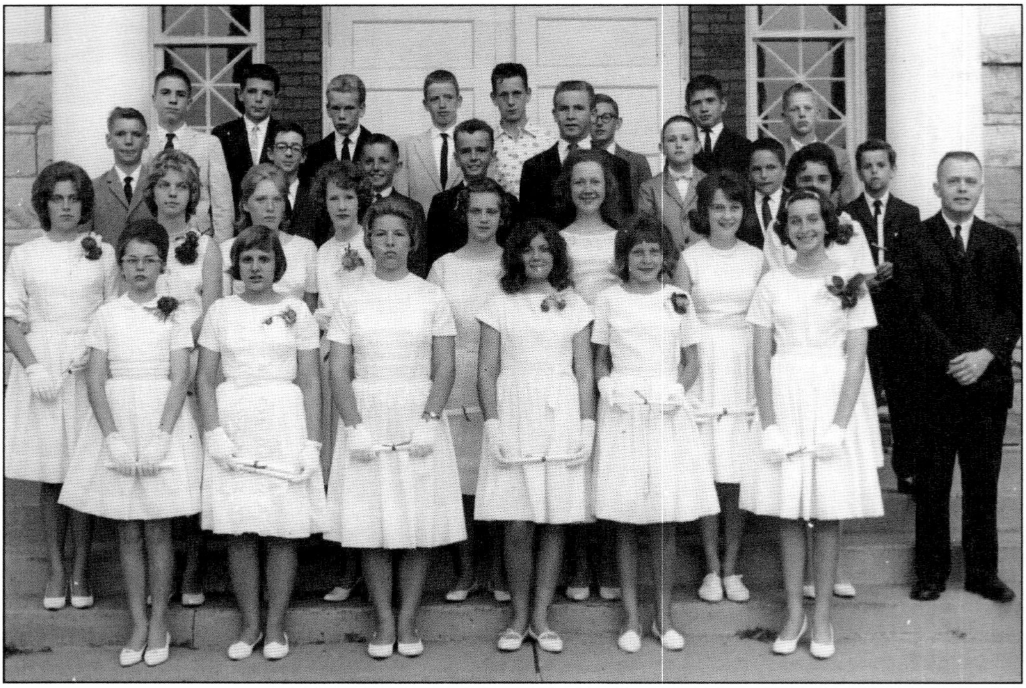

The graduating class of 1959–1960 is pictured here in front of Middletown High School. (Mary Lou Koontz.)

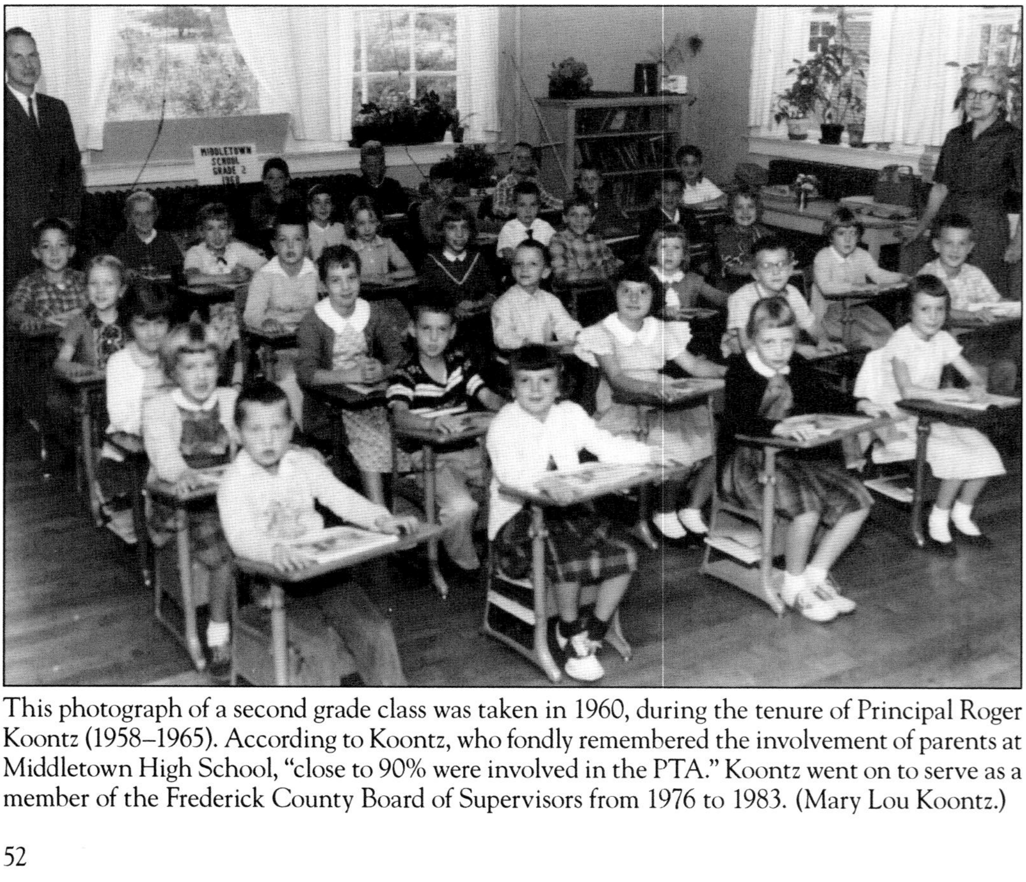

This photograph of a second grade class was taken in 1960, during the tenure of Principal Roger Koontz (1958–1965). According to Koontz, who fondly remembered the involvement of parents at Middletown High School, "close to 90% were involved in the PTA." Koontz went on to serve as a member of the Frederick County Board of Supervisors from 1976 to 1983. (Mary Lou Koontz.)

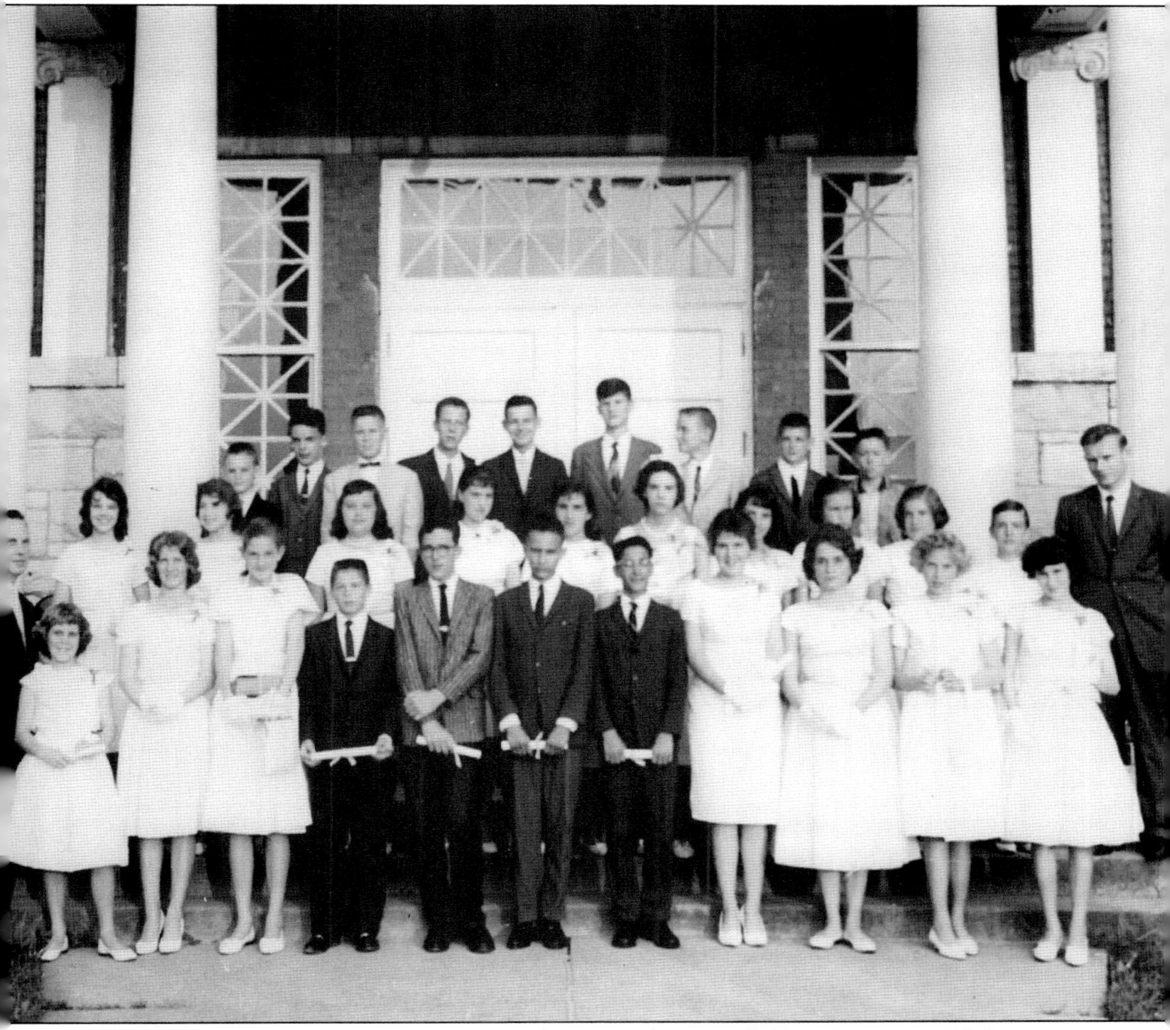

The graduating class of 1960–1961 is pictured with Principal Koontz (left) and instructor Holtzman Frazier (right). Future Middletown mayor Ray Steele (1988–1992) is seen in the first row, fifth from left. (Mary Lou Koontz.)

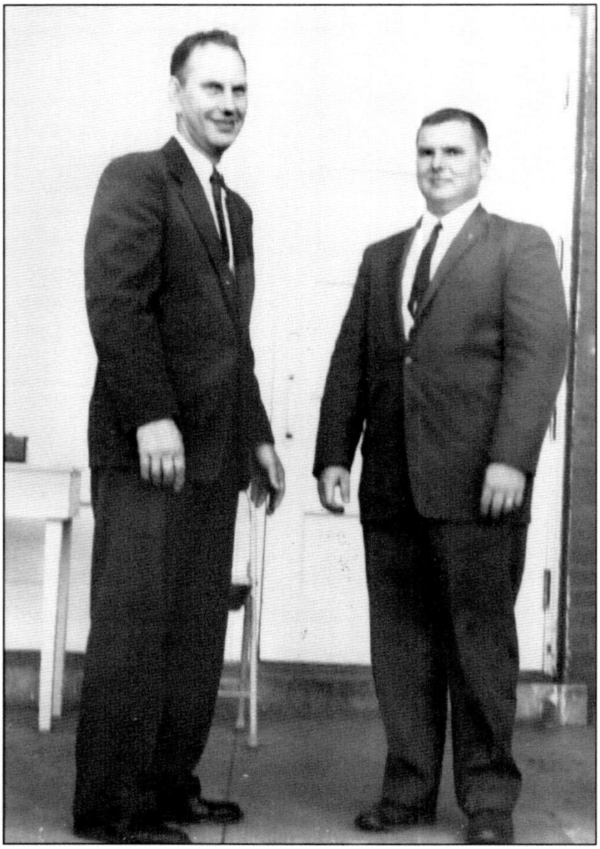

Principal Koontz and Middletown mayor Gene Dicks are pictured here in the early 1960s. (Mary Lou Koontz.)

Teachers and administrators pose for a picture in October 1960. (Mary Lou Koontz.)

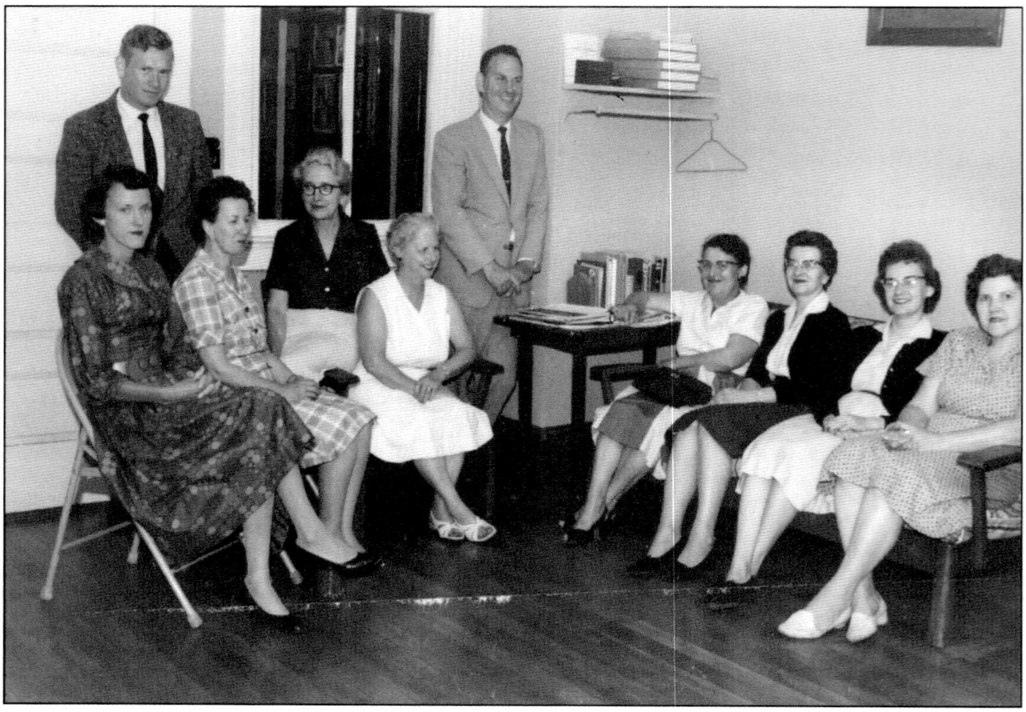

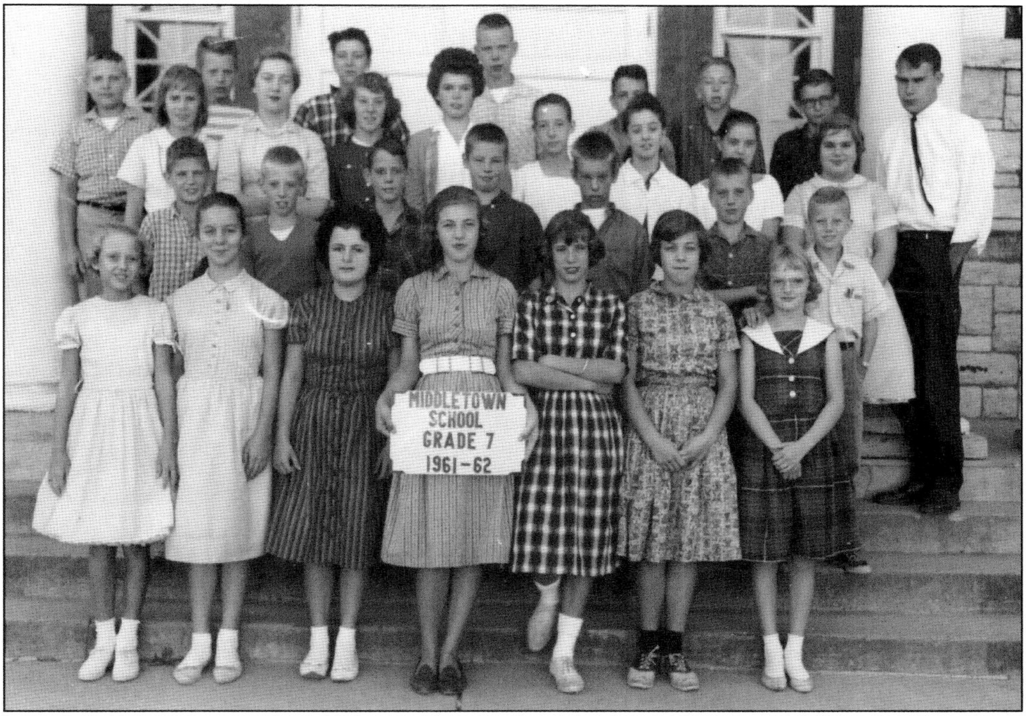

Here is the seventh grade class of Middletown High School in 1961–1962. (Mary Lou Koontz.)

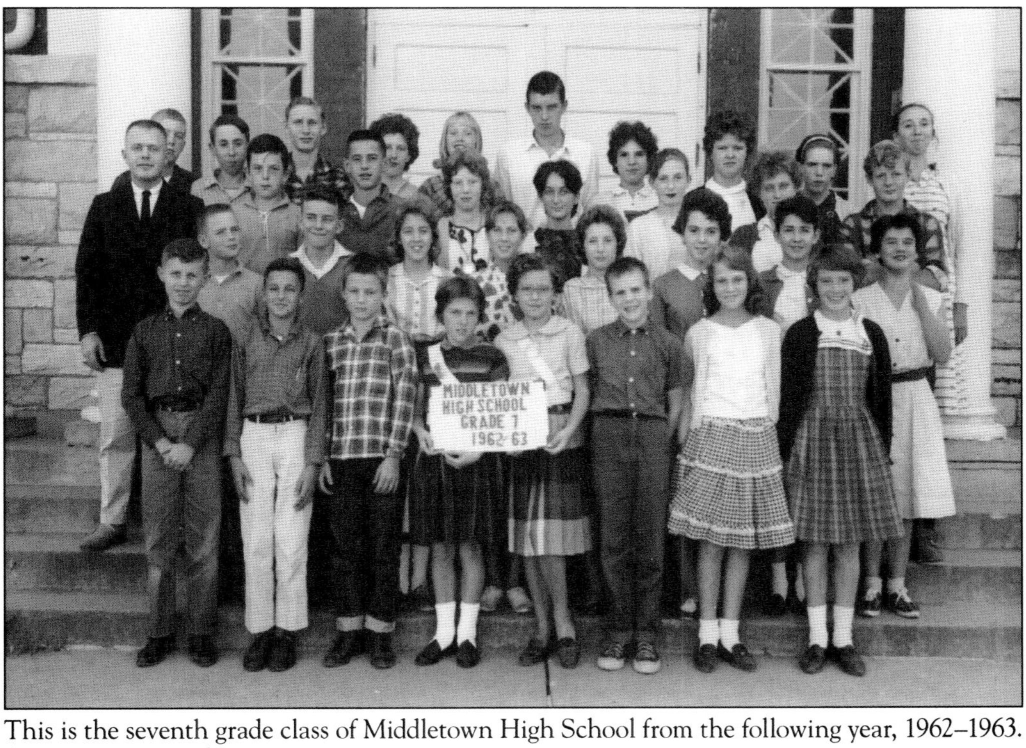

This is the seventh grade class of Middletown High School from the following year, 1962–1963. (Mary Lou Koontz.)

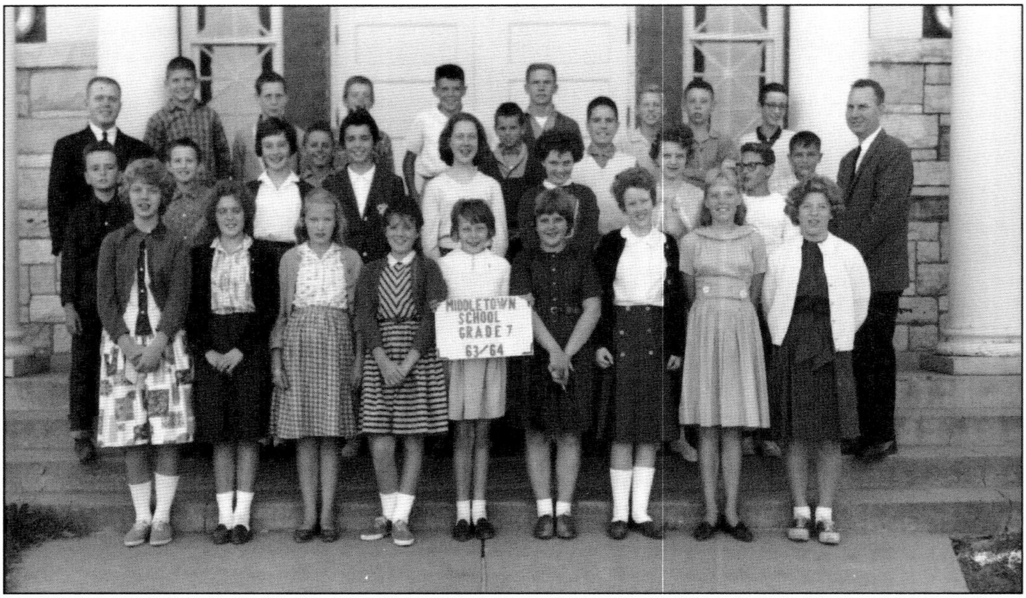

The 1963–1964 seventh grade class of Middletown High School is pictured here in front of the school. (Mary Lou Koontz.)

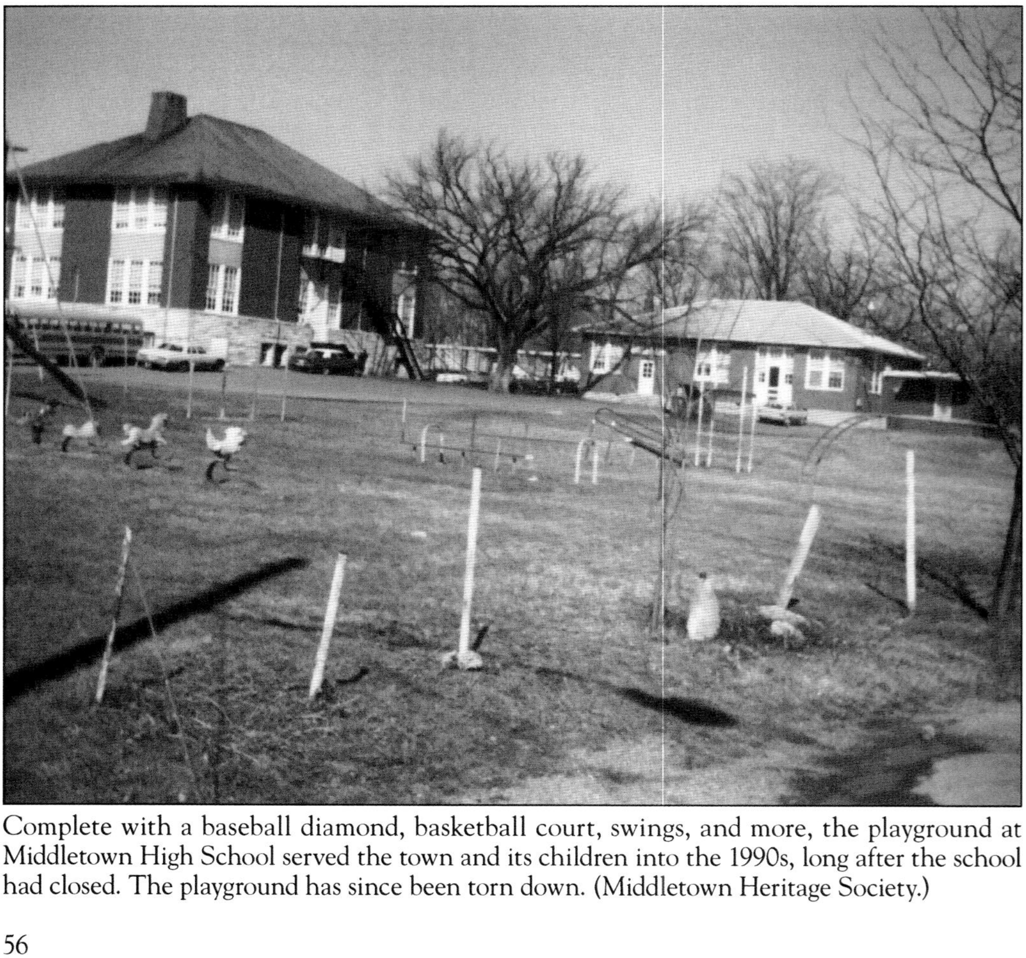

Complete with a baseball diamond, basketball court, swings, and more, the playground at Middletown High School served the town and its children into the 1990s, long after the school had closed. The playground has since been torn down. (Middletown Heritage Society.)

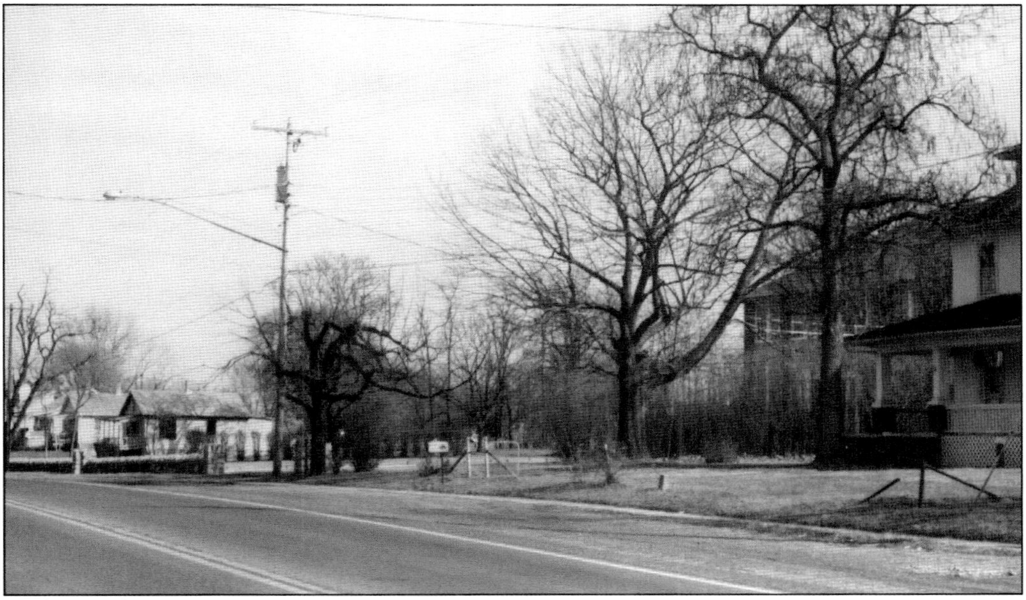

The row houses seen in this view north of Middletown High School have been demolished. (Helen Lee Fletcher.)

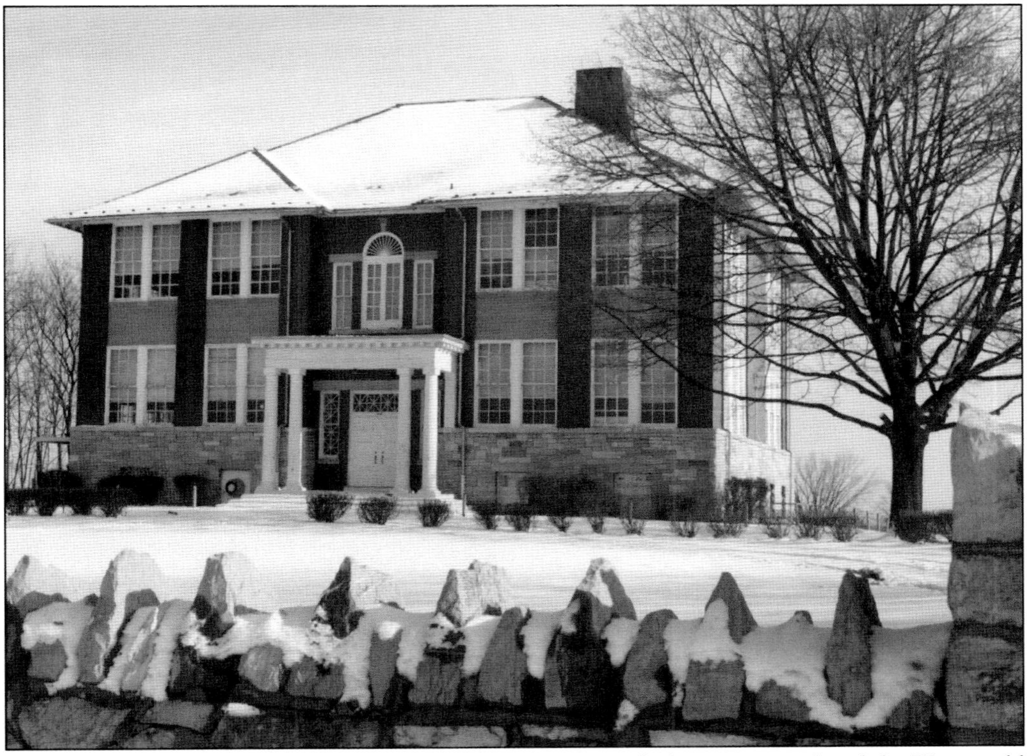

Despite many pleas and petitions, the Frederick County Board of Supervisors closed the 75-year-old school by a four-to-one vote in 1984, citing inefficiency. At the time, it was the oldest school still in operation in the county. The new Middletown Elementary School would open a few years later on Valley Pike. The old schoolhouse and the principal's house are now private residences. (Harold Gardenhour Jr.)

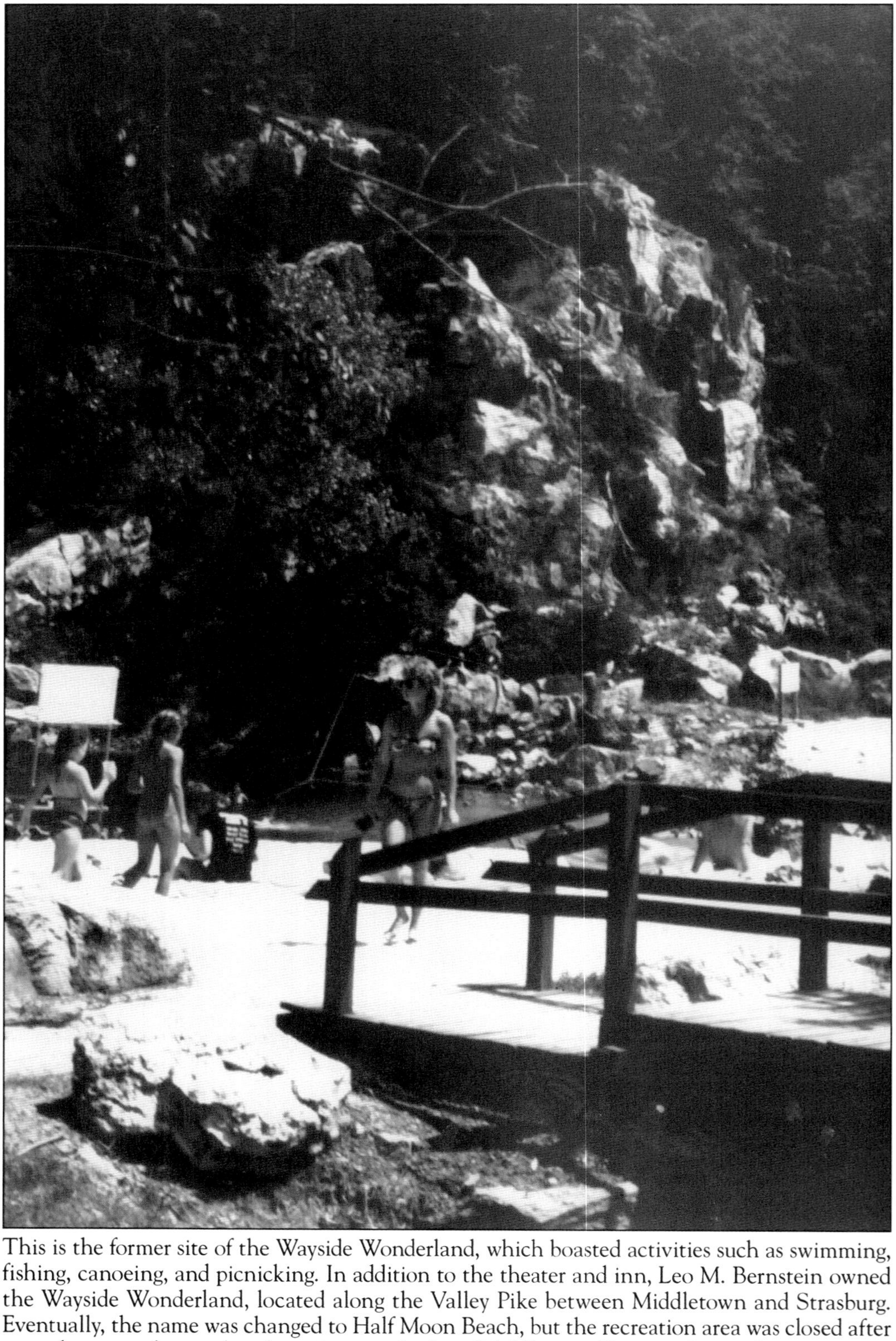

This is the former site of the Wayside Wonderland, which boasted activities such as swimming, fishing, canoeing, and picnicking. In addition to the theater and inn, Leo M. Bernstein owned the Wayside Wonderland, located along the Valley Pike between Middletown and Strasburg. Eventually, the name was changed to Half Moon Beach, but the recreation area was closed after several patrons drowned at the swimming facility. (Middletown Heritage Society.)

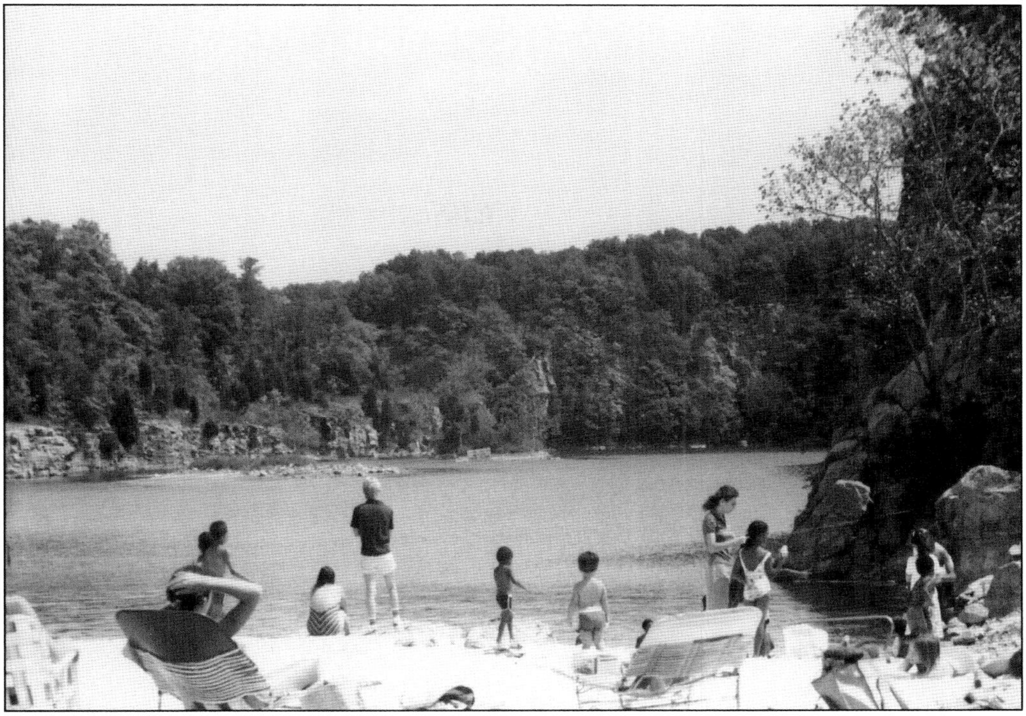

Tons of sand was brought in to create Half Moon Beach, making it a popular tourist destination, as seen in this summertime picture of the former quarry. (Middletown Heritage Society.)

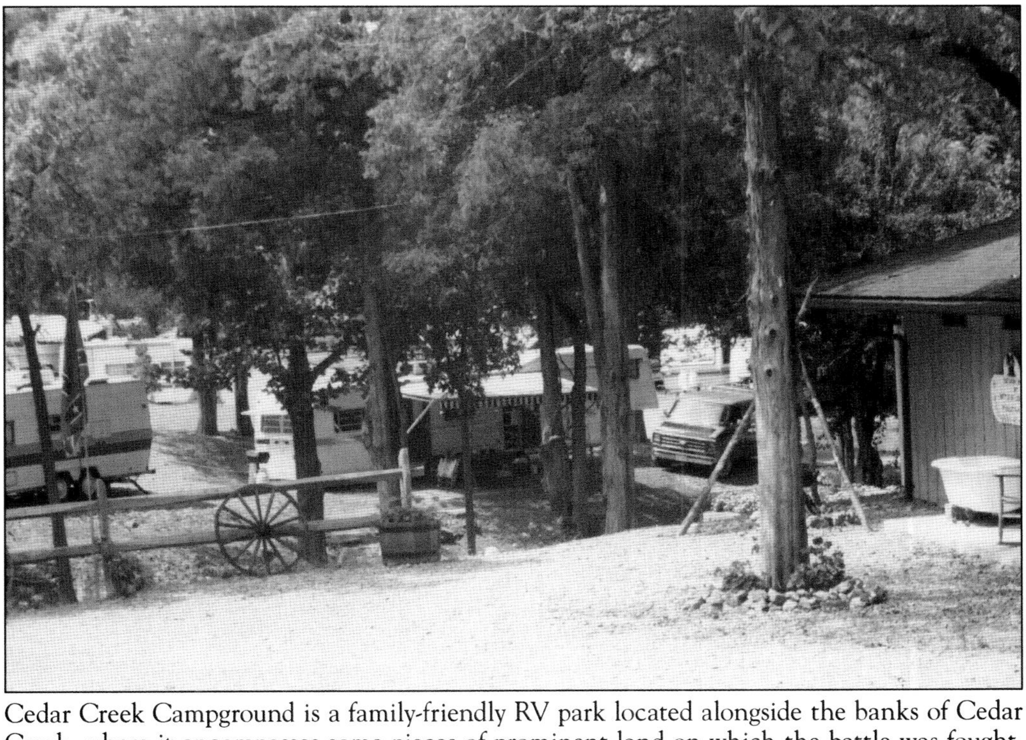

Cedar Creek Campground is a family-friendly RV park located alongside the banks of Cedar Creek, where it encompasses some pieces of prominent land on which the battle was fought. (Middletown Heritage Society.)

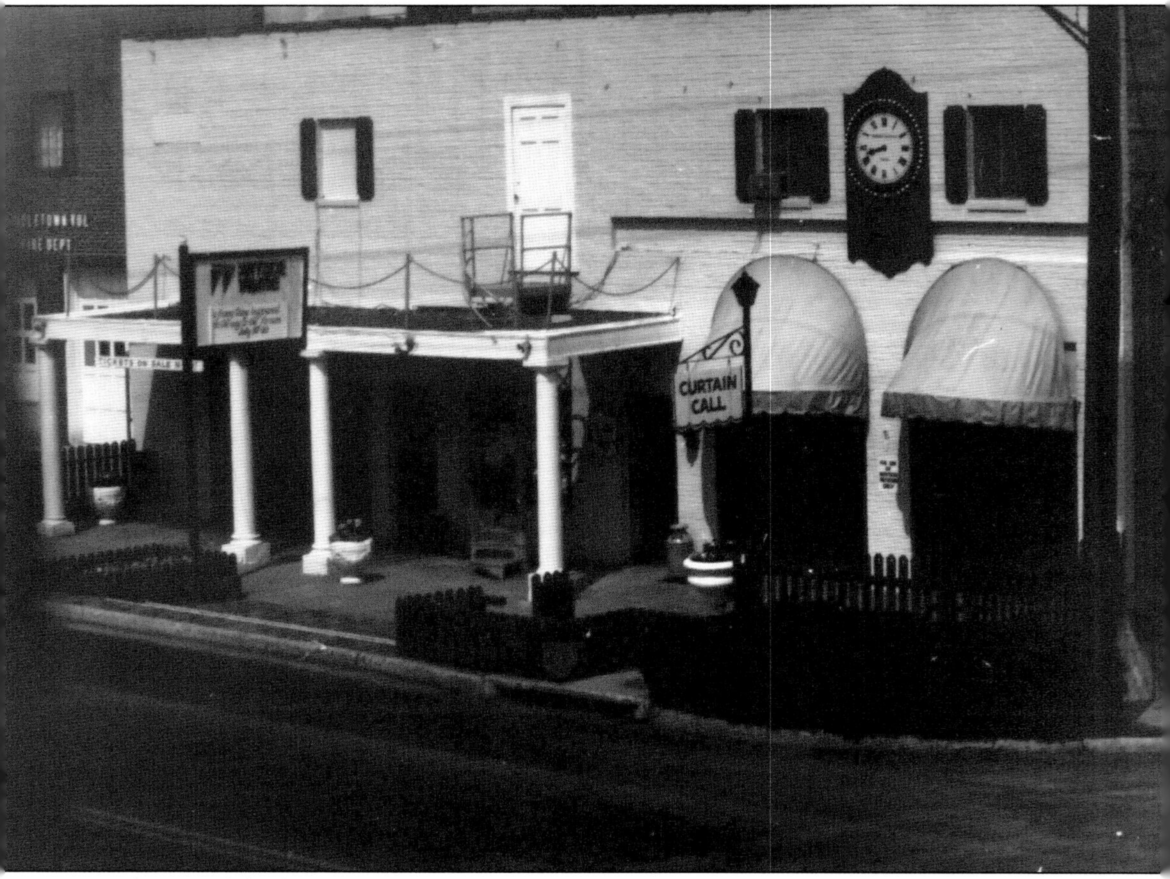

The site of this building has had a rich and colorful history on the corner of Main and Second Streets. The property first belonged to John Campbell in 1797. Ownership then transferred to Jacob Danner, who operated a store and hotel until 1903. In addition to the Shenandoah Normal College, it has housed a variety of establishments, including a town hall, jail, barbershop, dry cleaner, Middletown Movie Theatre, and Wayside Theatre (pictured). (Middletown Heritage Society.)

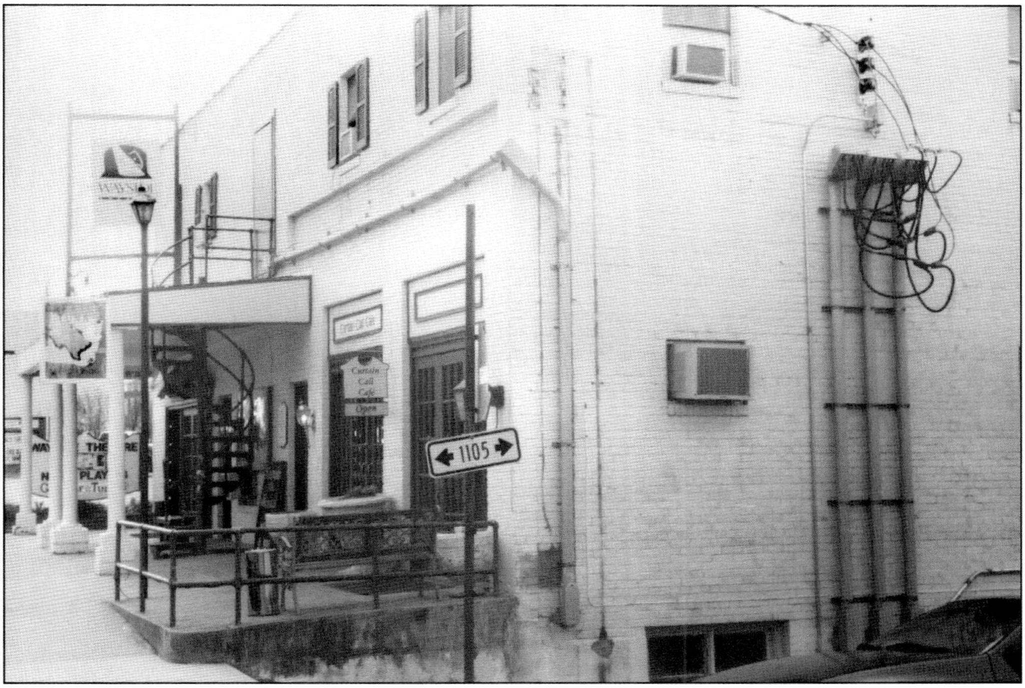

Shenandoah Gas donated the gaslight on the northeast corner (behind the pole and sign) to the Town of Middletown in honor of H.C. Borden, the area's first natural gas customer. Borden owned the property until a structure fire destroyed the building in 1941. (Helen Lee Fletcher.)

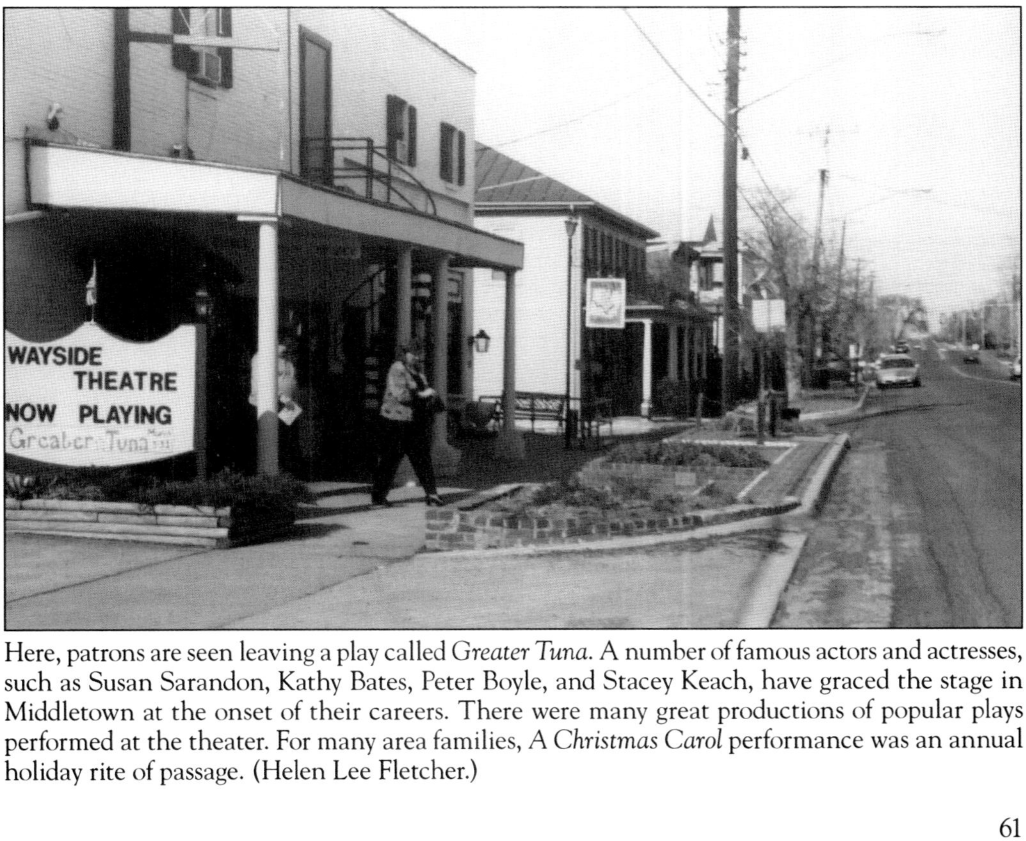

Here, patrons are seen leaving a play called *Greater Tuna*. A number of famous actors and actresses, such as Susan Sarandon, Kathy Bates, Peter Boyle, and Stacey Keach, have graced the stage in Middletown at the onset of their careers. There were many great productions of popular plays performed at the theater. For many area families, A *Christmas Carol* performance was an annual holiday rite of passage. (Helen Lee Fletcher.)

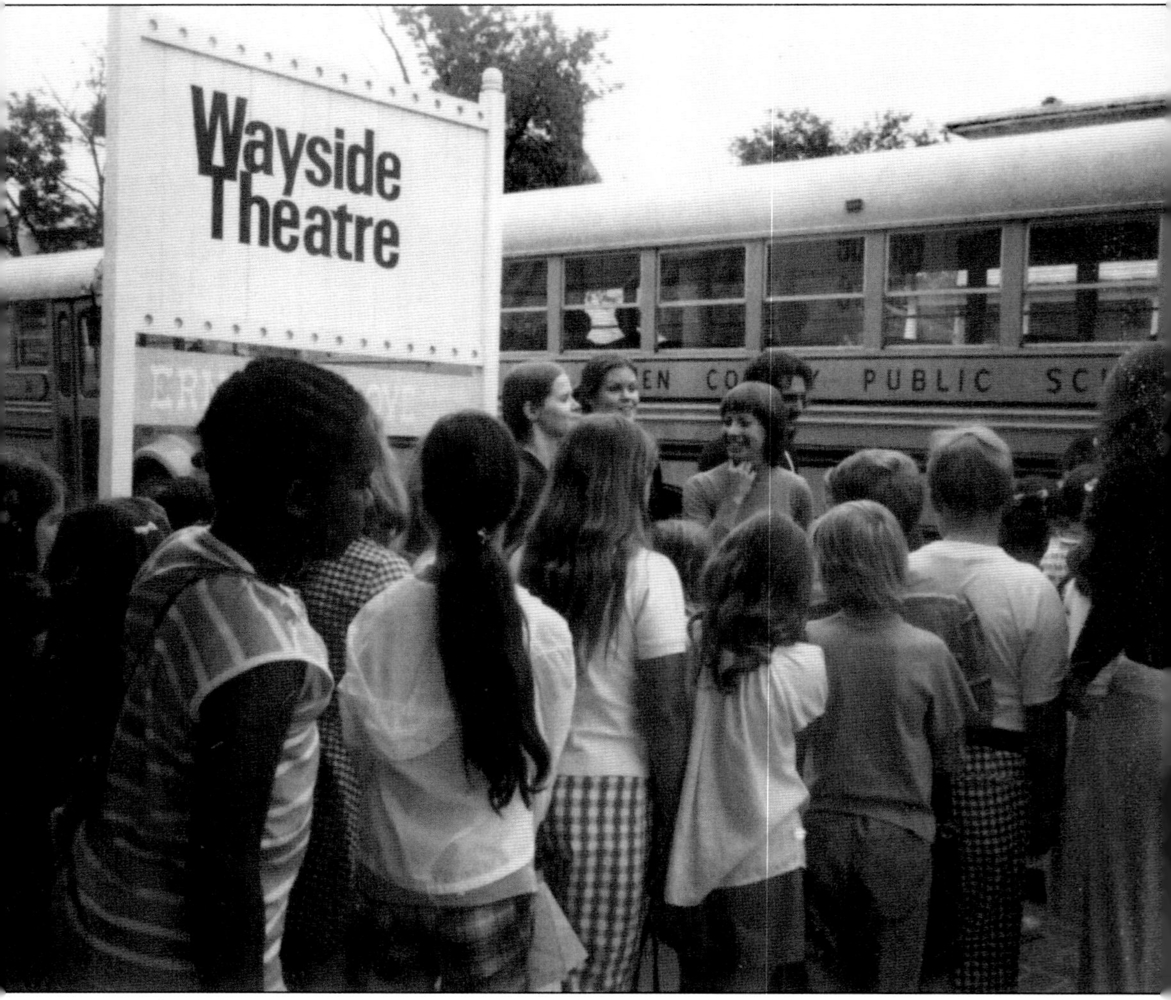

Students from Warren County are seen visiting the theater in the 1980s. The Wayside Theatre's matinees and educational programs made the theater a popular spot for adults and children alike. (Middletown Heritage Society.)

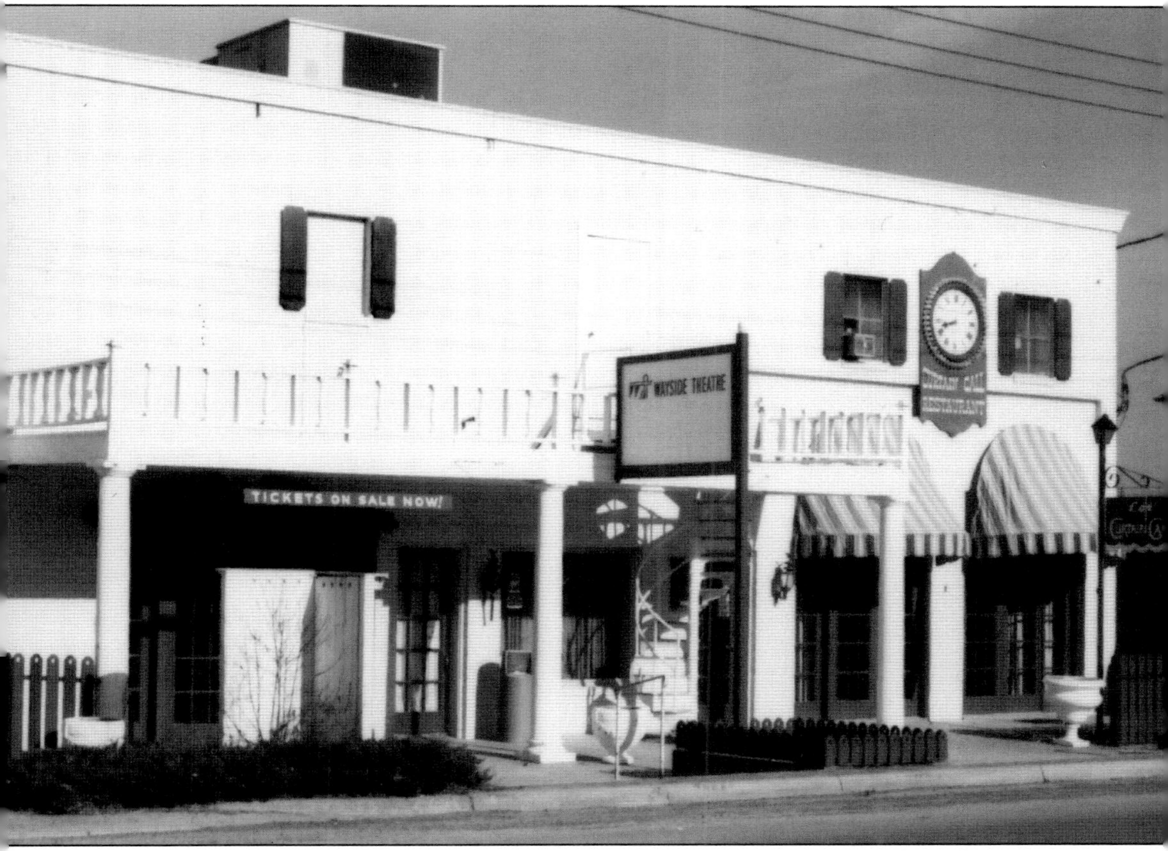

The Wayside Theatre was one of the oldest professional theaters in Virginia until its closing in 2013. It began as Maralarrick Players in 1961–1962. Leo M. Bernstein bought the building in 1963 and hired Owen Phillips as the first artistic director. The organization rose from a summer production company to a theater with year-round performances. The closing of the beloved little theater was difficult for many, and the hope is great that someone can return the theater to its glory days. (Middletown Heritage Society.)

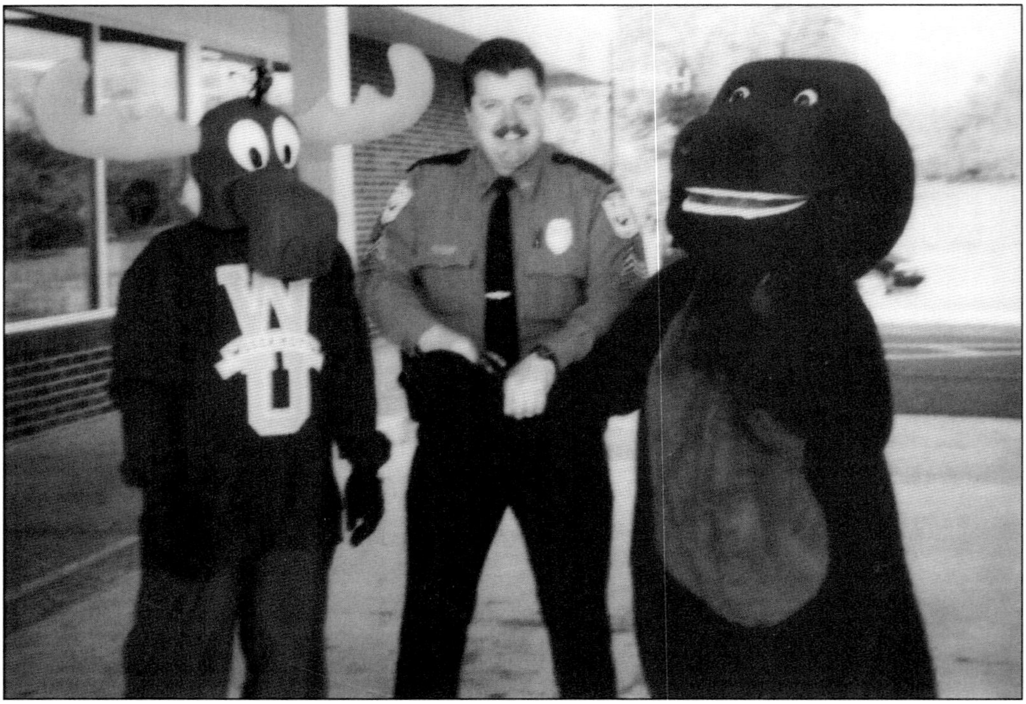

Former Middletown police chief Roger Ashley is pictured with the popular children's characters Bullwinkle (left) and Barney (right) at the opening of Liberty Gas Station off Interstate 81. (Middletown Heritage Society.)

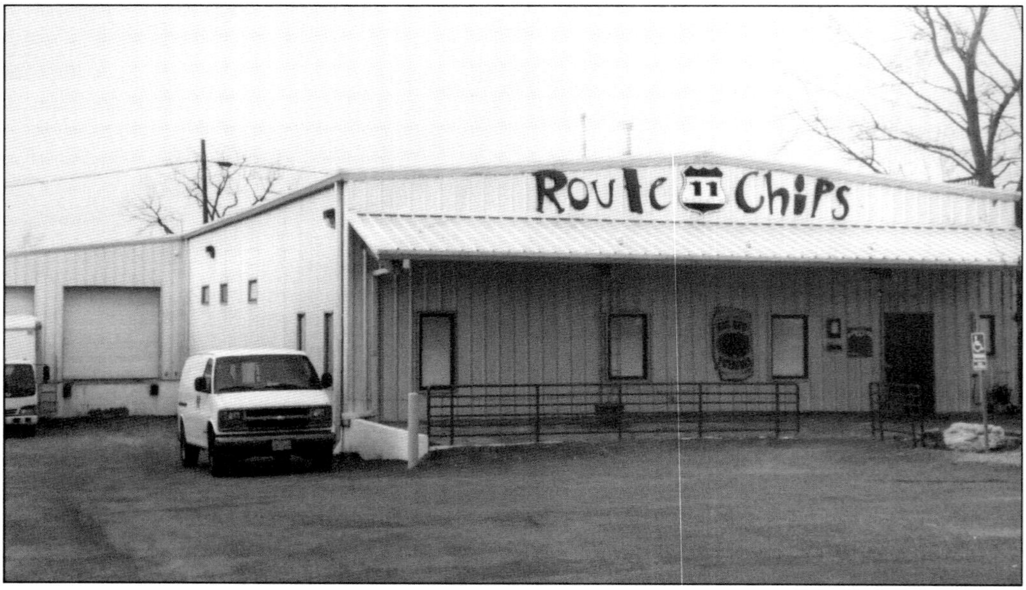

Route 11 Chips was started in Middletown in 1992 and quickly expanded out of the storefront adjacent to the newer warehouse pictured. As a big tourist attraction, Route 11 Chips received several awards from high-profile industries, such as O, *The Oprah Magazine*, the *Washington Post*, *Southern Living*, and *The Today Show*. As the chip factory grew so did the need for a bigger warehouse. Sadly, Route 11 Chips moved its operations down the valley to Mount Jackson. (Middletown Heritage Society.)

Three

HOUSES OF WORSHIP

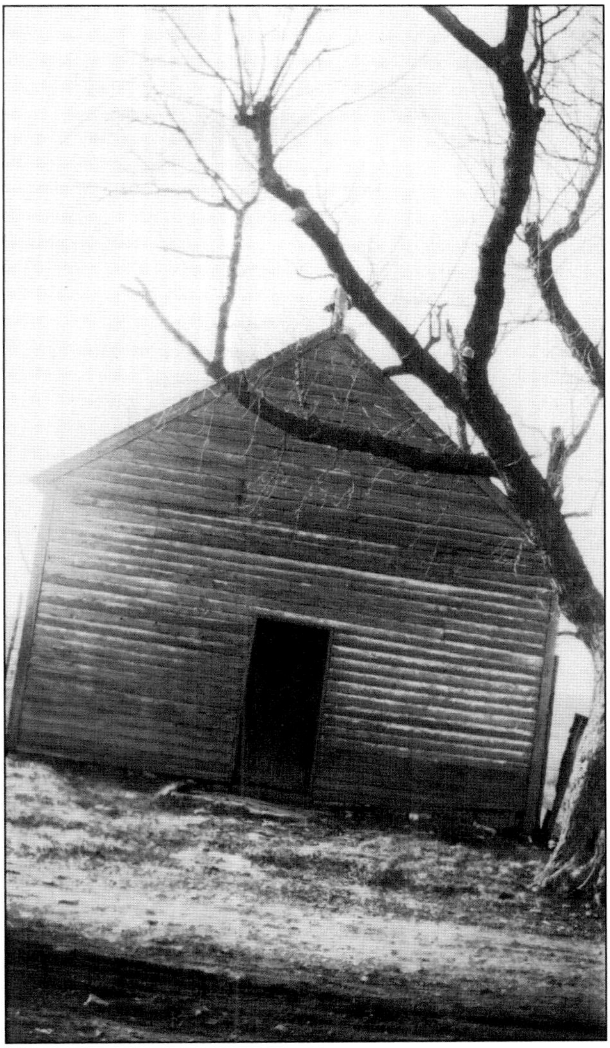

The Wright family gave a former schoolhouse for "white inhabitants" to the African American population of Middletown, provided they would always use it as a church. Its location on what was once called Back Street is now Senseney Avenue. (Joyce D. Tucker.)

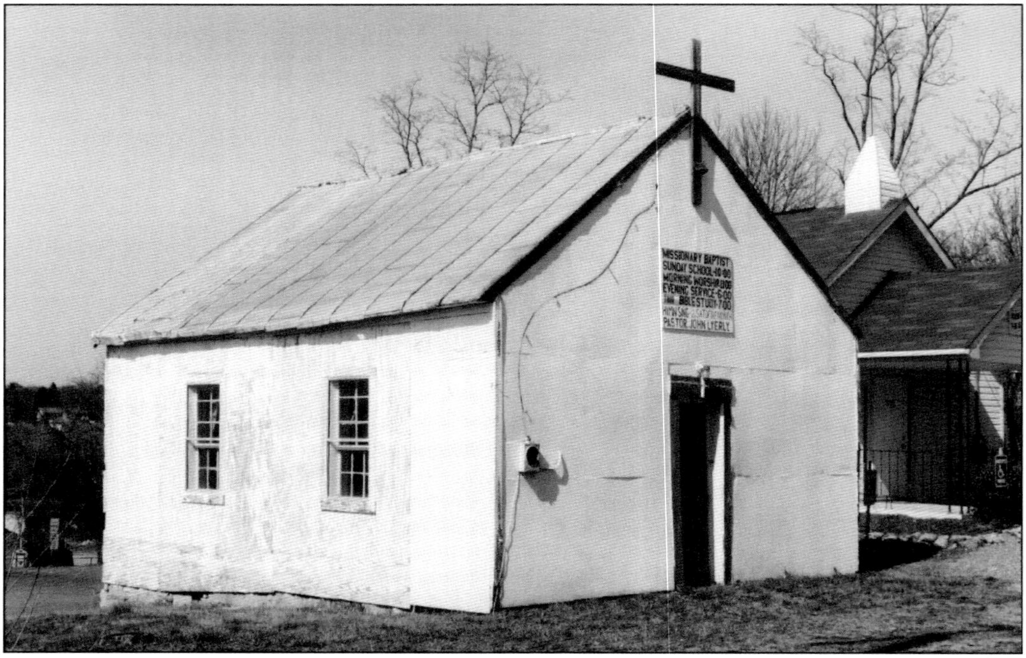

When the Methodist congregation outgrew its first church constructed in 1818, this building still saw use among the African American community. The structure, as it still stands today, has avoided attempts of demolition because of the integral part it has played in the town's history. A larger, newer church stands at right in the photograph. (Helen Lee Fletcher.)

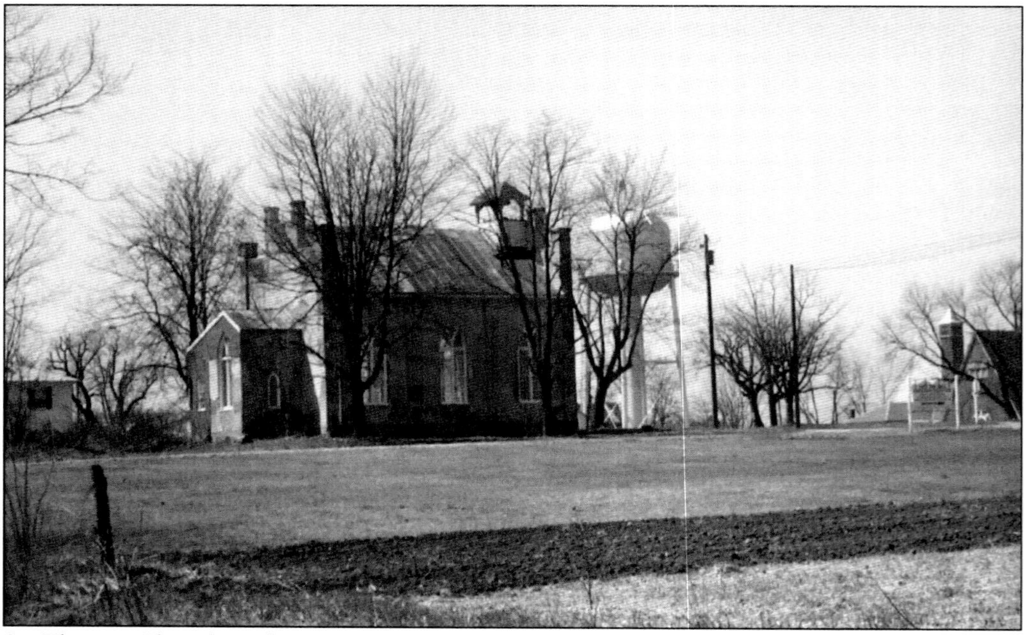

St. Thomas Chapel, or the Episcopal church, was designed after a cathedral in York, England, and around that time, three others were built nearby in Berryville, Millwood, and Winchester. Recorded on April 17, 1834, its small corner lot was purchased for $50, and the Bishop Meade consecrated the chapel in 1836. Note the cupola, which has since undergone several changes. (Middletown Heritage Society.)

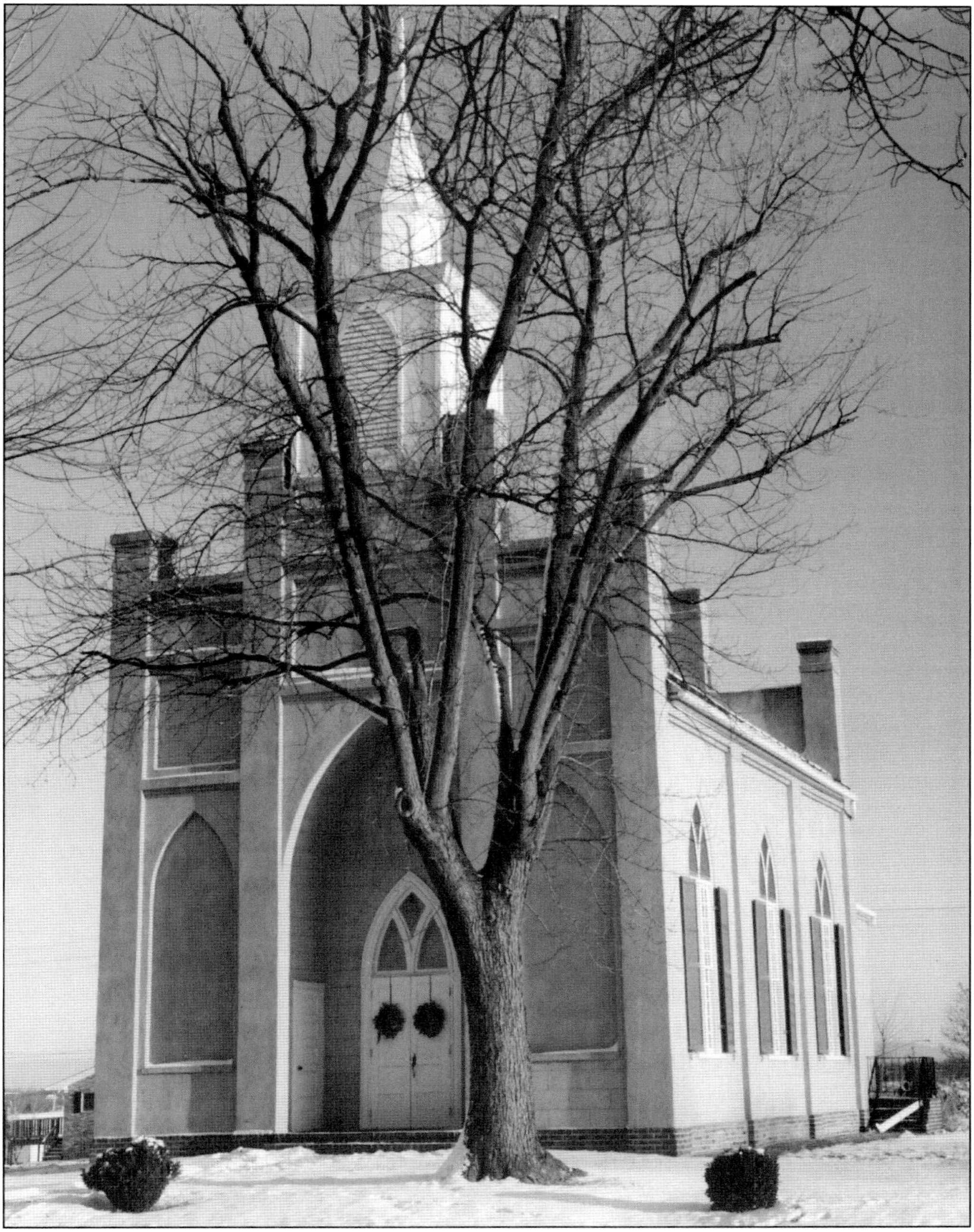

Inside St. Thomas Chapel is seating for about 100 individuals, above which hangs a four-tier chandelier that has been beautifully restored, along with a wind organ in the nave. The parish of the same name covered Frederick and Warren Counties in the 1830s. The chapel was abandoned in the 1930s, and in the 1960s, a trust was established to administer the building. (Harold Gardenhour Jr.)

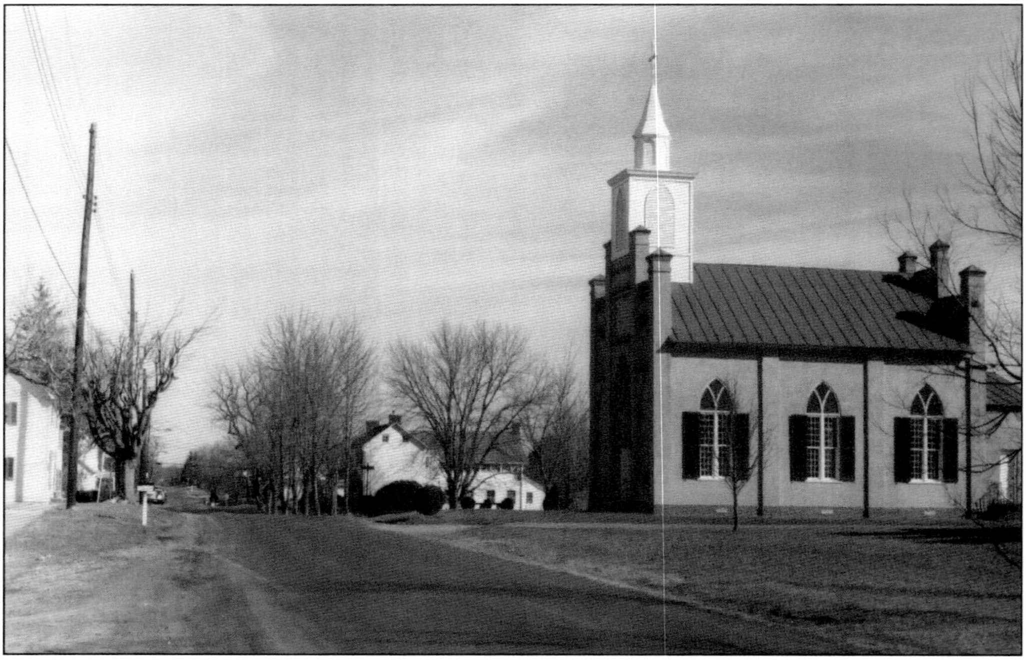

St. Thomas Chapel saw many uses during the Civil War as a commissary and stable under Union general Nathaniel Banks as well as an infirmary where Dr. Guyer (whose house is the white structure in the background) first tended to the Confederate wounded, then Union soldiers from the 1864 engagement. Soldiers were buried behind the chapel and later exhumed for reburial in Winchester, Virginia. (Helen Lee Fletcher.)

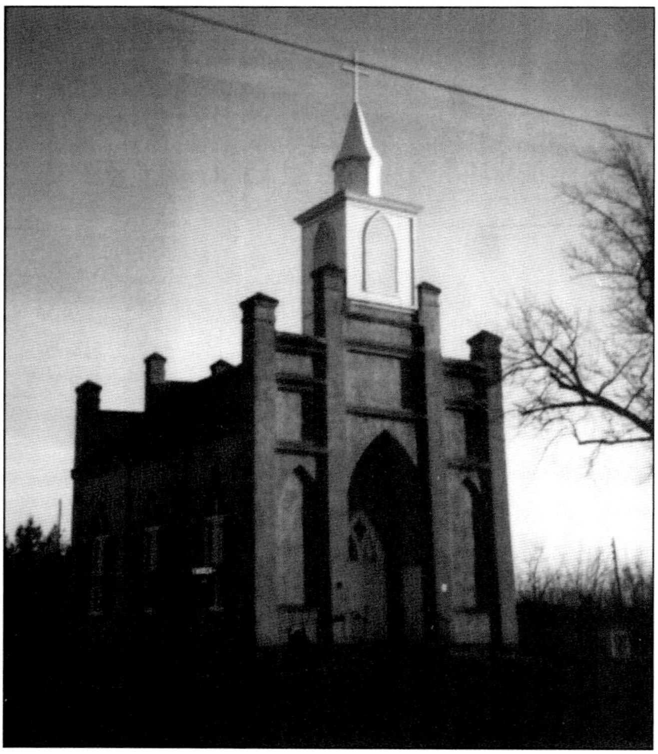

This early-1980s image exhibits the beauty of the original structure, along with the renovations from the 1960s. St. Thomas Chapel is now used as a venue for special events, such as weddings and holiday services. (Middletown Heritage Society.)

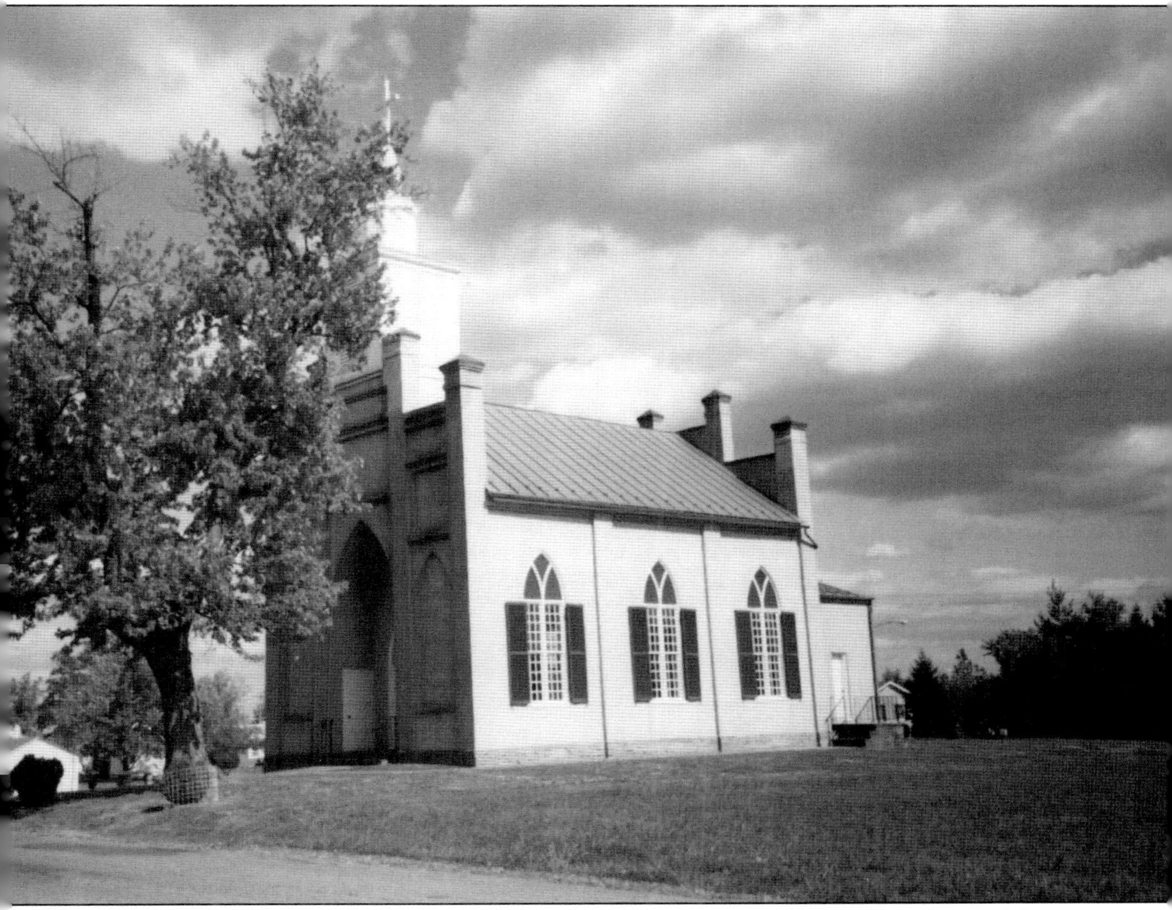

In January 1973, St. Thomas Chapel was registered as a Virginia Landmark, and in April of that year, it was added to the National Register of Historic Places. (Helen Lee Fletcher.)

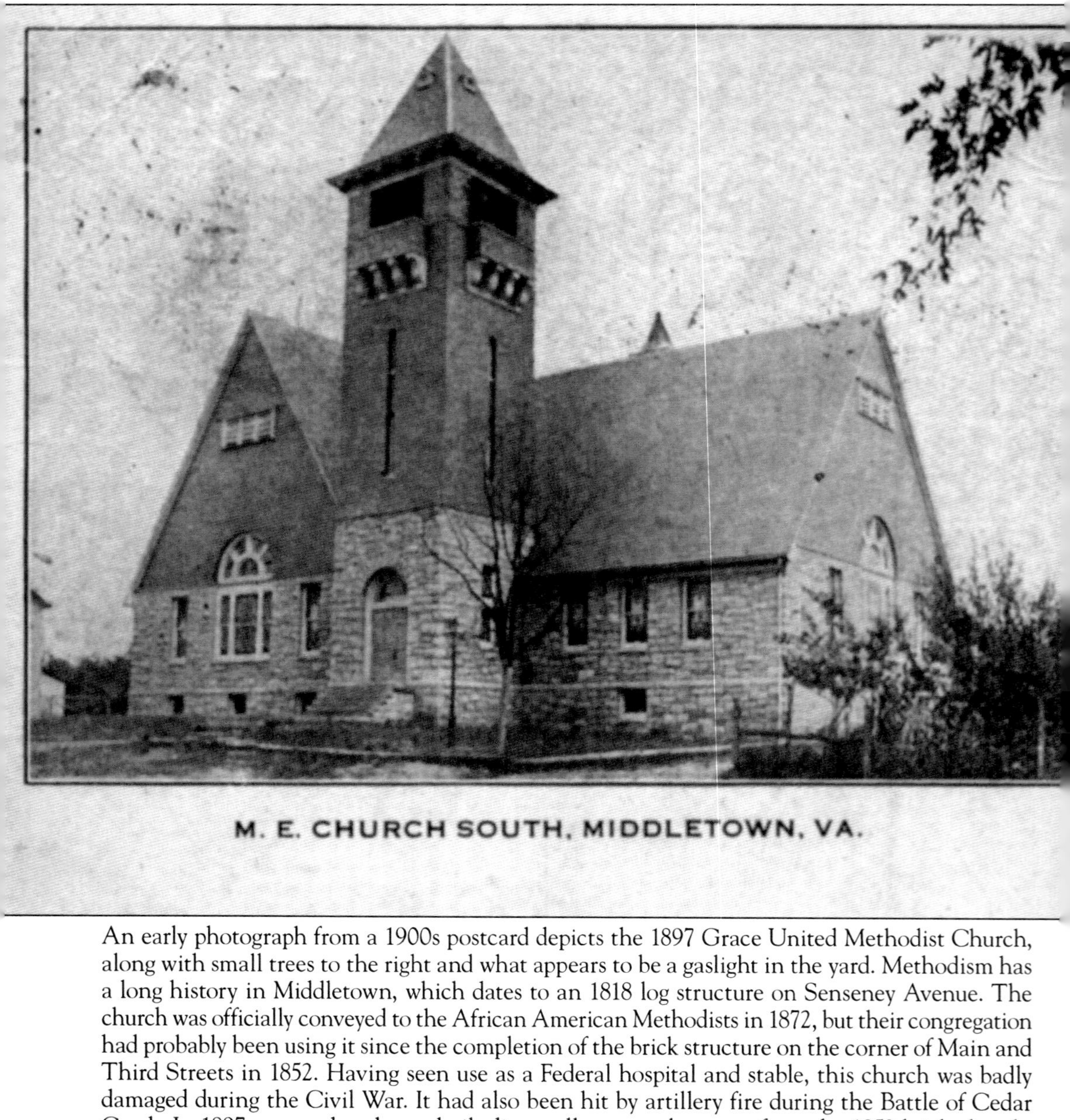

An early photograph from a 1900s postcard depicts the 1897 Grace United Methodist Church, along with small trees to the right and what appears to be a gaslight in the yard. Methodism has a long history in Middletown, which dates to an 1818 log structure on Senseney Avenue. The church was officially conveyed to the African American Methodists in 1872, but their congregation had probably been using it since the completion of the brick structure on the corner of Main and Third Streets in 1852. Having seen use as a Federal hospital and stable, this church was badly damaged during the Civil War. It had also been hit by artillery fire during the Battle of Cedar Creek. In 1897, a new church was built diagonally across the street from the 1852 brick church. According to the *Baltimore Sun*, "About 2500 people attended all day church services to dedicate the new 1897 church to Christian work." (Joyce D. Tucker.)

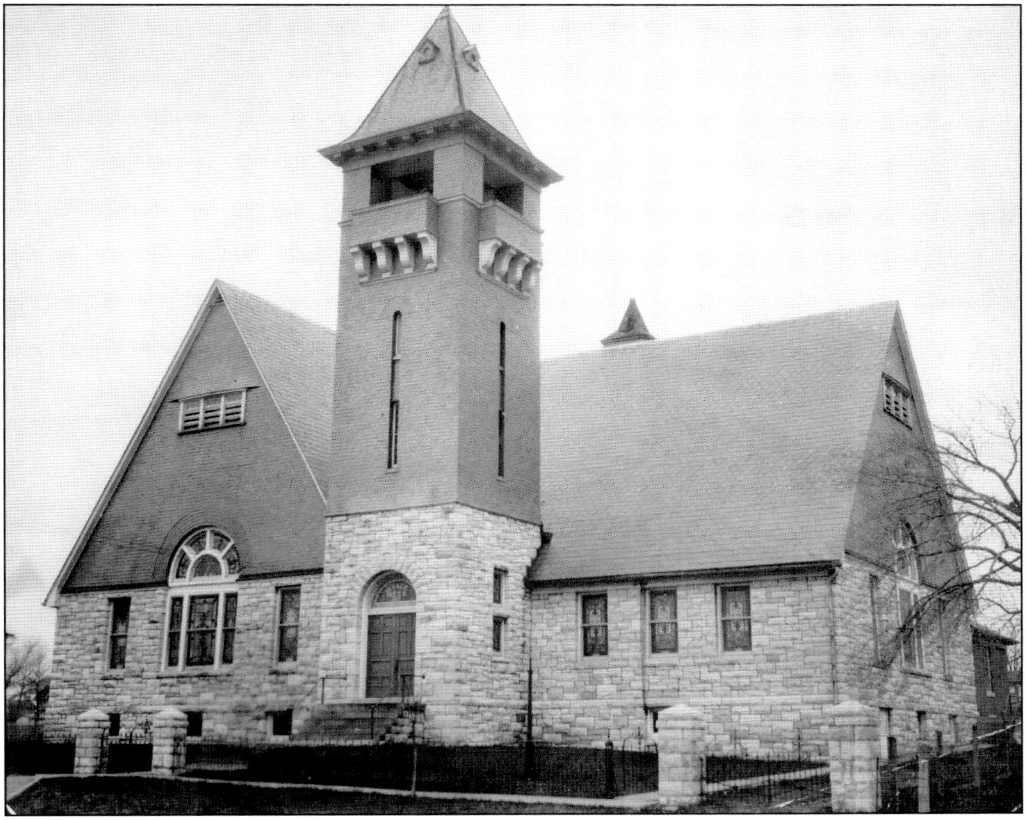

In this 1930s view of Grace United Methodist Church, the globe is missing from the lamp in the front yard, and the tree to the right is much larger than that in the earlier print. One striking feature of this church is the beautiful stained-glass windows, which cast a serene glow during evening events. Many of these windows were inscribed with the names of patrons, sponsors, and prominent members of the church during the era of its construction. At 75 feet tall, the bell tower is still the most dominant structure in town. (Middletown Heritage Society.)

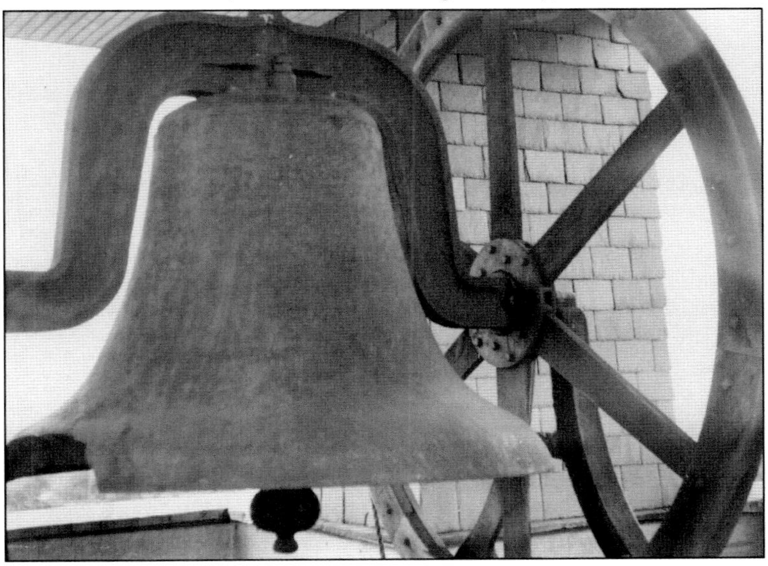

The original bell of the Methodist church is seen at right as it appeared in the bell tower at Grace United Methodist Church in 1938. The large piece missing from its left side is likely the damage from a passing artillery shell during the Battle of Cedar Creek. (Middletown Heritage Society.)

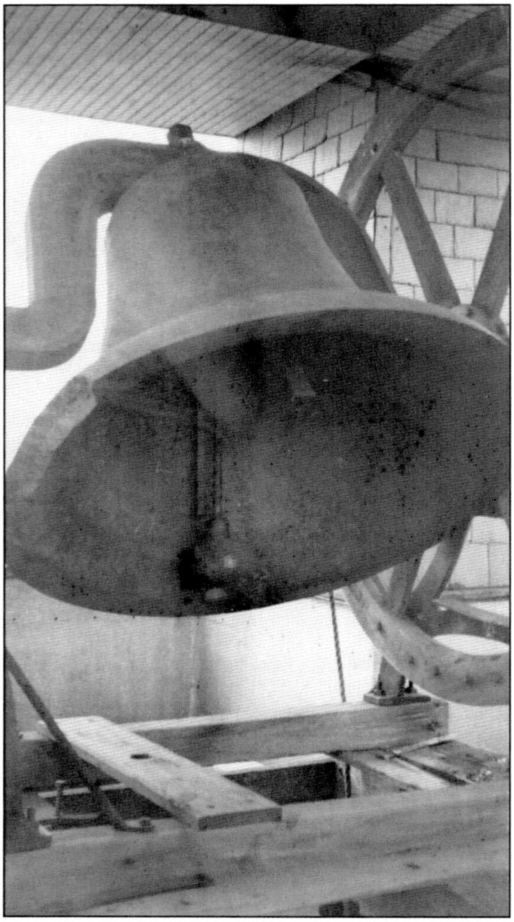

The original bell in the tower of the Grace United Methodist Church has been readied for removal by hand using ancient techniques of block and tackle. (Middletown Heritage Society.)

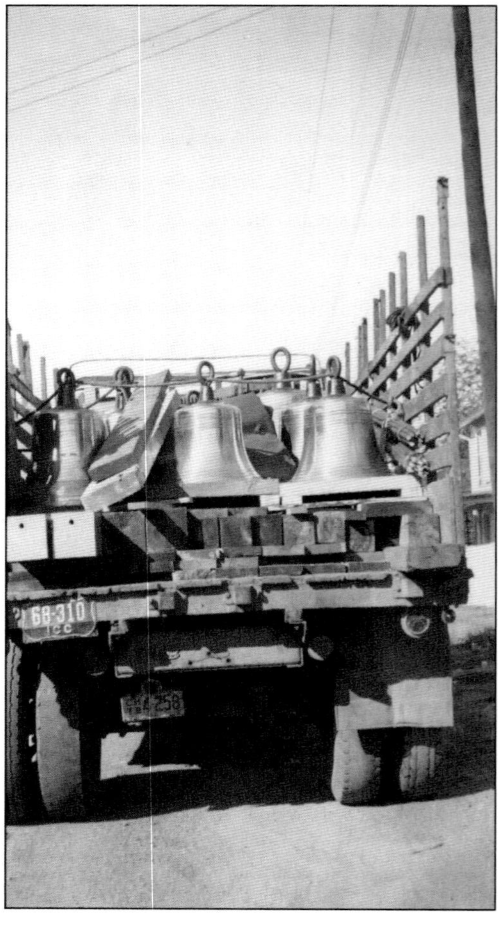

In July 1938, a monumental event occurred in Middletown when the old bell was prepared for removal and the new chime system comprised of multiple bells arrived by flatbed truck at Grace United Methodist Church. (Middletown Heritage Society.)

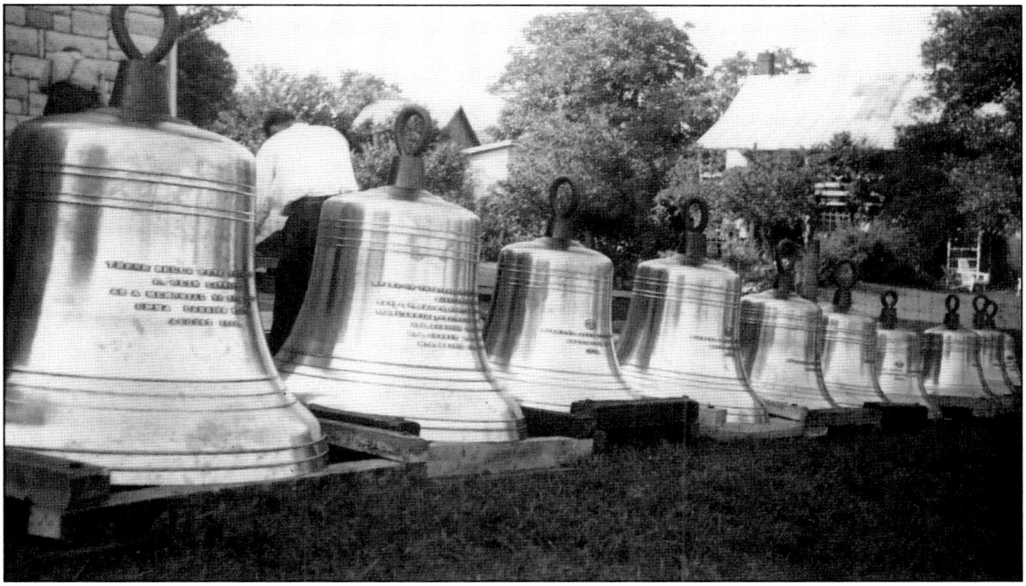

Awaiting installation, the new chimes were laid out in the front yard of the church. Each bell was inscribed with the names of sponsors and benefactors of this project. This view looks south, showing the neighboring homes beyond. (Middletown Heritage Society.)

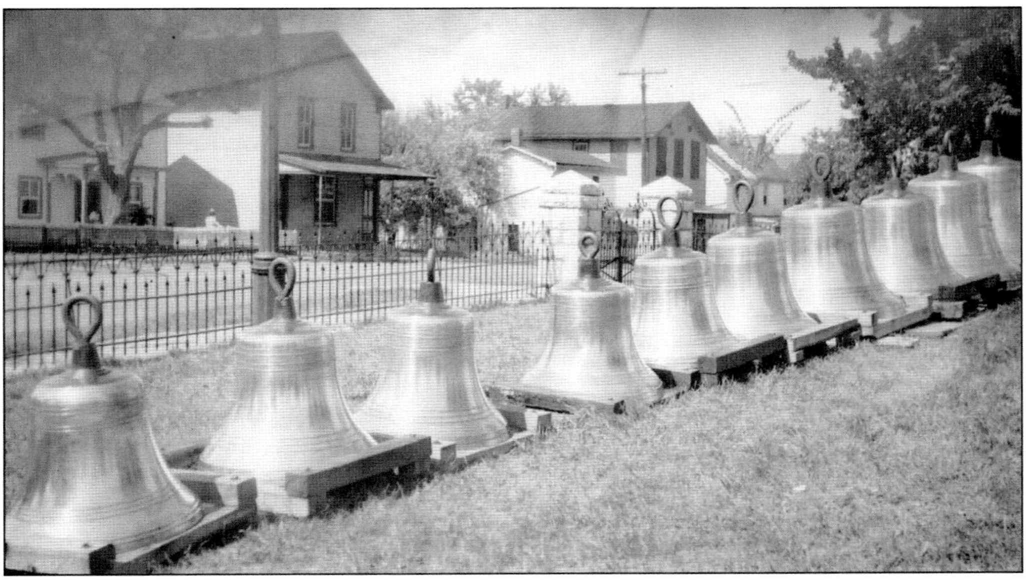

In another view of the chimes in the yard, the homes across the street are now visible. At the far right is the house that once stood on the site of today's fire station. (Middletown Heritage Society.)

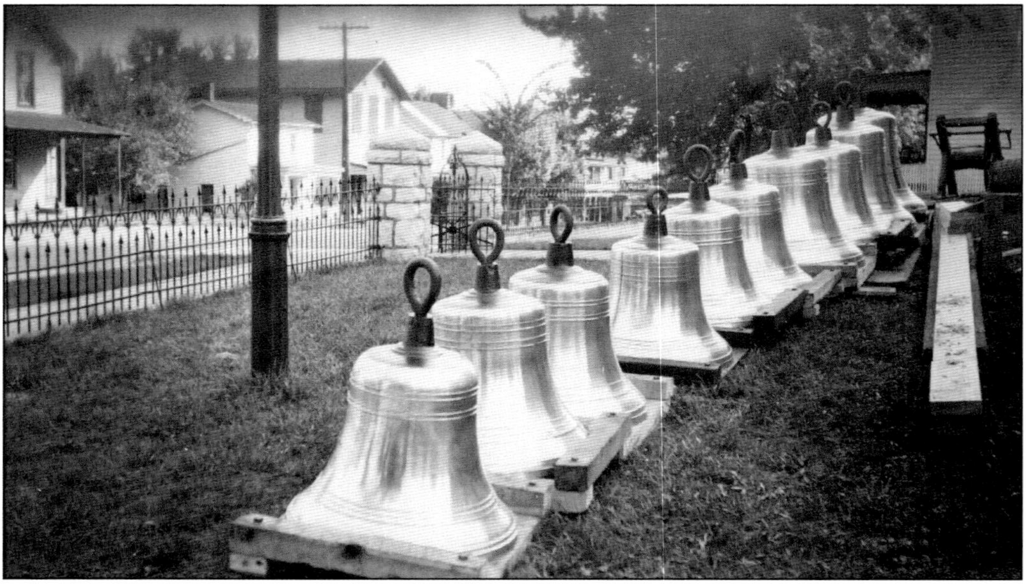

Looking north, the neighboring houses can be seen beyond the construction equipment in this view of the new chime system, which has been arranged by size and order of their installation. (Middletown Heritage Society.)

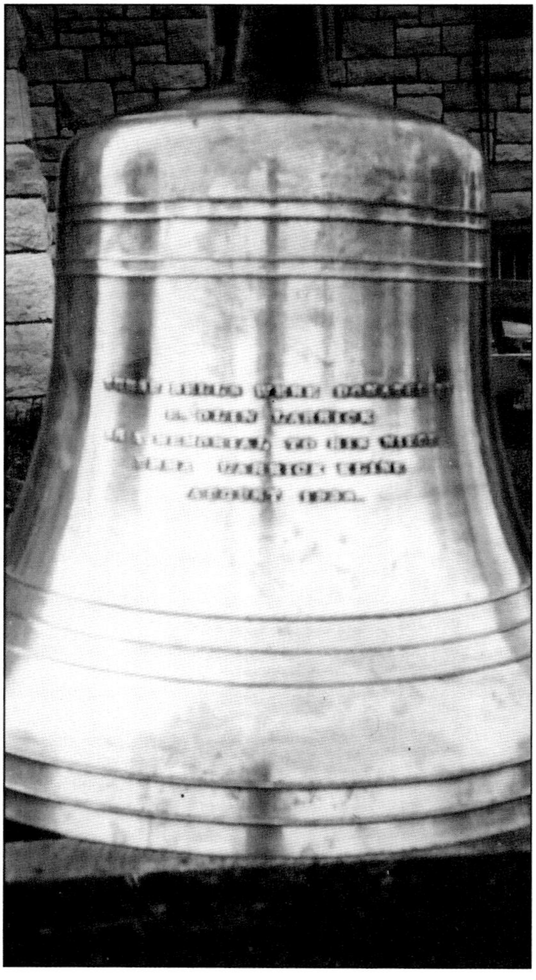

It appears that Olin Larrick has donated this bell. The Larrick family was well known in town as the owners of the Wayside Inn, formerly Wilkenson's Tavern during the Civil War and later Larrick's Hotel. (Middletown Heritage Society.)

A gentleman poses with the "Larrick Bell." Prominent families like the Larricks had sufficient wealth to contribute and made great sacrificial gifts to the church while still in the midst of the Great Depression. (Middletown Heritage Society.)

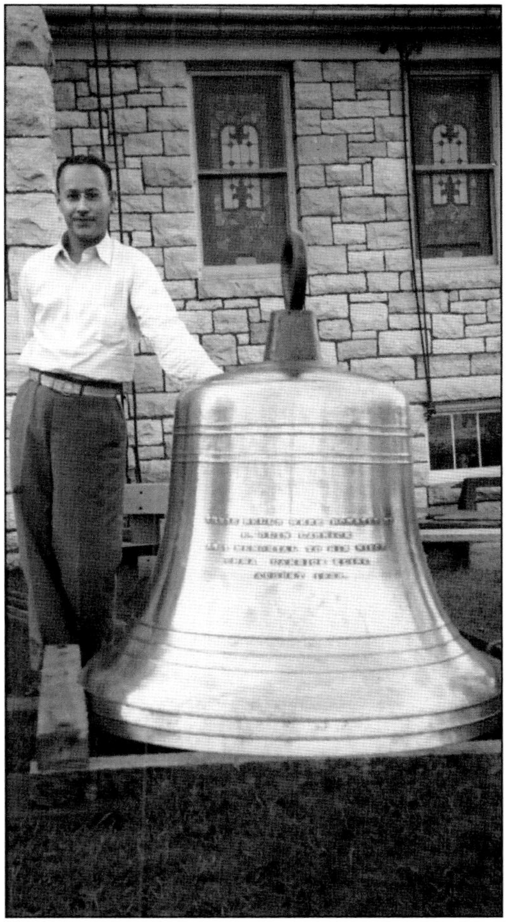

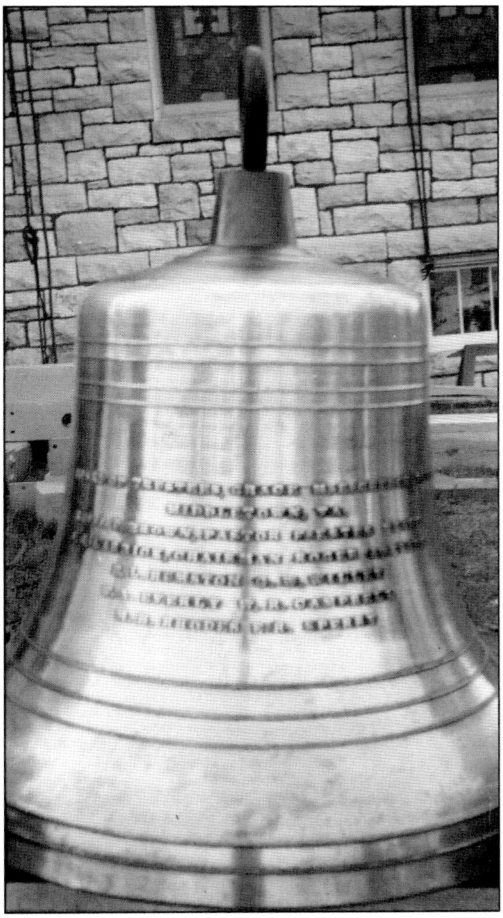

Here is a different chime with the inscriptions of several contributing families and noteworthy Middletown residents, including the Sperry, Rhodes, Campbell, Willey, and Everly families. (Middletown Heritage Society.)

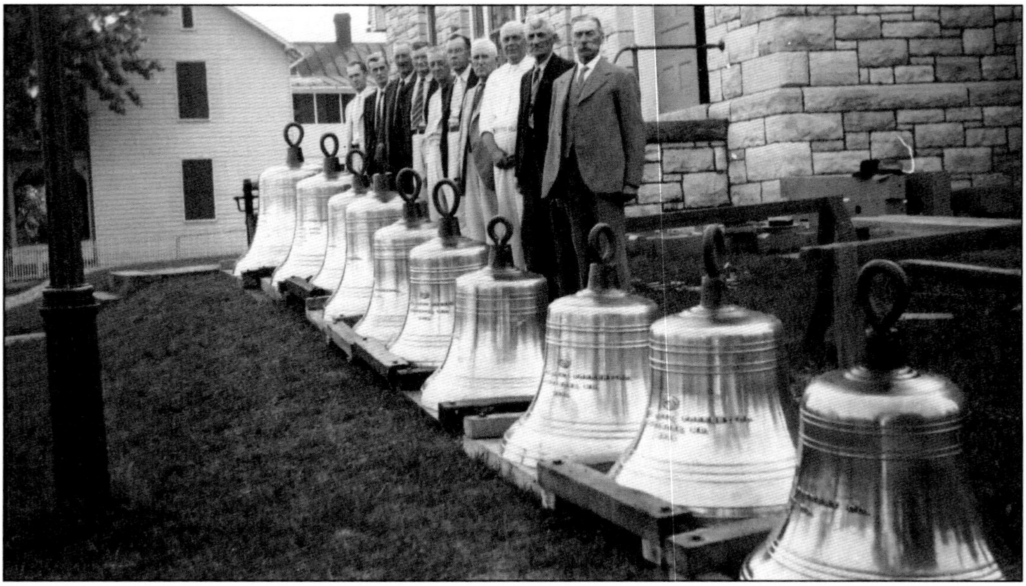

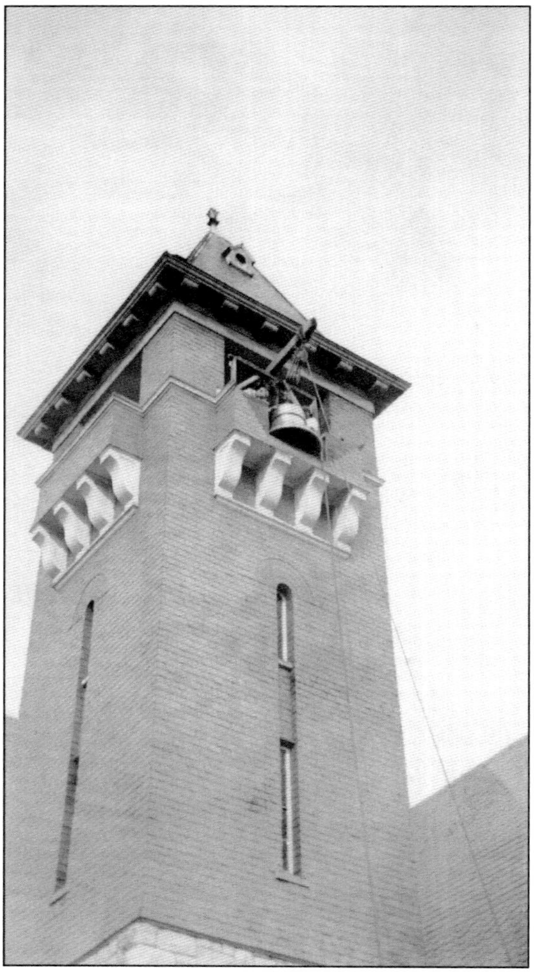

A group of church leaders pose with the chimes as they await installation. This was a joyous day for the Grace United Methodist Church congregation, but these men of faith were keeping with earlier photographic etiquette, which held that smiles were not allowed, as they would distort one's true likeness. (Middletown Heritage Society.)

Once the festivities and photographs ended, it was time for the men to get to work, several of whom can be seen guiding the old bell as it is cautiously and slowly moved toward the opening of the 75-foot tower. (Middletown Heritage Society.)

The workers have moved out of the way, as the bell is nearly halfway out of the tower. (Middletown Heritage Society.)

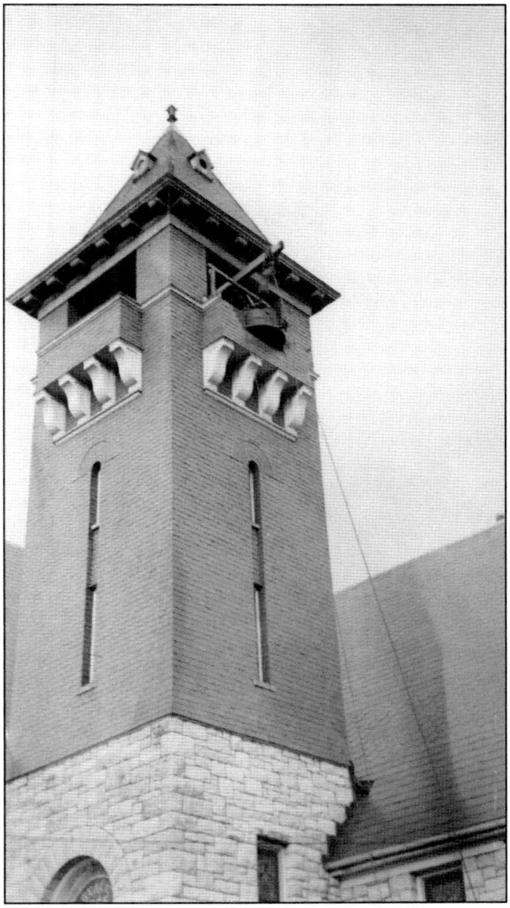

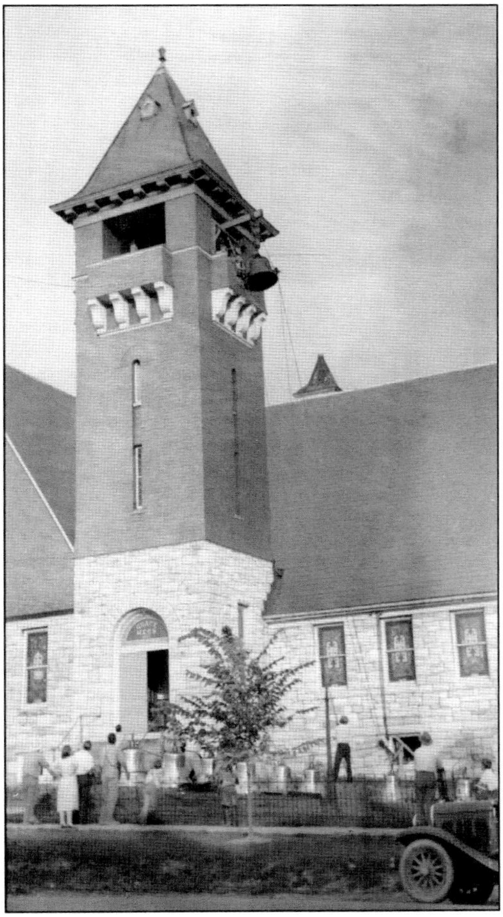

Being held by rope, the bell has finally emerged from the tower. Onlookers gaze up at the bell as it is prepared for descent. (Middletown Heritage Society.)

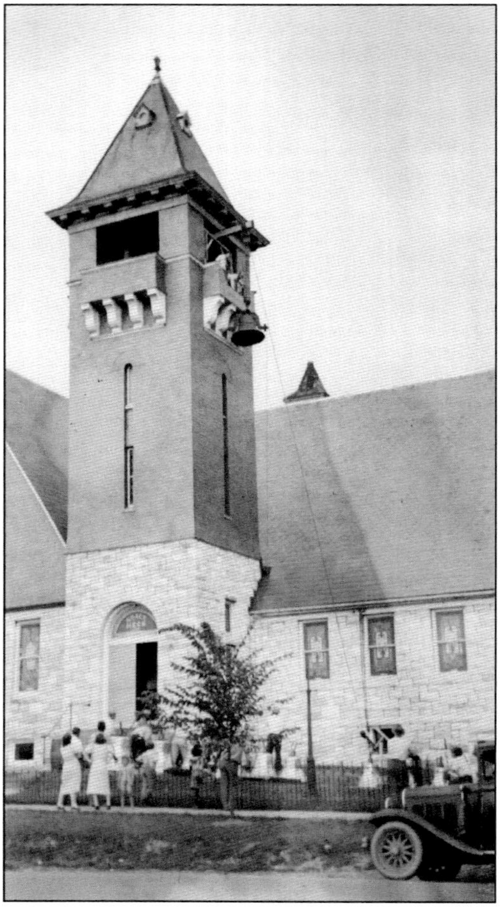

The bell has begun its descent as it angles away from the tower structure. (Middletown Heritage Society.)

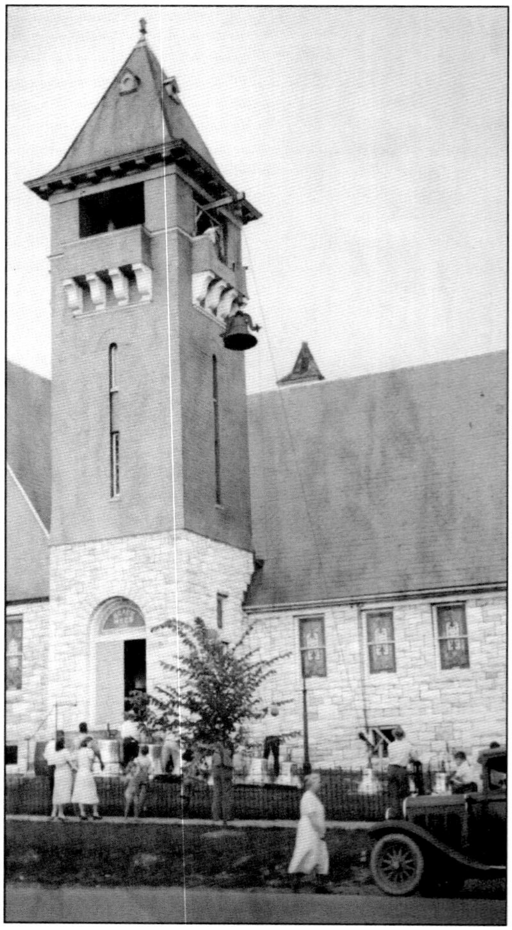

This image, taken from the Valley Pike, shows the bell at a slightly lower position. The lady walking in the road is Mae Ginn, and the boy on the bike beyond the vehicle is a young Harry McCauley. (Middletown Heritage Society.)

Crowds remain riveted as the bell reaches the halfway mark of its descent. Gazing down from the tower, workers seem concerned about the clearance between the bell and the tower. (Middletown Heritage Society.)

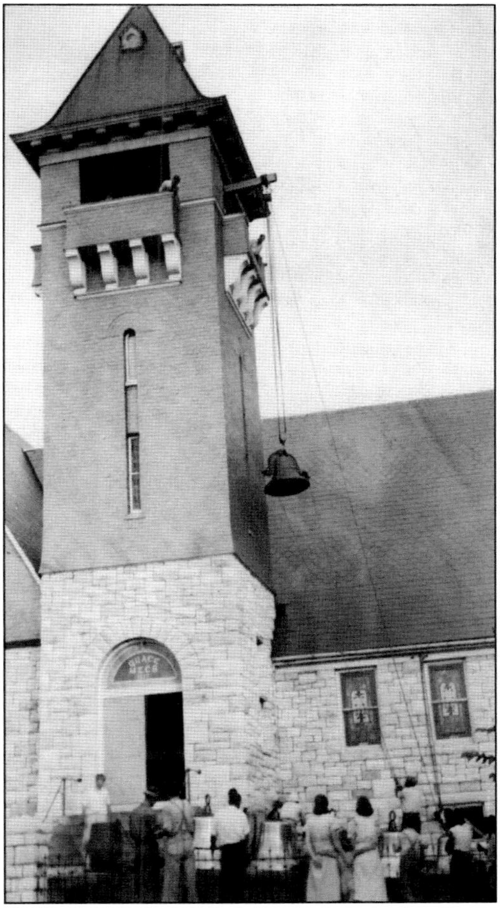

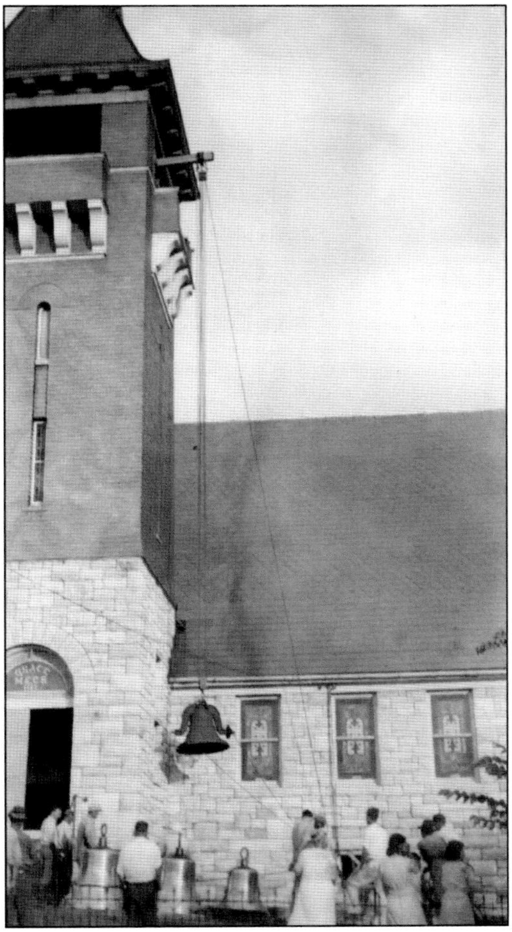

The bell finally nears the ground as onlookers continue to watch this laborious process. (Middletown Heritage Society.)

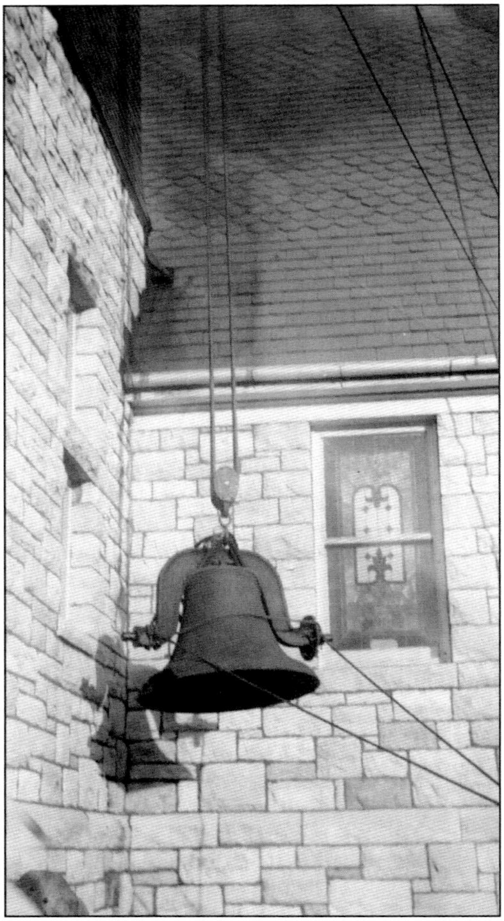

A closer view shows the reason for concern, as the path of descent nearly intersects with the corner between the tower and the sanctuary. (Middletown Heritage Society.)

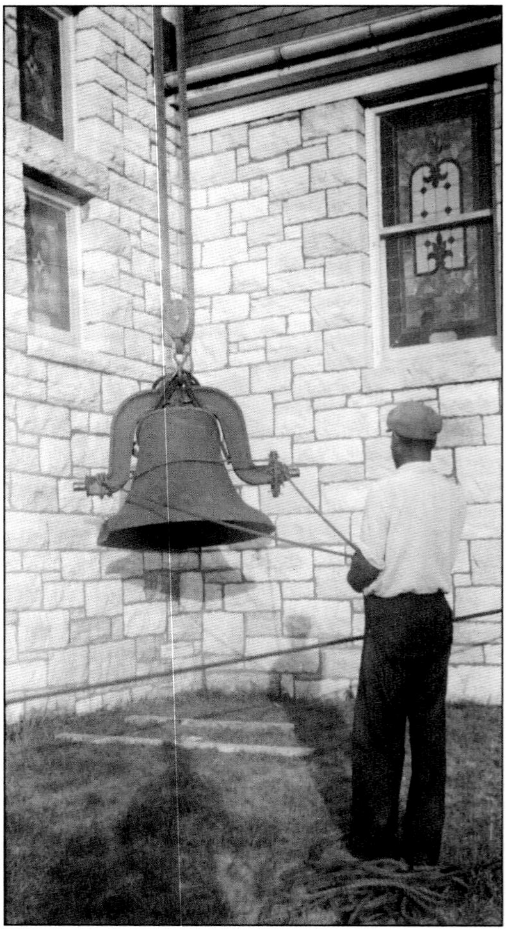

Holmes Butler had the difficult task of working the control line of the bell as it neared its landing point. (Middletown Heritage Society.)

The same process is now reversed as the first of the new chimes is hauled upward, one at a time. This time, however, it was twice as difficult because now the workers had to haul up the chimes against gravity. (Middletown Heritage Society.)

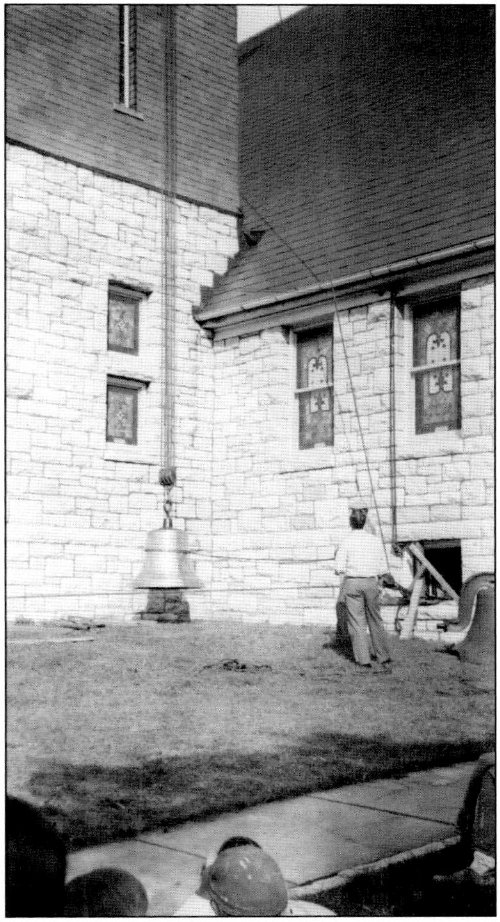

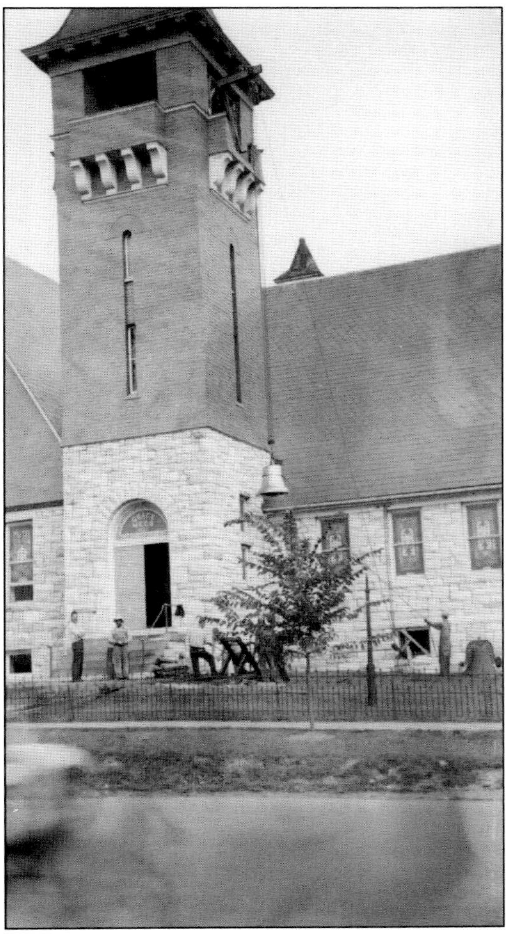

The chime begins its ascent, but the onlookers have appeared to lose interest and have dispersed. (Middletown Heritage Society.)

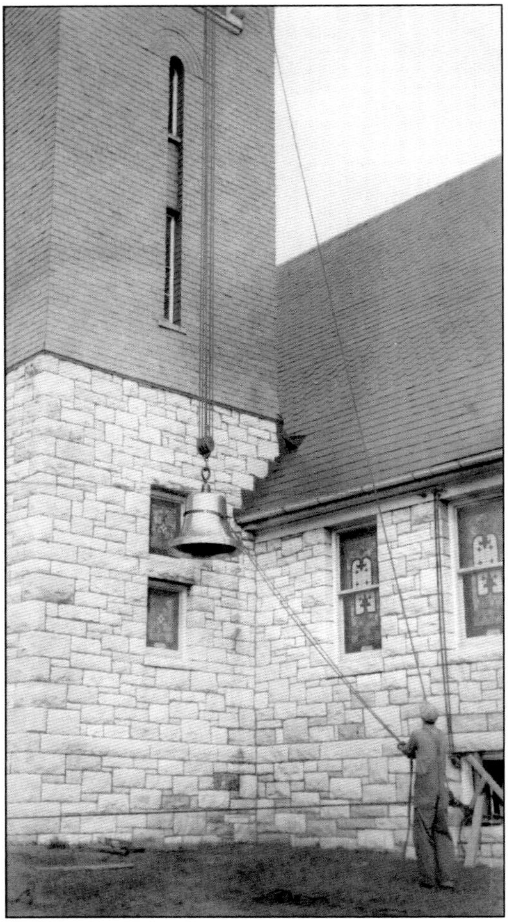

As Holmes Butler holds the chime in place, other workers adjust the rigging before continuing to raise the chime. (Middletown Heritage Society.)

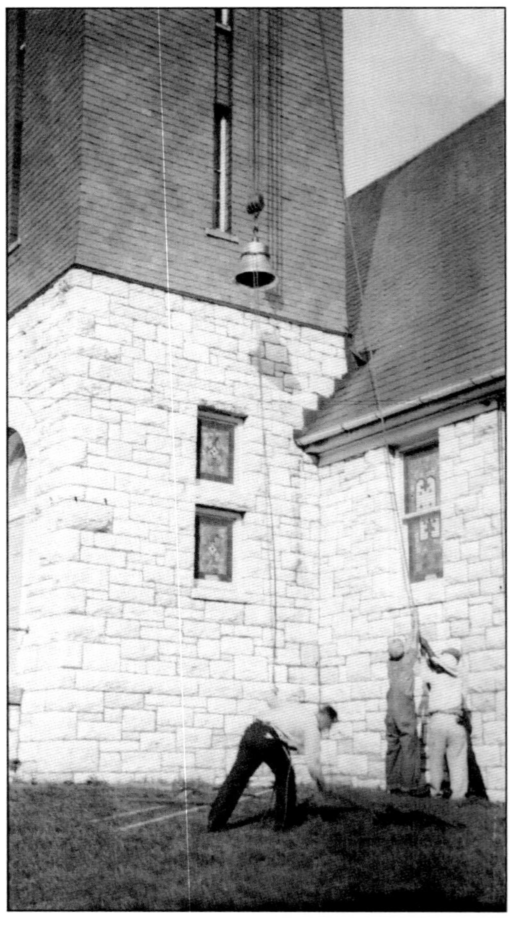

A man holds the control line and adjusts the excess cable on the ground as three other men work together to hoist the chime. (Middletown Heritage Society.)

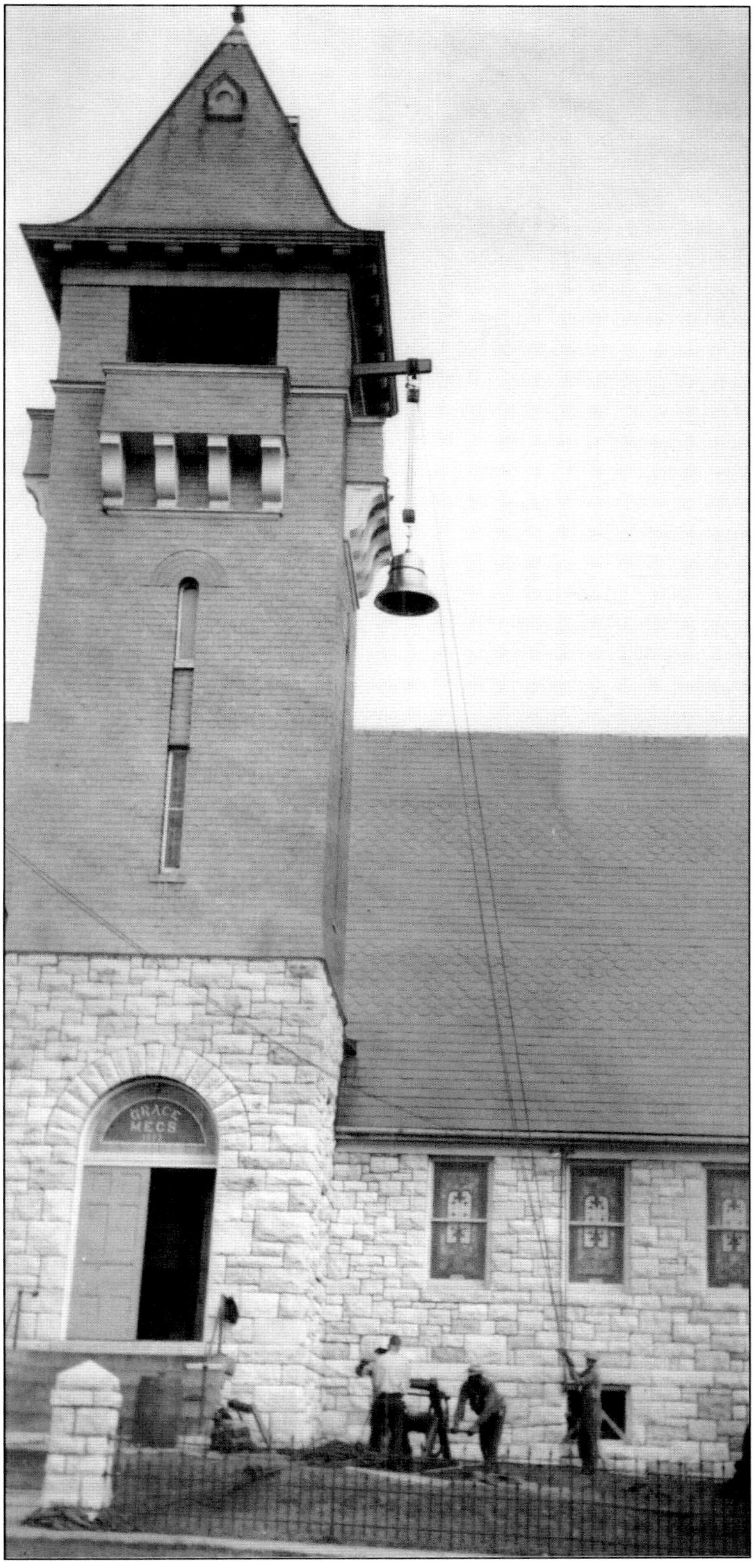

Here, one of the chimes is nearly to the top of the tower. Several men seem to be operating some type of cable winder and hand-operated wench. All successfully installed, the chimes are still a staple of Sunday mornings in Middletown, starting at 9:30 a.m. each week. The old bell was graciously donated to an African American congregation in Frederick County, Virginia. (Middletown Heritage Society.)

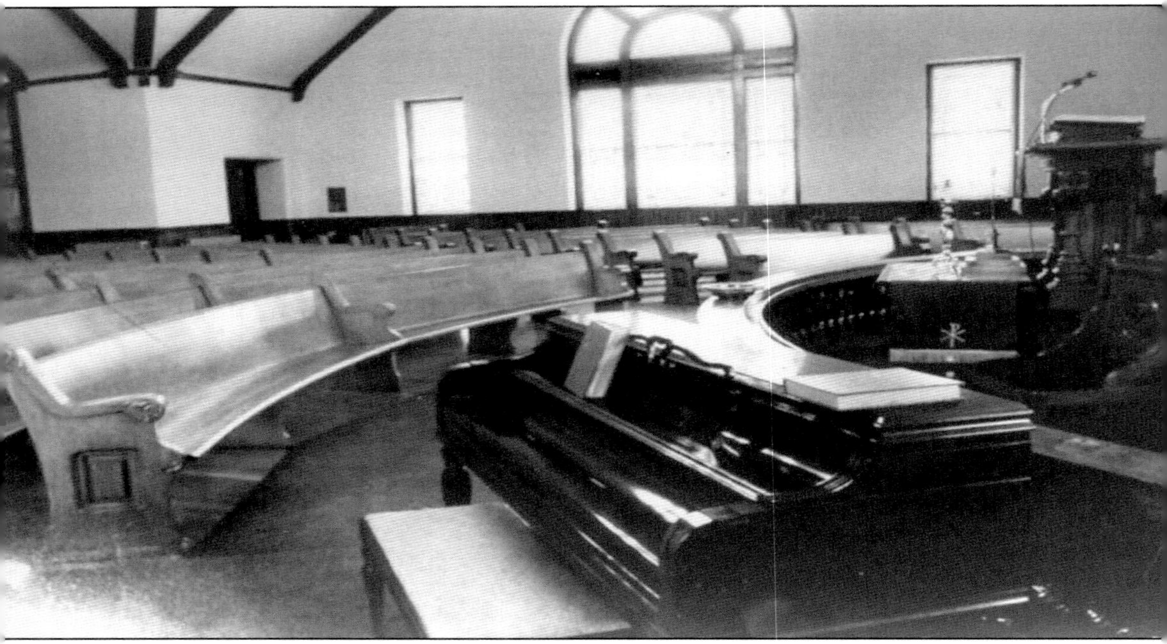

An early interior photograph of Grace United Methodist Church shows an unorthodox semiround seating arrangement, which is more common today. The exquisite woodwork on the pews, altar rails, chairs, and lectern is still retained today as part of its original character. (Stewart Bell Jr. Archives.)

Four

FACES OF MIDDLETOWN

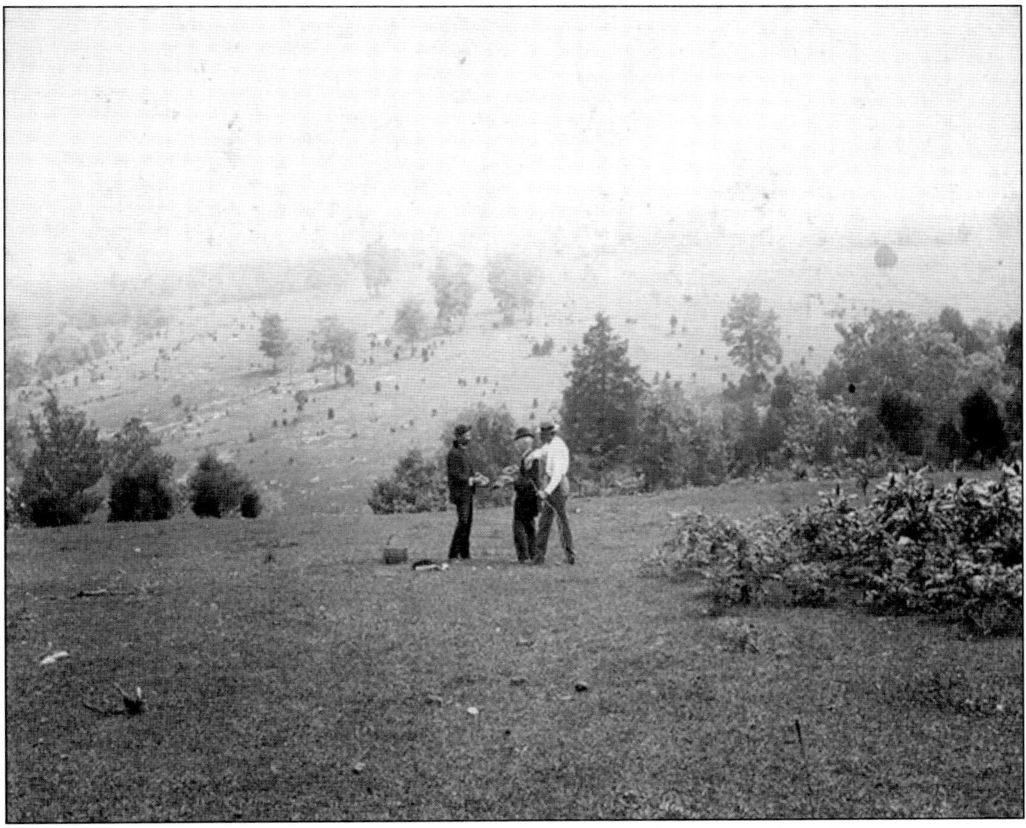

Civil War tourism began with veterans returning to honor their comrades. Here, veterans tour the Cedar Creek Battlefield, near where the climactic battle began. The man in the white shirt appears to be holding part of a relic musket with the bayonet attached. This view is south of Waterplant Road, just east of the turnpike and roughly 1.5 miles south of town. (Stewart Bell Jr. Archives.)

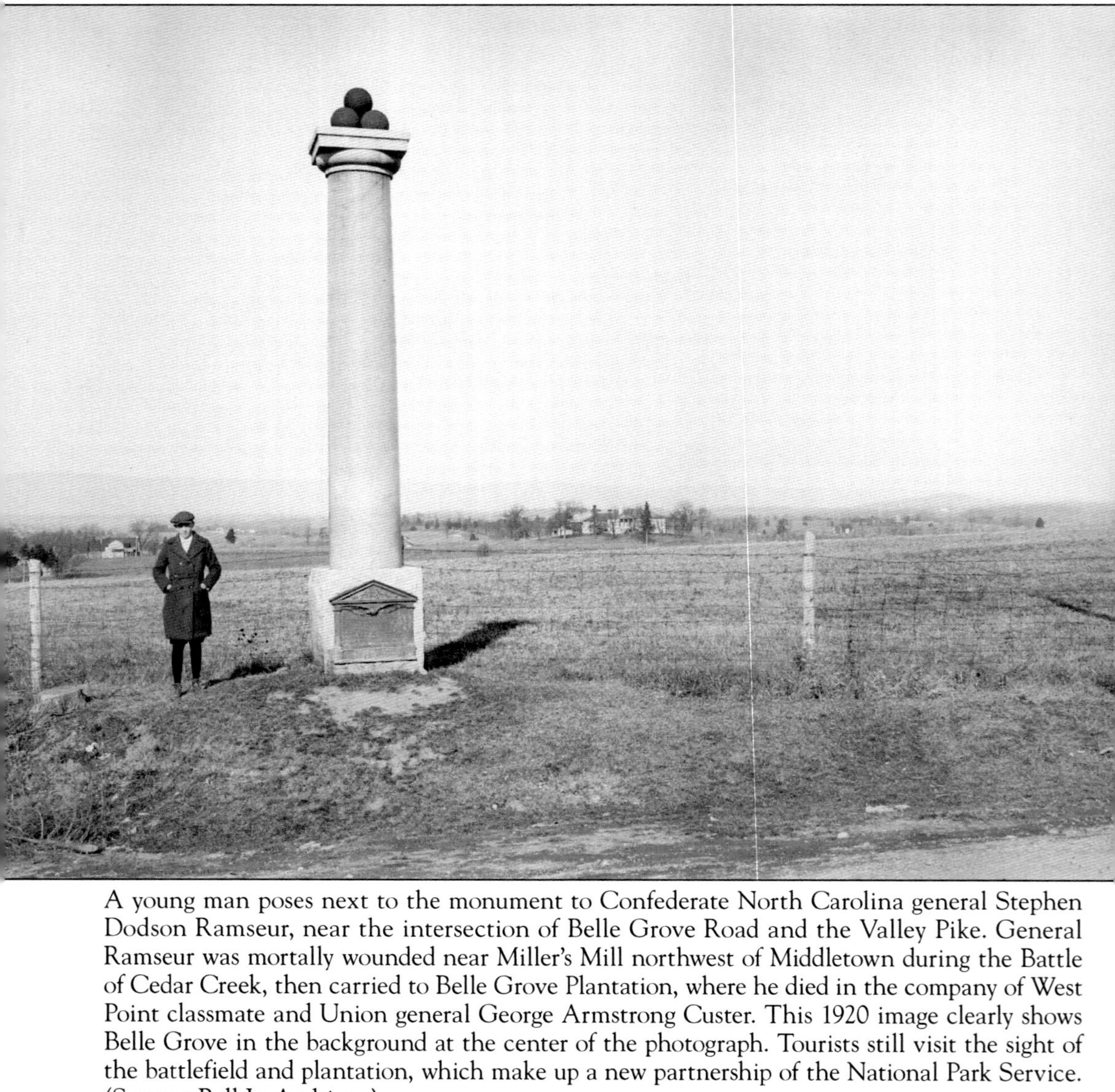

A young man poses next to the monument to Confederate North Carolina general Stephen Dodson Ramseur, near the intersection of Belle Grove Road and the Valley Pike. General Ramseur was mortally wounded near Miller's Mill northwest of Middletown during the Battle of Cedar Creek, then carried to Belle Grove Plantation, where he died in the company of West Point classmate and Union general George Armstrong Custer. This 1920 image clearly shows Belle Grove in the background at the center of the photograph. Tourists still visit the sight of the battlefield and plantation, which make up a new partnership of the National Park Service. (Stewart Bell Jr. Archives.)

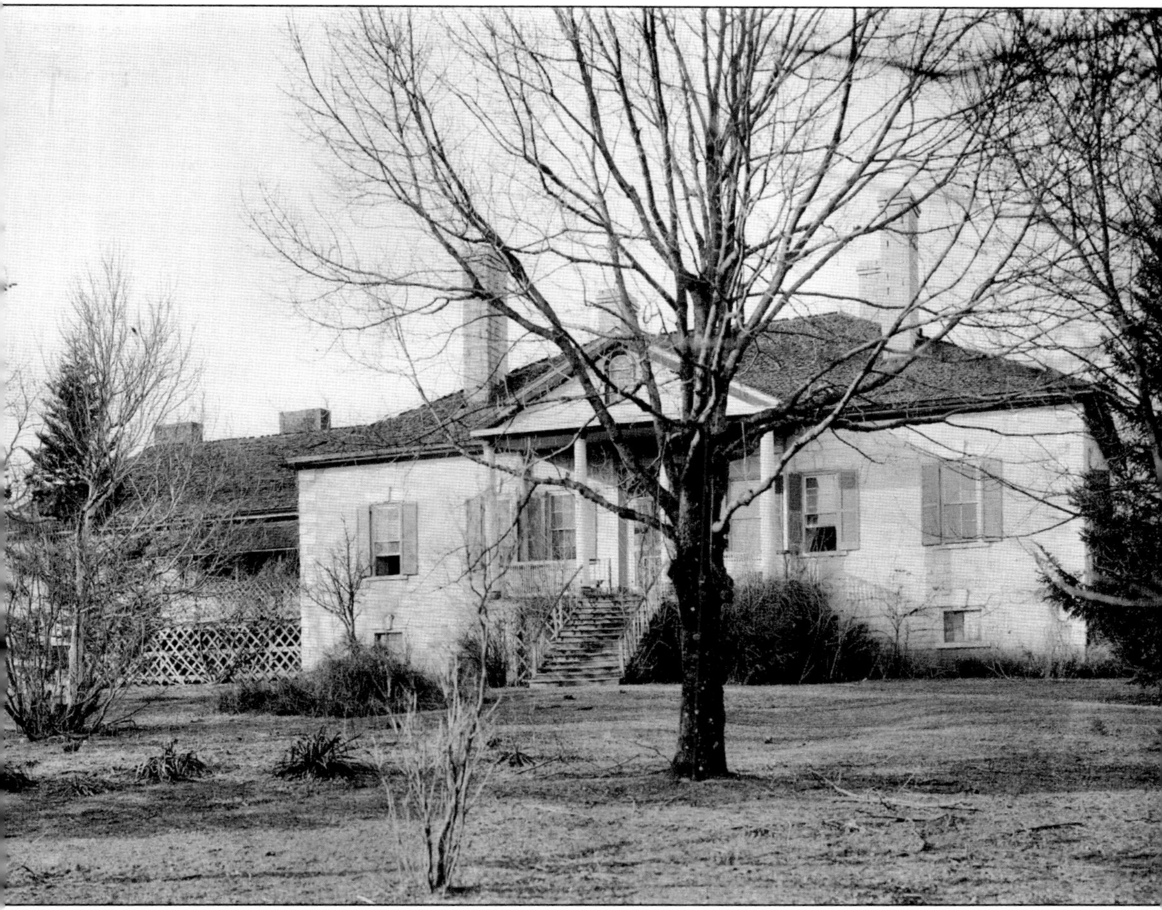

Pictured is an early 1900s view of the Belle Grove Plantation, which had served as Gen. Phil Sheridan's headquarters during the Battle of Cedar Creek. It was captured by the Confederates on the morning of the battle and retaken in the afternoon. It is said that bullets bounced off the building and littered the surrounding yard.

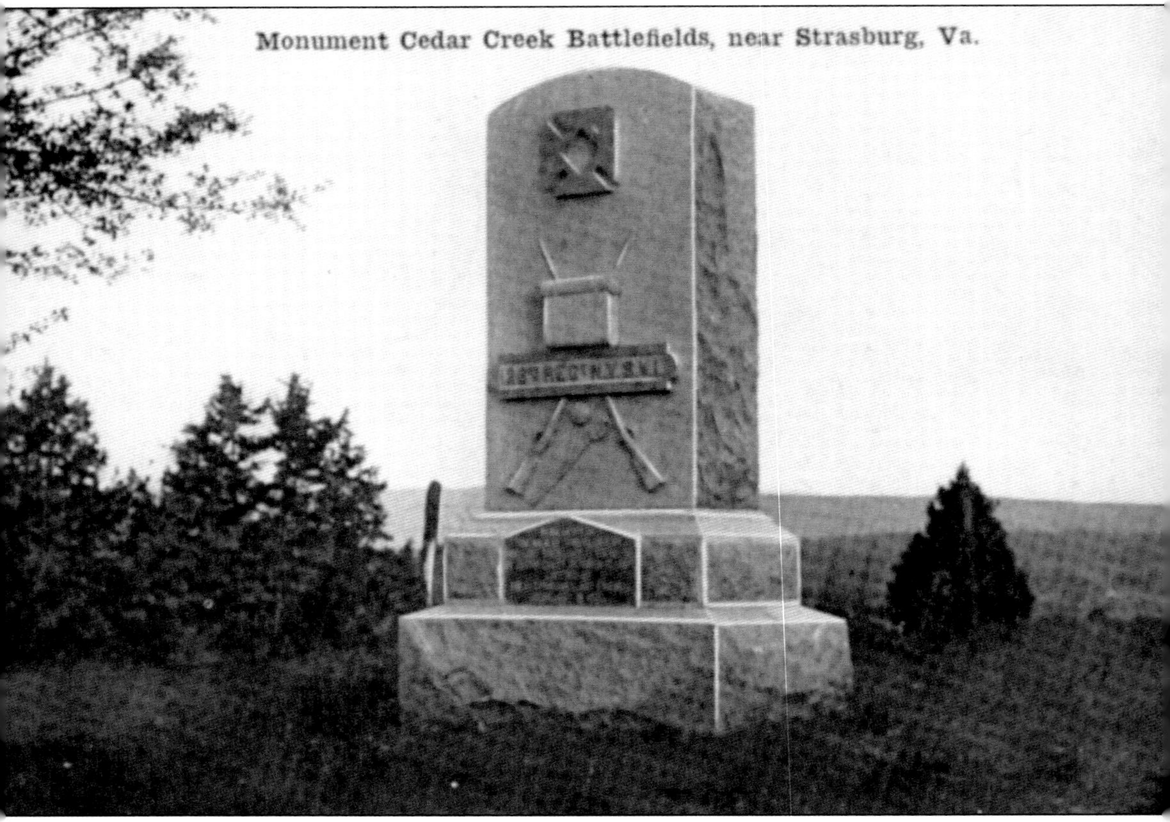

This misprinted postcard should actually read "near Middletown" rather than Strasburg. This monument to the 128th New York Volunteer Infantry marks the extreme right end of the Federal lines the 19th Corps attempted to repulse in the Confederate surprise attack. As soon as the battle was joined, Gen. Horatio Wright left headquarters to determine the situation and found himself in the midst of this Empire State Regiment. He then received a slight facial wound but continued his command of the Federal army until General Sheridan arrived from Winchester. This monument stands west of the turnpike, near the present-day Cedar Creek Campground. (Stewart Bell Jr. Archives.)

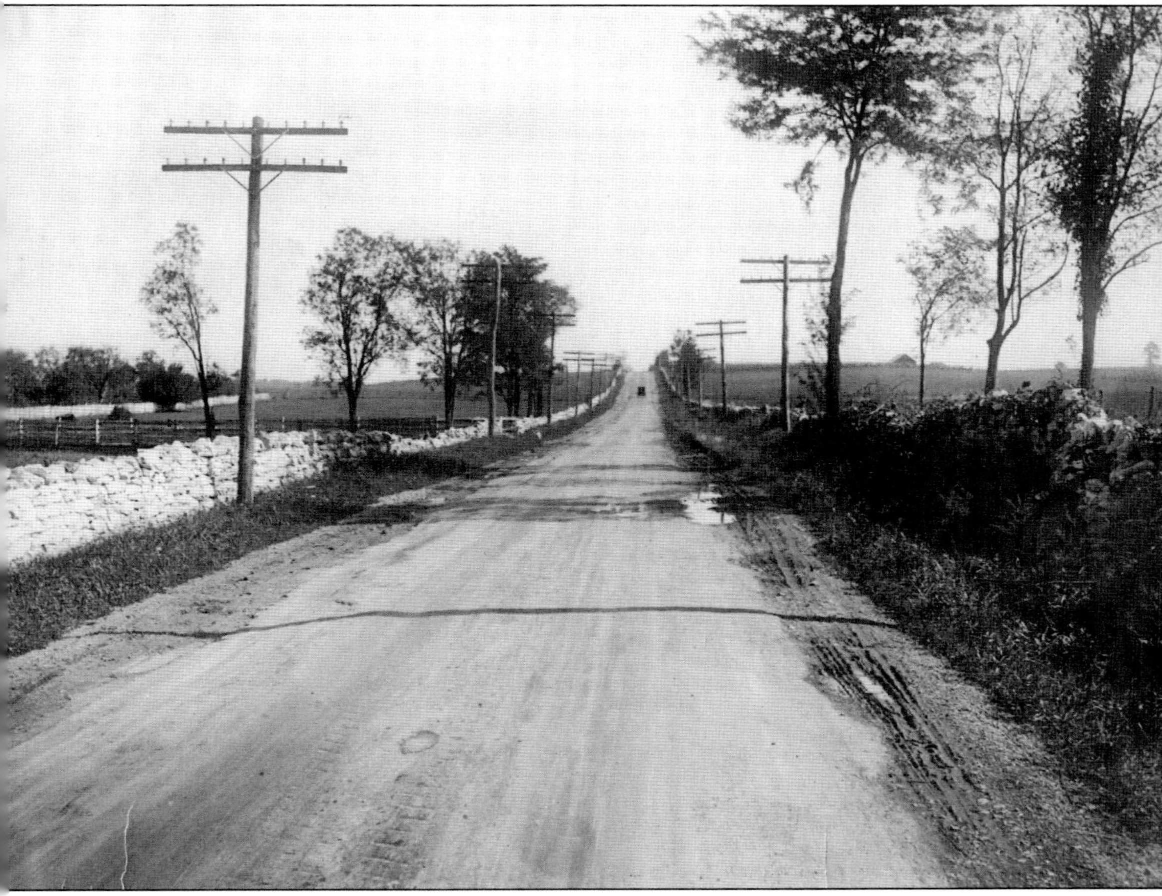

This 1928 image of the Valley Pike looks north toward Vaucluse and Stephens City from where the Lord Fairfax Community College is now located. A vintage "horseless carriage" clatters along the pike between its stone walls. Named for Union general Phillip Sheridan's horse, the Reinzi Knoll elevation at center marks the appropriate end of Sheridan's famous ride from Winchester to rally his troops at Cedar Creek. The road and path have changed little since the Civil War. (Stewart Bell Jr. Archives.)

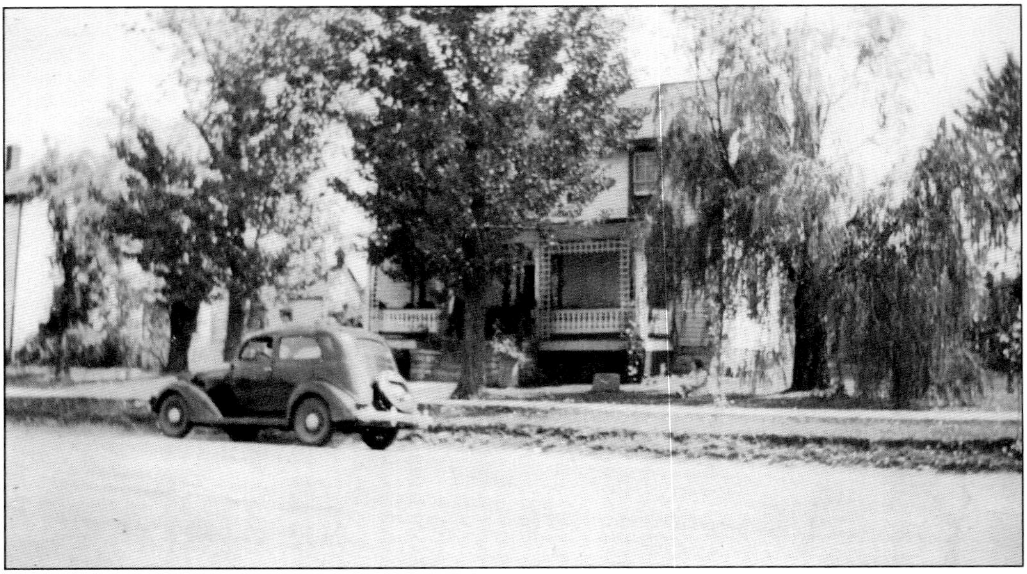

The 1940s home of James Lawson Willey is seen in this view of Main Street, along with the George William Willey home next door, to the left. (Nancy Keaton.)

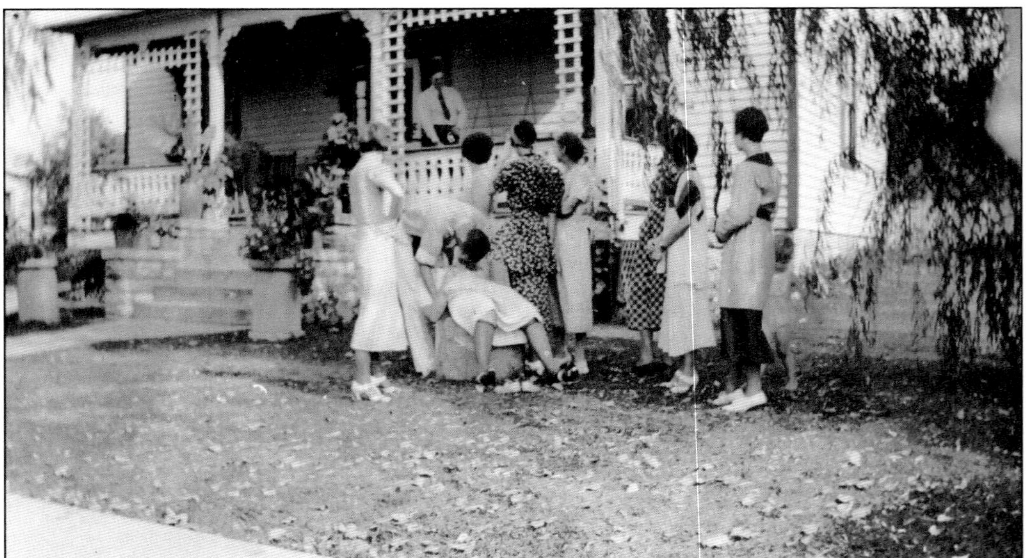

A Willey family gathering takes place at the home of James Lawson Willey—and someone is getting kissed! The full porch has been shortened in renovations by later owners and now includes only the center section. (Nancy Keaton.)

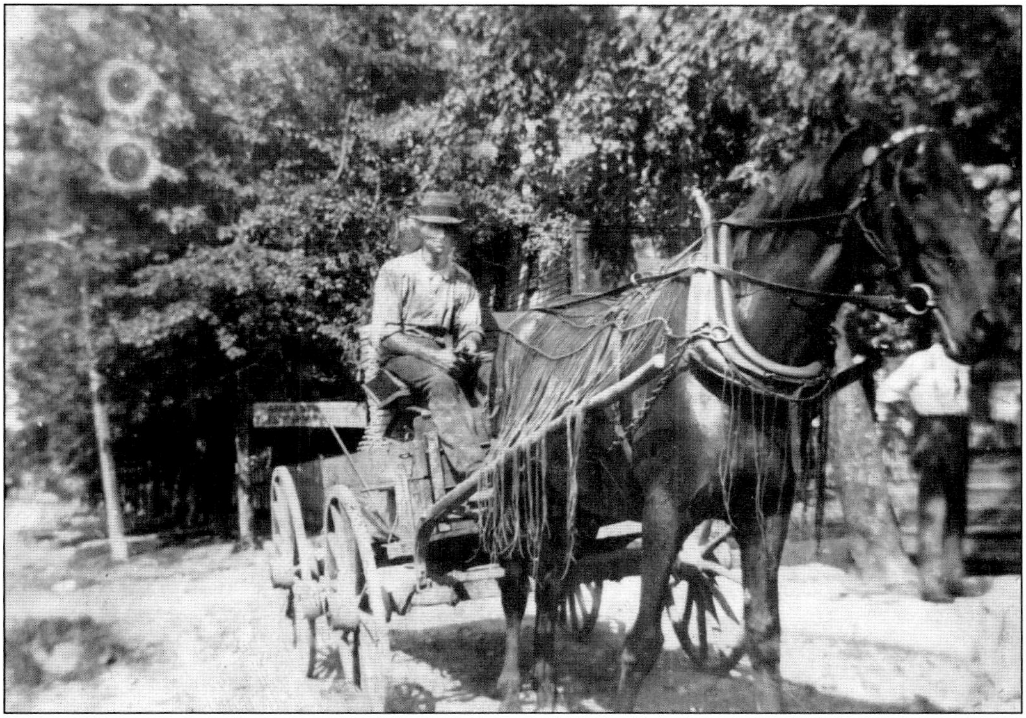

James "Jim" Lawson Willey is pictured driving his "huckster" wagon. A huckster was someone who sold various sundry goods and, often, edible items. A Willey relative, Nancy Keaton, said much of his huckster business centered on the railroad station on the west side of Middletown. (Nancy Keaton.)

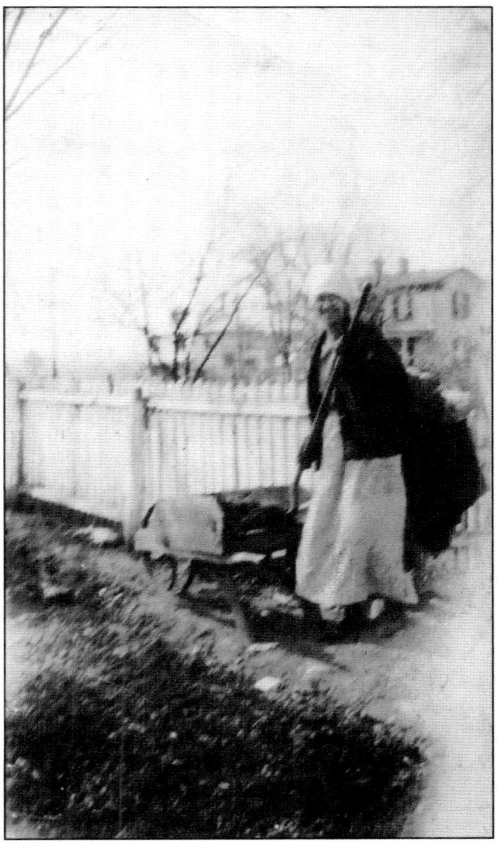

Mary Elizabeth "Lilly" Willey (1877–1950), the wife of James Lawson Willey, is captured doing yard work outside her Main Street home. Note the old wheelbarrow in which she moved dirt. (Nancy Keaton.)

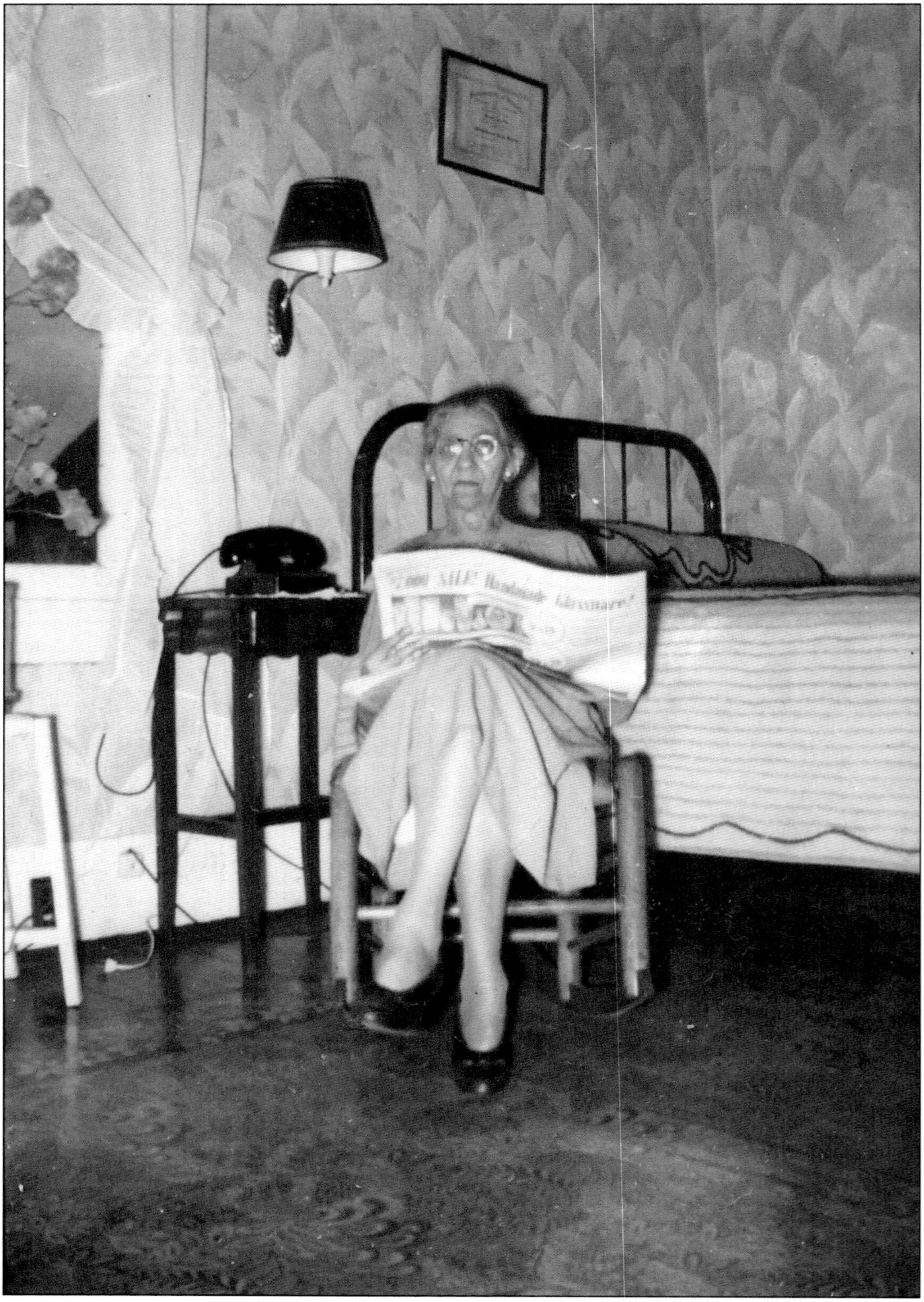

Lilly Willey is pictured here in her bedroom later in life. The Willey home still stands on the old Valley Pike, between Fifth and Sixth Streets. (Nancy Keaton.)

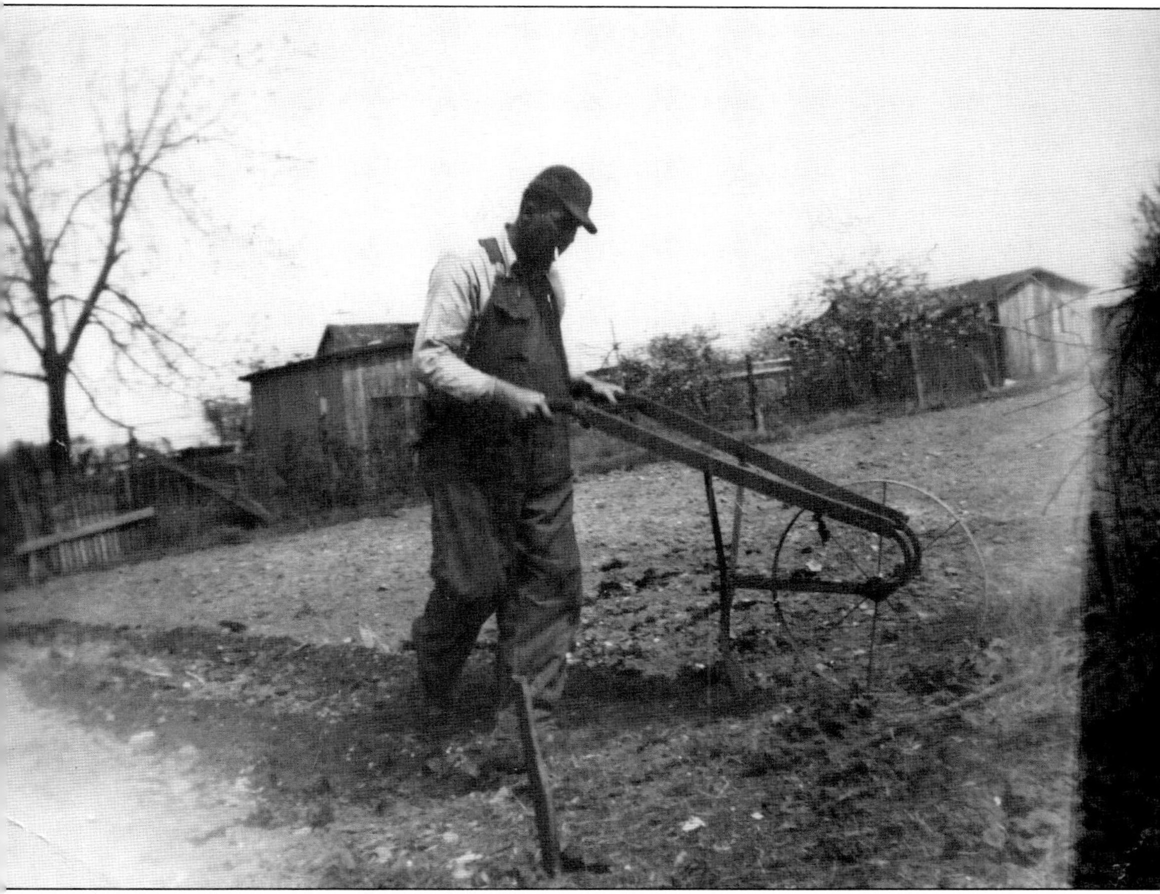

Lacy Coverstone works an old hand plow behind the George William Willey house on South Main Street. Coverstone had married into the Willey family; his wife was the former Eleanor Jean Willey who later served on Middletown's town council. This photograph demonstrates the self-reliance among the Willey family and many valley residents of past generations. A garden was an essential part of life and sometimes meant survival during the lean times in the Shenandoah Valley. (Nancy Keaton.)

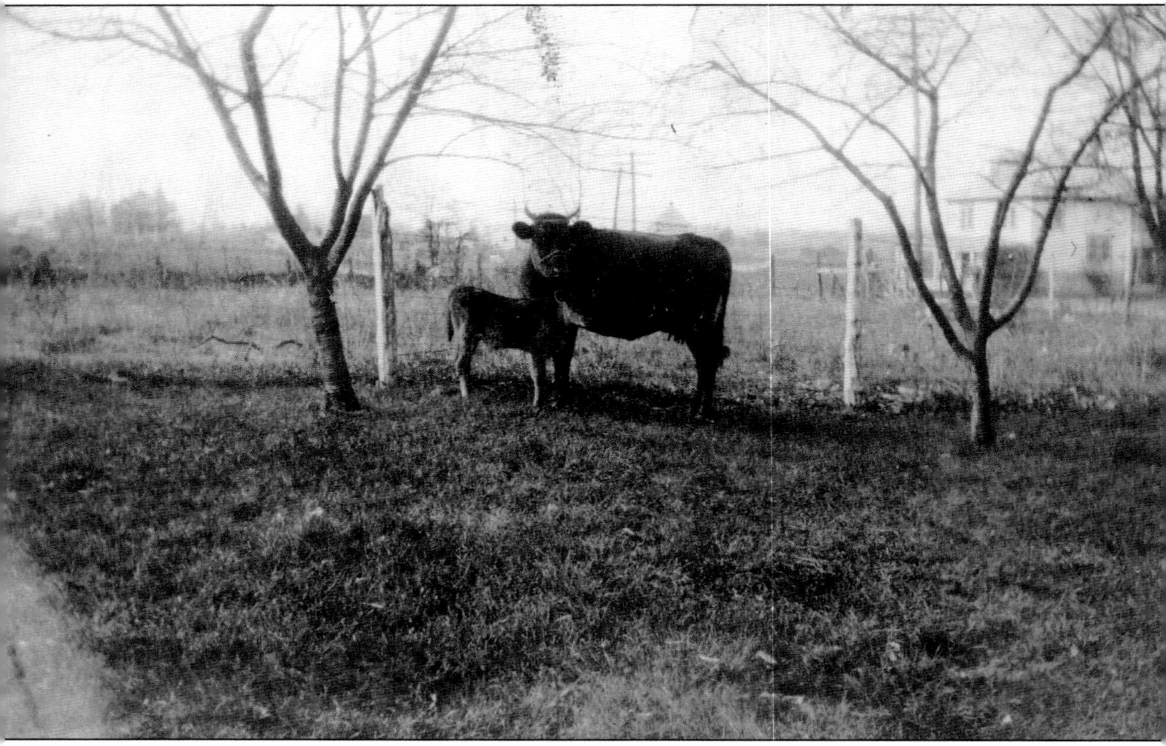

Families in Middletown like the Willeys often kept livestock, as seen by this cow and her calf shown behind the home of James Lawson Willey. Next to the property of George William Willey, they kept chickens and hogs, along with eight flourishing pear trees. One of these trees is still yielding fruit at the time of this writing. (Nancy Keaton.)

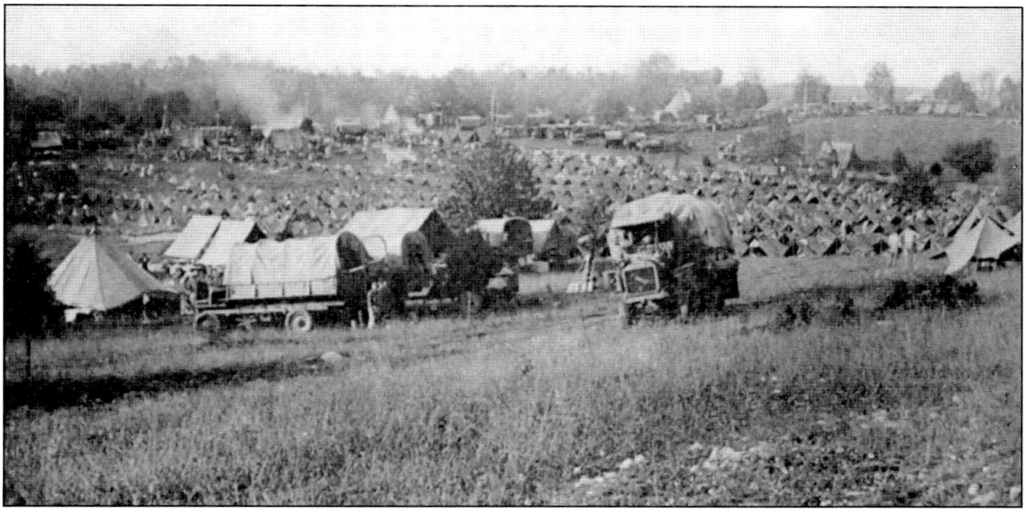

In 1923, US Marines encamped at the Cedar Creek Battlefield to practice maneuvers. Gen. Smedley D. Butler commanded the troops, which were headed to a Civil War reenactment at the nearby New Market Battlefield. (Stewart Bell Jr. Archives.)

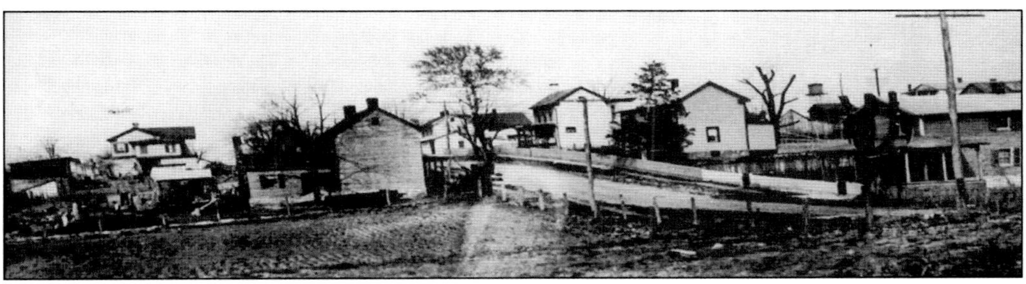

A 1941 image of Main Street shows the Riding family's homes on the crest of the hill. (Middletown Heritage Society.)

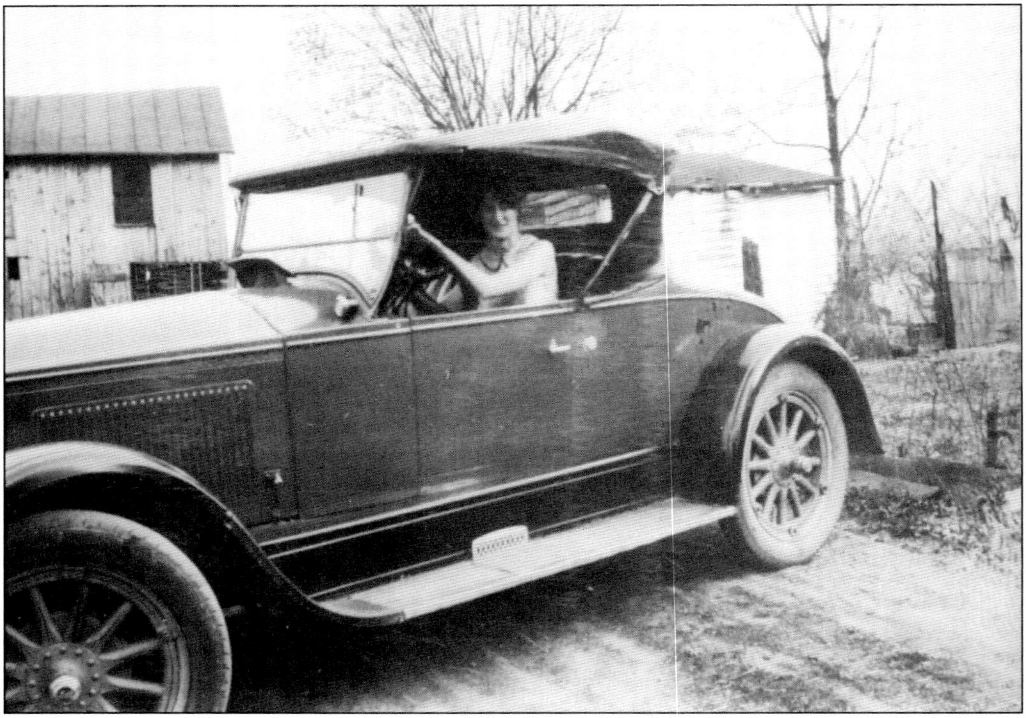

Ruby Campbell, seated in a 1914 Chevrolet, drove this vehicle to California when she was 23 years old. (Middletown Heritage Society.)

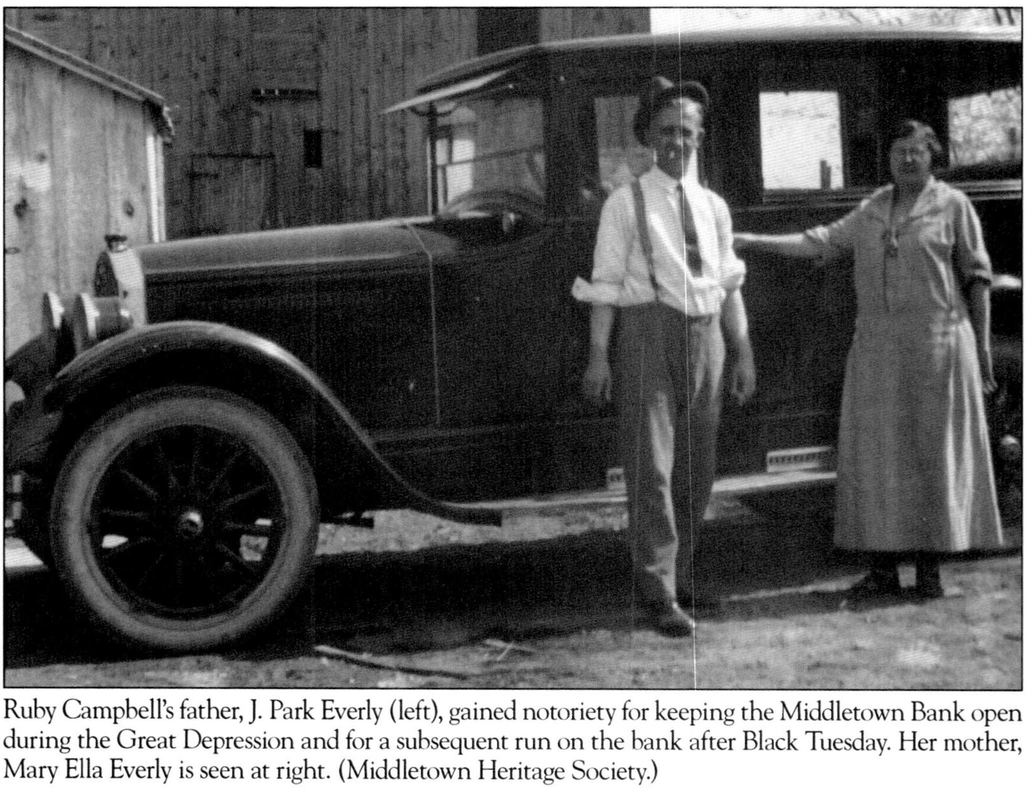

Ruby Campbell's father, J. Park Everly (left), gained notoriety for keeping the Middletown Bank open during the Great Depression and for a subsequent run on the bank after Black Tuesday. Her mother, Mary Ella Everly is seen at right. (Middletown Heritage Society.)

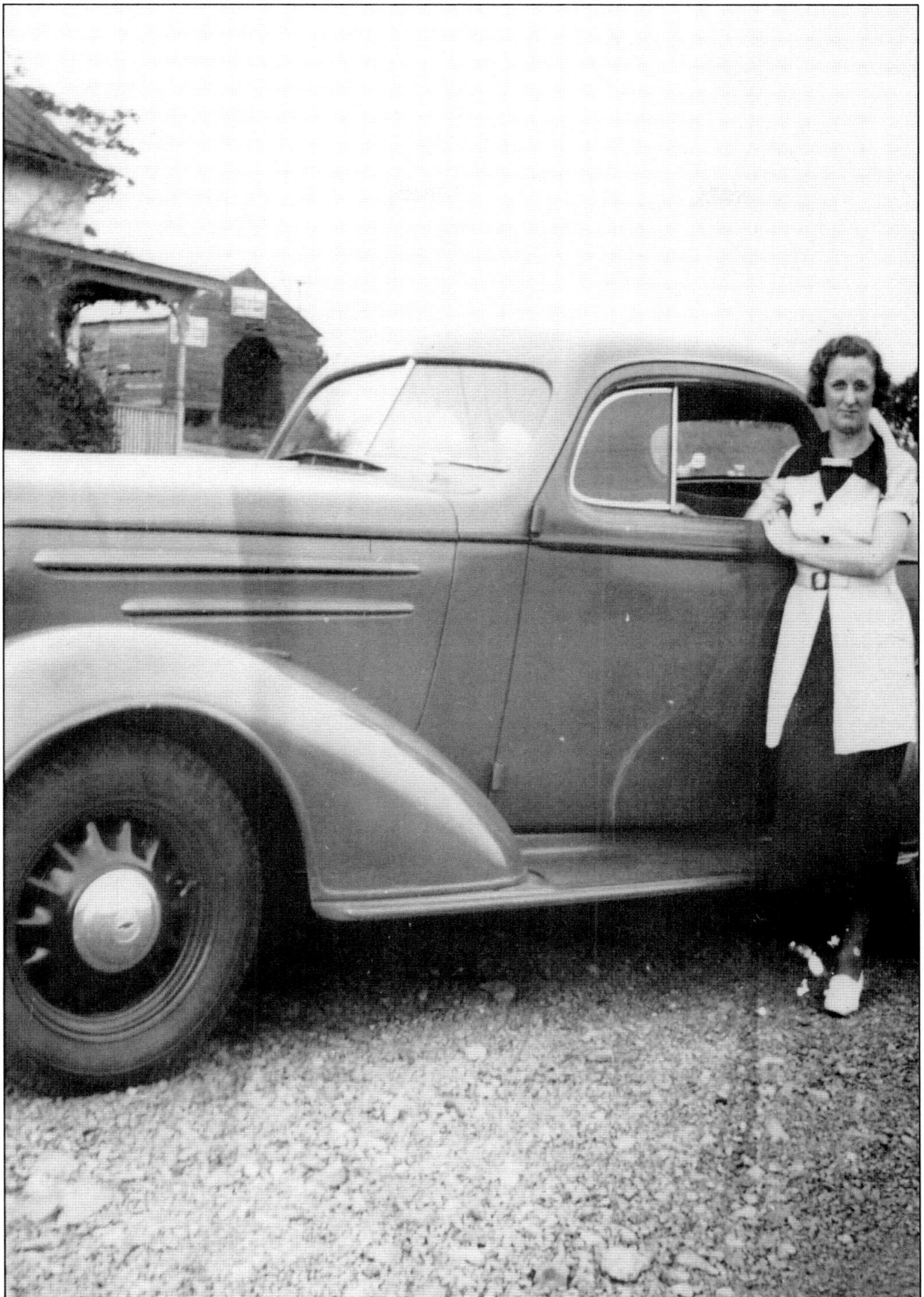

Considered an authority on Middletown's storied past, Ruby Campbell had the distinction of marching as a Native American in the first Apple Blossom Festival parade in 1924. (Middletown Heritage Society.)

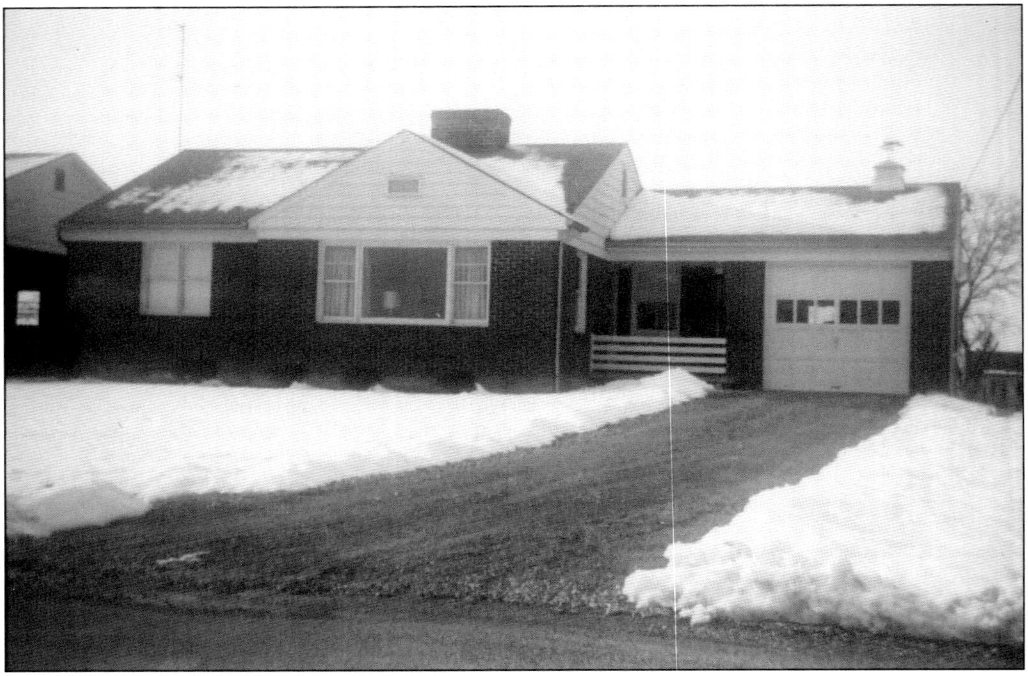

Here is a 1966 image of Ruby Campbell's Church Street home. (Middletown Heritage Society.)

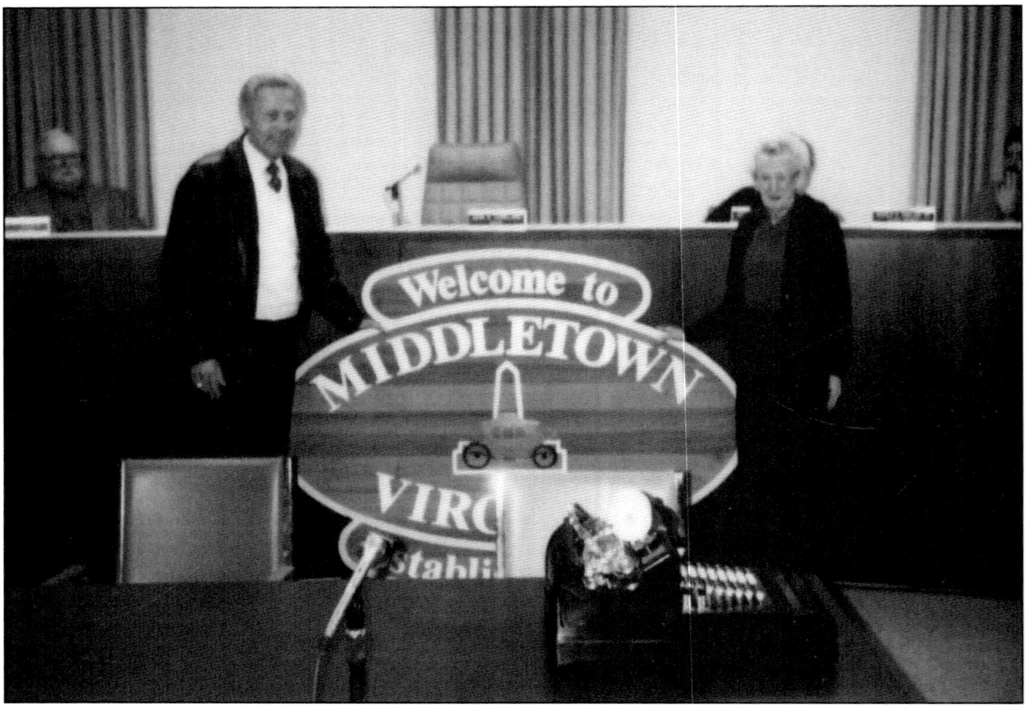

On February 12, 1999, Ruby Campbell was honored by Middletown mayor John Copeland at the unveiling of the new "Welcome to Middletown" signage; Campbell was instrumental in their creation. Commissioned at a town office meeting, the new signs remain in use today as just one of the many accomplishments Copeland achieved in his 12-year tenure as mayor. (Middletown Heritage Society.)

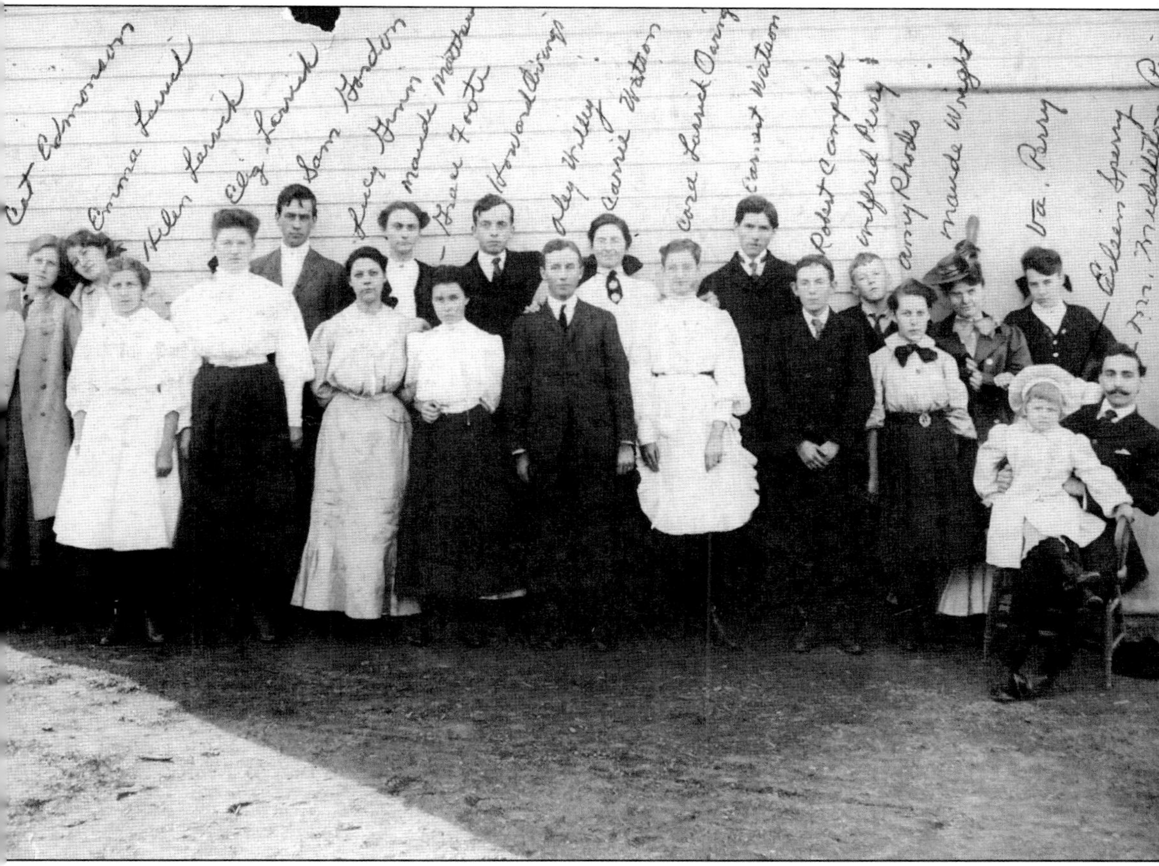

According to the handwritten names on this 1909 class photograph of Middletown High School, from left to right are Cat Edmonson, Emma Larrick, Helen Larrick, Elig Larrick, Sam Gordon, Lucy Ginn, Maude Matthews, Grace Foote, Howard Owings, Oley Willey, Carrie Watson, Cora Larrick Owings, Earnest Watson, Robert Campbell, Alfred Perry, Amy Rhodes, Maude Wright, Virginia Perry, Eileen Sperry (little girl), and a Mr. Middleton (principal). Carrie Watson's family owned a large tract of land that bordered the high school property. Also among those pictured are three girls from the first graduating class: Cora Larrick, Emma Larrick, and Maude Matthews. (John Owings.)

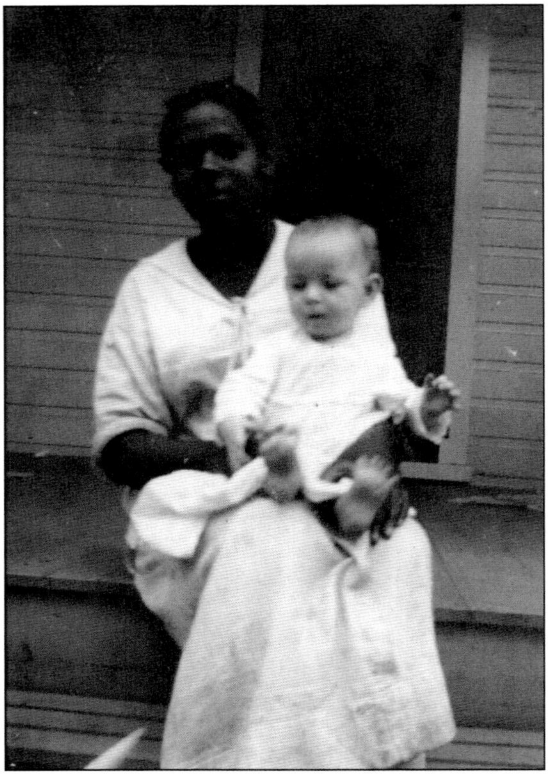

Will Owings is pictured here as an infant in 1917, along with one of his caretakers known only as "Cedie." (John Owings.)

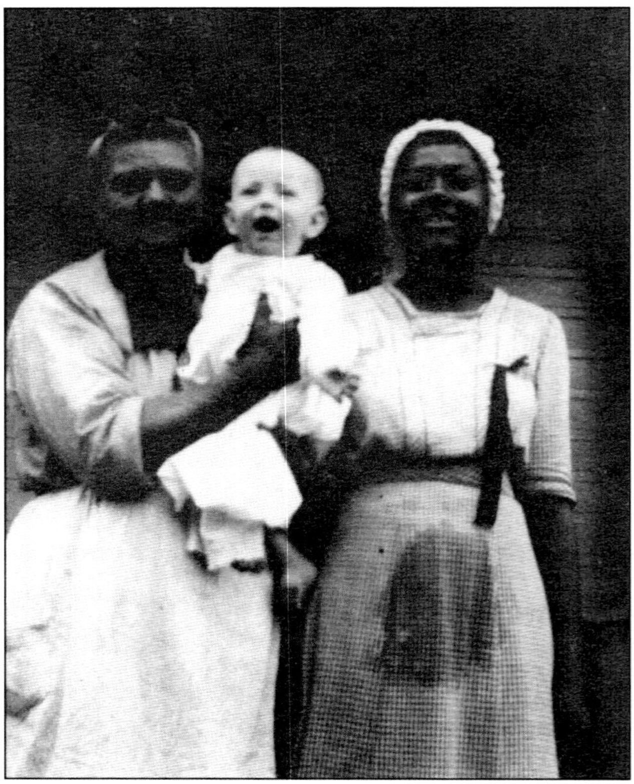

"Aunt" Lucy Walker holds infant Will Owings, again pictured here with Cedie. The Walker family, who lived off East Fourth Street, employed the women to look after Will and the house. (John Owings.)

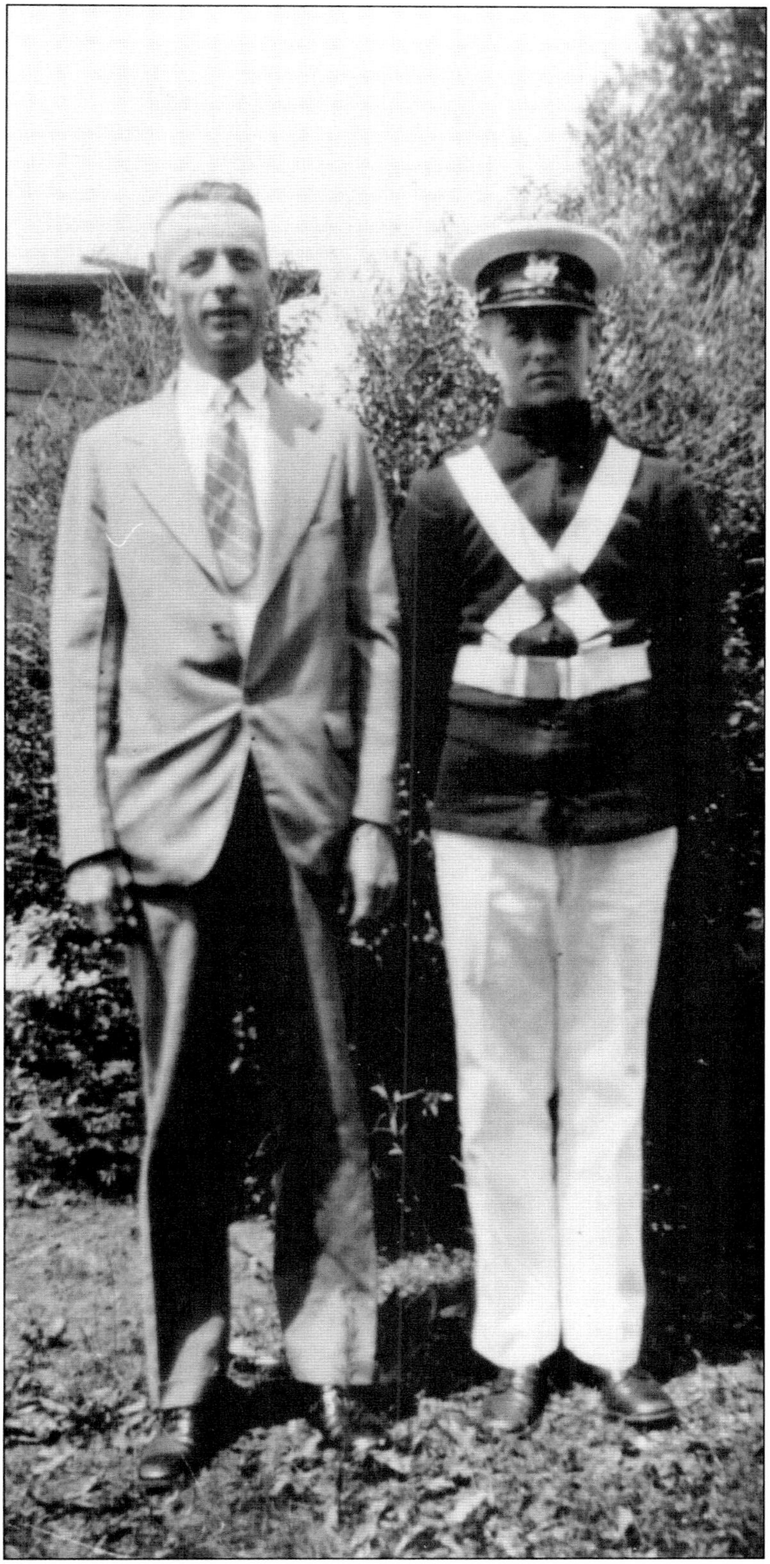

Seen here in the early 1930s are Howard W. Owings, who was a prominent merchant in town, and his son Will L. Owings, dressed in his band uniform from Handley High School in Winchester, Virginia. (John Owings.)

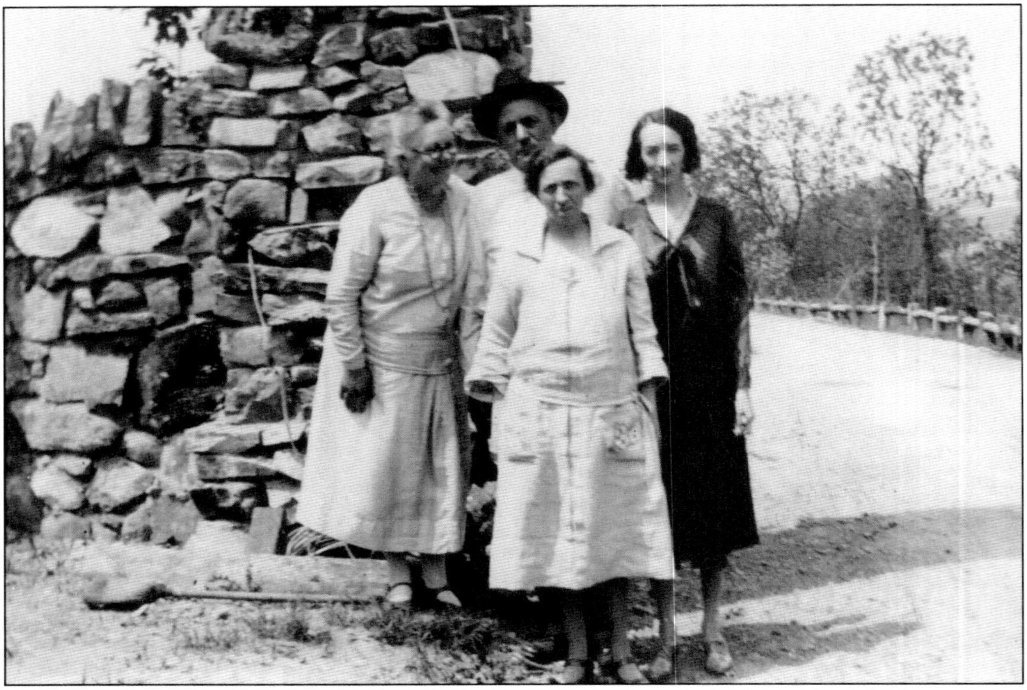

Pictured here are Mr. and Mrs. Jim Smith (left), Julia Owings Wright (center), and Edna Owings Long (right). Julia lived in the Peck-Wright house near the Wayside Inn, which later incorporated the home as office space. (John Owings.)

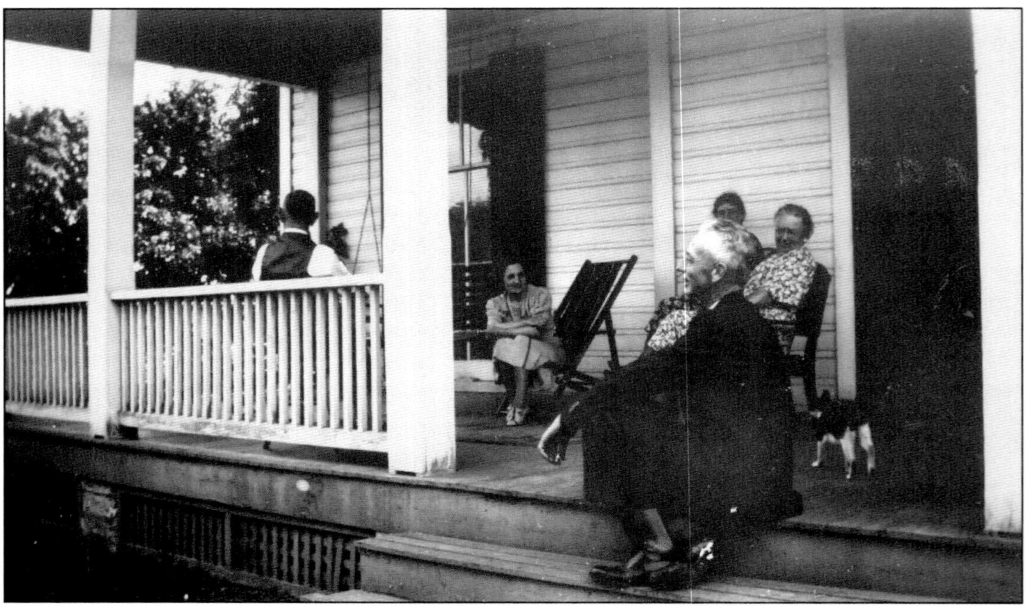

Howard W. Owings and family are pictured on the porch of their 7913 Church Street home in the 1940s. (John Owings.)

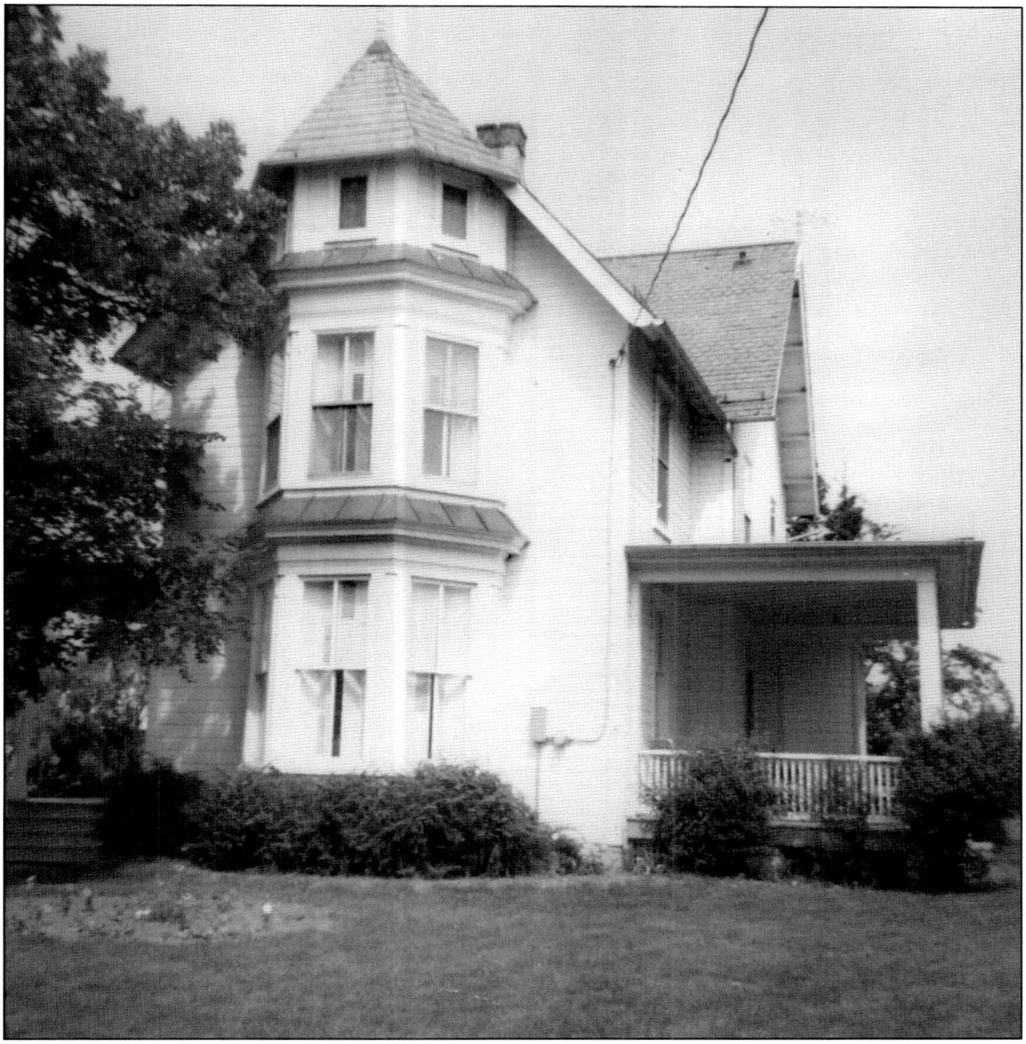

Here is a 1950s view of the Larrick-Owings house on Church Street. This home was unique in that it was the first house in town to have indoor plumbing. Previously, the home was also the office of Dr. G.W. Larrick. (John Owings.)

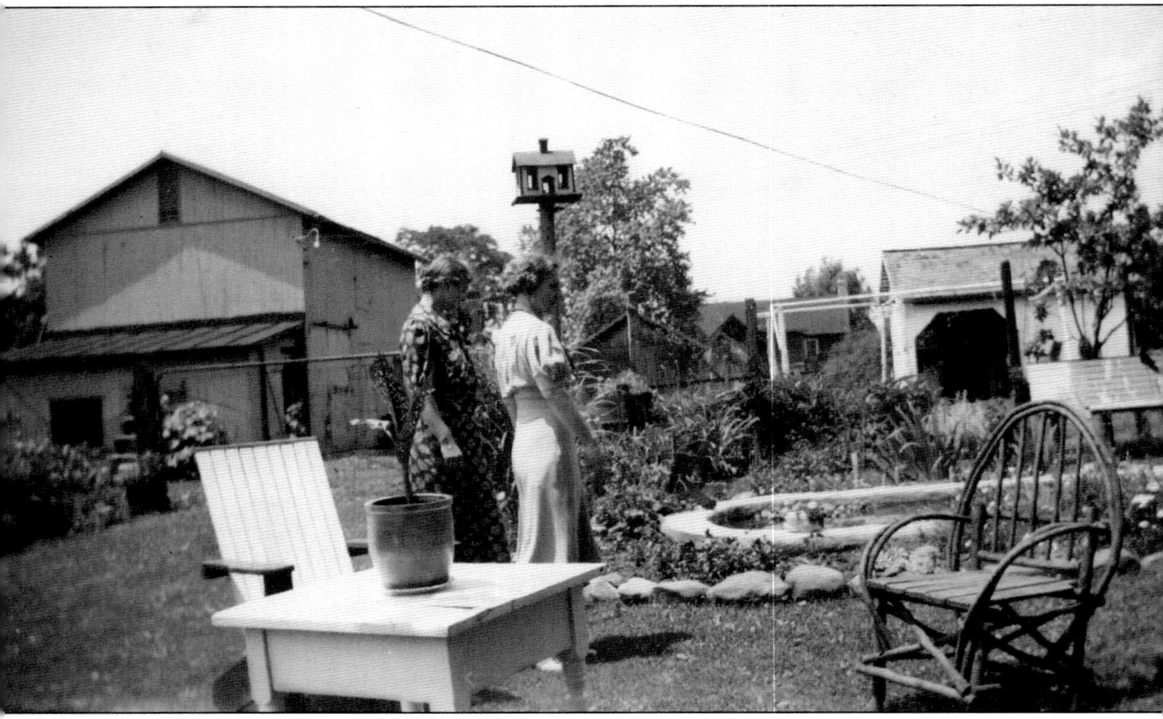

Rachel Owings (right), the wife of Will Owings, helped tend to the working farm of Howard and Cora Owings. The farm had a corncrib, chicken house, pigpen, smokehouse, and fishpond, which was well known to every child in Middletown for years to come. The woman at left is unidentified. (John Owings.)

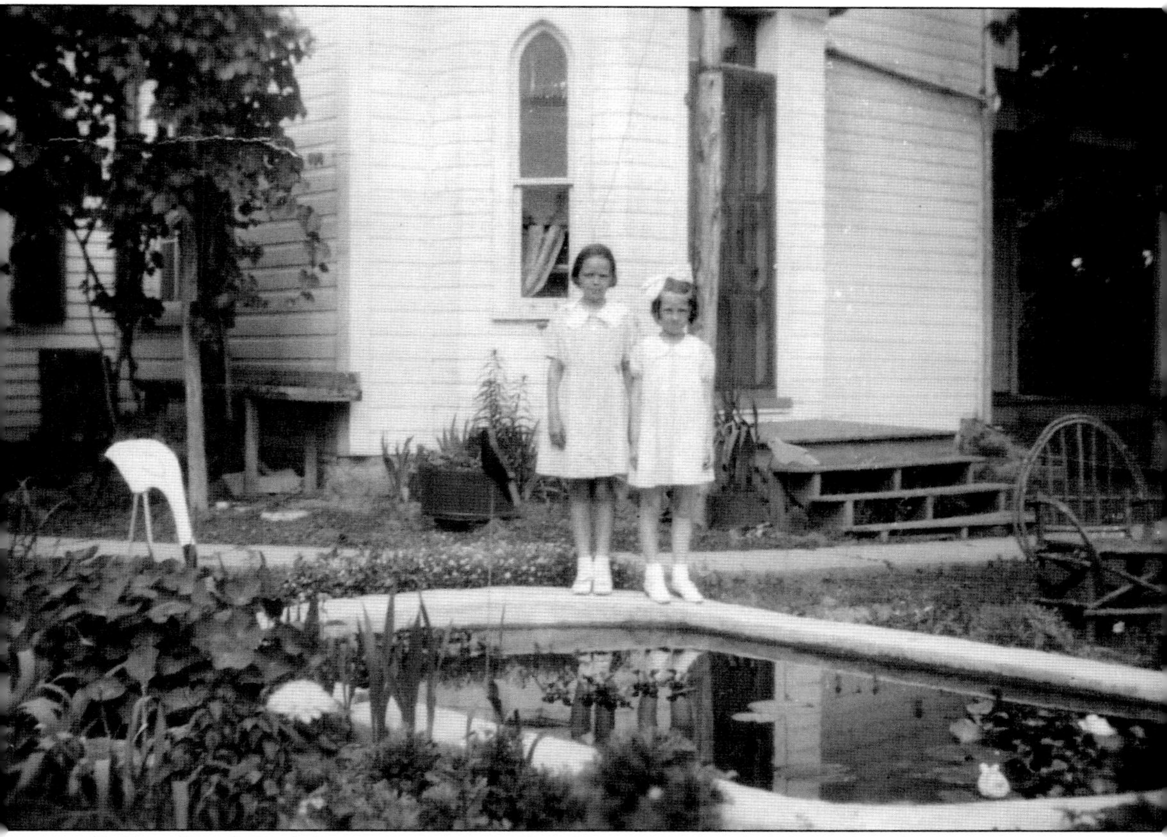

Lois (left) and Ruth (right) Sperry are pictured at the Owings family fishpond in the 1930s. Note the small porch at right that was the entrance to G.W. Larrick's doctor's office. (John Owings.)

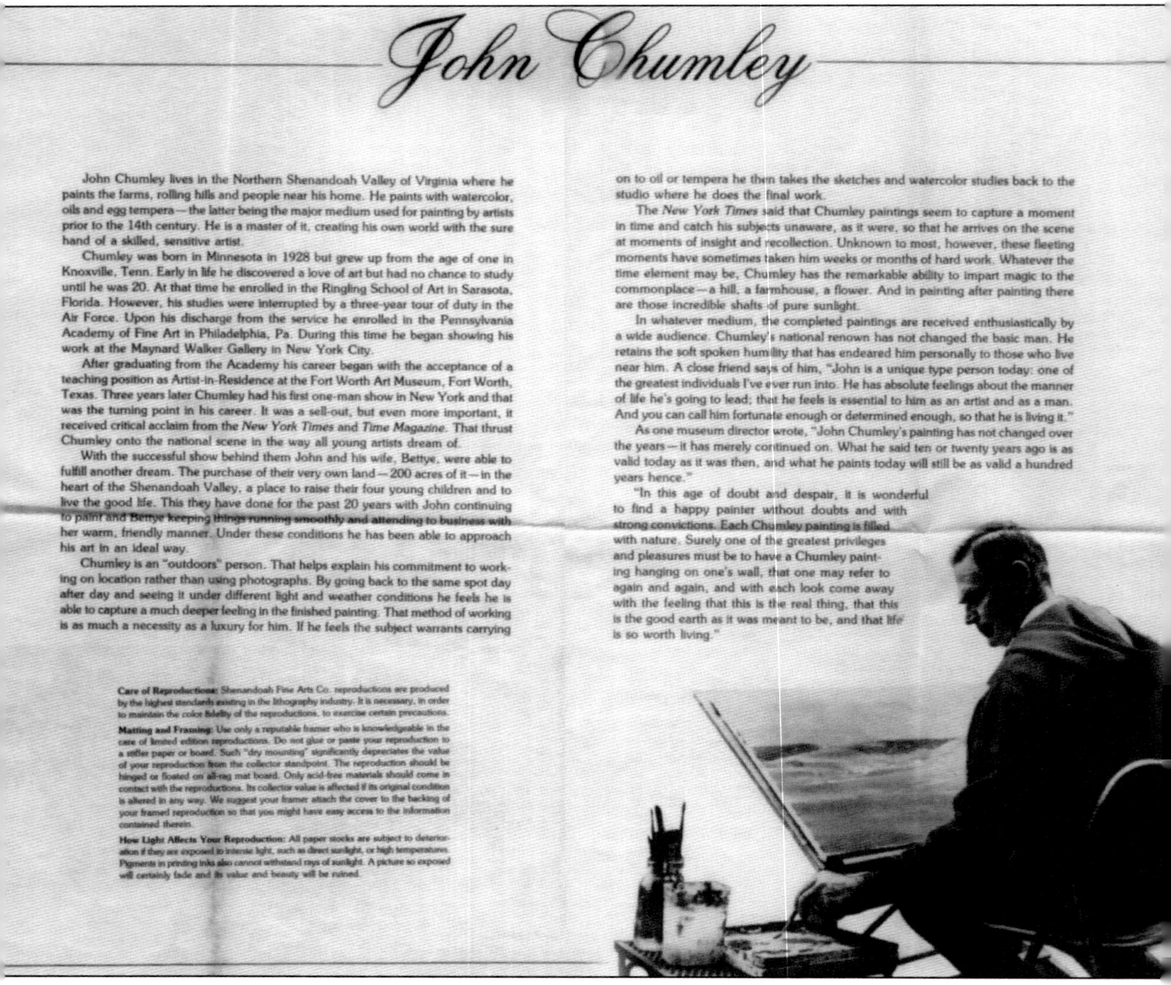

John Chumley

John Chumley lives in the Northern Shenandoah Valley of Virginia where he paints the farms, rolling hills and people near his home. He paints with watercolor, oils and egg tempera—the latter being the major medium used for painting by artists prior to the 14th century. He is a master of it, creating his own world with the sure hand of a skilled, sensitive artist.

Chumley was born in Minnesota in 1928 but grew up from the age of one in Knoxville, Tenn. Early in life he discovered a love of art but had no chance to study until he was 20. At that time he enrolled in the Ringling School of Art in Sarasota, Florida. However, his studies were interrupted by a three-year tour of duty in the Air Force. Upon his discharge from the service he enrolled in the Pennsylvania Academy of Fine Art in Philadelphia, Pa. During this time he began showing his work at the Maynard Walker Gallery in New York City.

After graduating from the Academy his career began with the acceptance of a teaching position as Artist-in-Residence at the Fort Worth Art Museum, Fort Worth, Texas. Three years later Chumley had his first one-man show in New York and that was the turning point in his career. It was a sell-out, but even more important, it received critical acclaim from the *New York Times* and *Time Magazine*. That thrust Chumley onto the national scene in the way all young artists dream of.

With the successful show behind them John and his wife, Bettye, were able to fulfill another dream. The purchase of their very own land—200 acres of it—in the heart of the Shenandoah Valley, a place to raise their four young children and to live the good life. This they have done for the past 20 years with John continuing to paint and Bettye keeping things running smoothly and attending to business with her warm, friendly manner. Under these conditions he has been able to approach his art in an ideal way.

Chumley is an "outdoors" person. That helps explain his commitment to working on location rather than using photographs. By going back to the same spot day after day and seeing it under different light and weather conditions he feels he is able to capture a much deeper feeling in the finished painting. That method of working is as much a necessity as a luxury for him. If he feels the subject warrants carrying on to oil or tempera he then takes the sketches and watercolor studies back to the studio where he does the final work.

The *New York Times* said that Chumley paintings seem to capture a moment in time and catch his subjects unaware, as it were, so that he arrives on the scene at moments of insight and recollection. Unknown to most, however, these fleeting moments have sometimes taken him weeks or months of hard work. Whatever the time element may be, Chumley has the remarkable ability to impart magic to the commonplace—a hill, a farmhouse, a flower. And in painting after painting there are those incredible shafts of pure sunlight.

In whatever medium, the completed paintings are received enthusiastically by a wide audience. Chumley's national renown has not changed the basic man. He retains the soft spoken humility that has endeared him personally to those who live near him. A close friend says of him, "John is a unique type person today: one of the greatest individuals I've ever run into. He has absolute feelings about the manner of life he's going to lead; that he feels is essential to him as an artist and as a man. And you can call him fortunate enough or determined enough, so that he is living it."

As one museum director wrote, "John Chumley's painting has not changed over the years—it has merely continued on. What he said ten or twenty years ago is as valid today as it was then, and what he paints today will still be as valid a hundred years hence."

"In this age of doubt and despair, it is wonderful to find a happy painter without doubts and with strong convictions. Each Chumley painting is filled with nature. Surely one of the greatest privileges and pleasures must be to have a Chumley painting hanging on one's wall, that one may refer to again and again, and with each look come away with the feeling that this is the real thing, that this is the good earth as it was meant to be, and that life is so worth living."

Care of Reproductions: Shenandoah Fine Arts Co. reproductions are produced by the highest standards existing in the lithography industry. It is necessary, in order to maintain the color fidelity of the reproductions, to exercise certain precautions.

Matting and Framing: Use only a reputable framer who is knowledgeable in the care of limited edition reproductions. Do not glue or paste your reproduction to a stiffer paper or board. Such "dry mounting" significantly depreciates the value of your reproduction from the collector standpoint. The reproduction should be hinged or floated on all-rag mat board. Only acid-free materials should come in contact with the reproductions. Its collector value is affected if its original condition is altered in any way. We suggest your framer attach the cover to the backing of your framed reproduction so that you might have easy access to the information contained therein.

How Light Affects Your Reproduction: All paper stocks are subject to deterioration if they are exposed to intense light, such as direct sunlight, or high temperatures. Pigments in printing inks also cannot withstand rays of sunlight. A picture so exposed will certainly fade and its value and beauty will be ruined.

John Chumley moved from Knoxville, Tennessee, to the Maplewood Farm at Sixth and Church Streets in Middletown. As a renowned watercolor artist, Chumley depicted life in and around Middletown from his Maplewood home in many of his paintings. Later in life, he moved to nearby Vaucluse. (John Owings.)

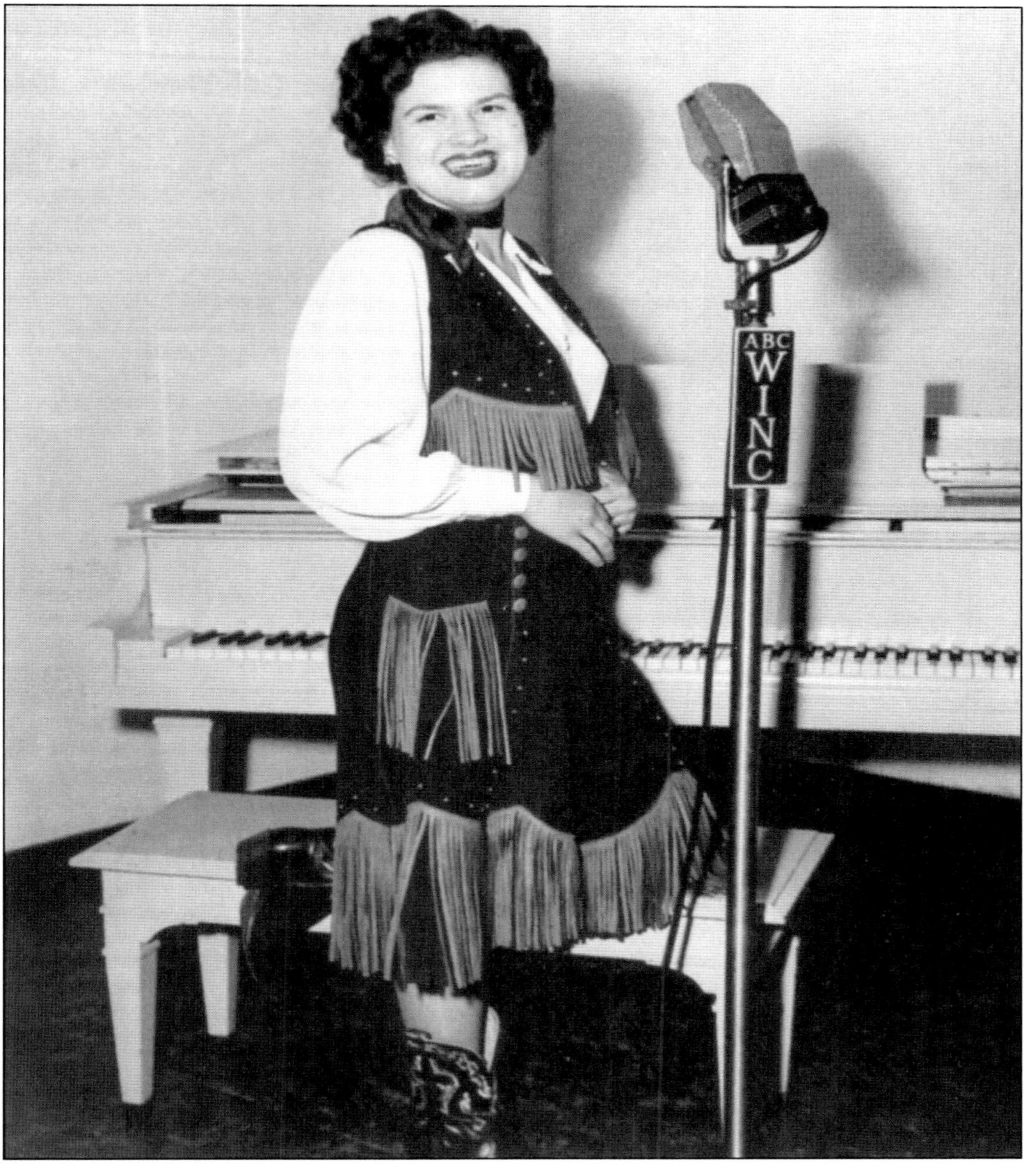

Country Music Hall of Famer Patsy Cline poses behind the WINC microphone. WINC had its beginnings in a space at the Wayside Inn. Patsy often stayed at the home of a friend in Middletown when playing venues in southern Frederick County, Warren County, and Shenandoah County. (Stewart Bell Jr. Archives.)

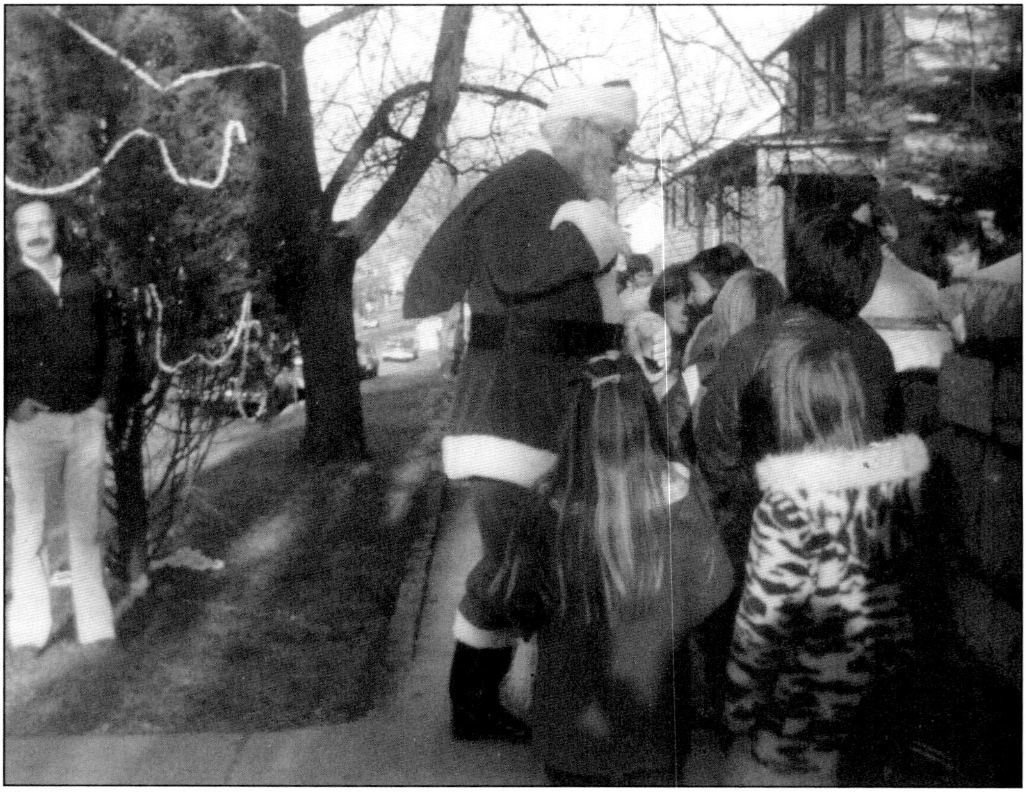

Here comes Santa Claus, this time right down Main Street to the gates of Grace United Methodist Church, where eager children await his arrival in the 1960s. (Middletown Heritage Society.)

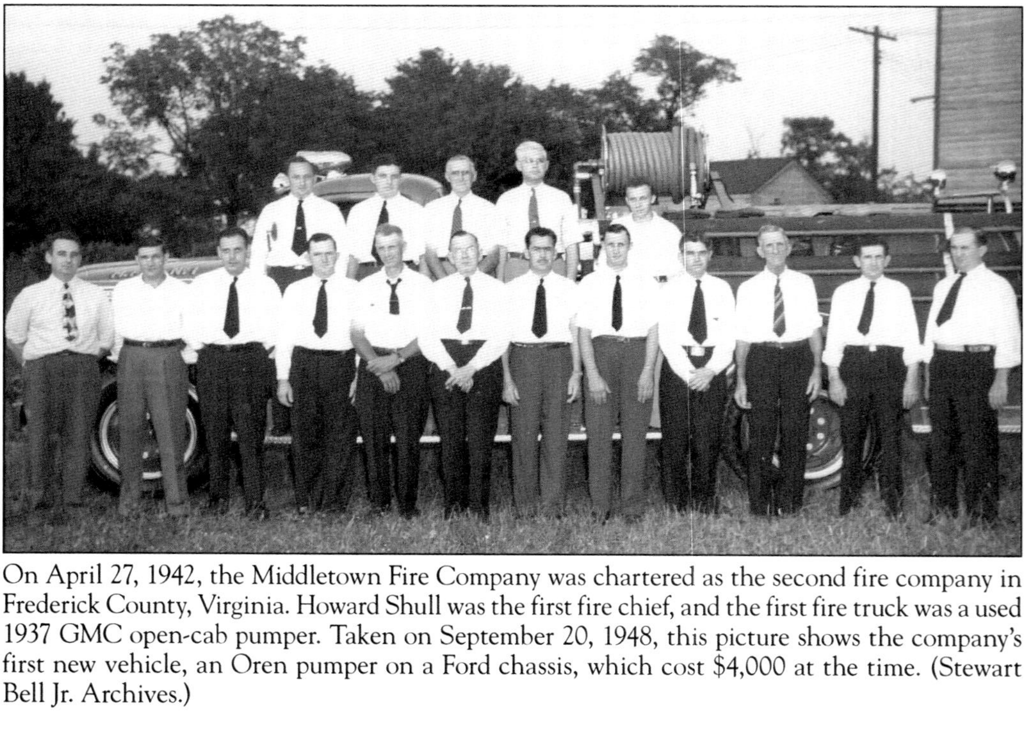

On April 27, 1942, the Middletown Fire Company was chartered as the second fire company in Frederick County, Virginia. Howard Shull was the first fire chief, and the first fire truck was a used 1937 GMC open-cab pumper. Taken on September 20, 1948, this picture shows the company's first new vehicle, an Oren pumper on a Ford chassis, which cost $4,000 at the time. (Stewart Bell Jr. Archives.)

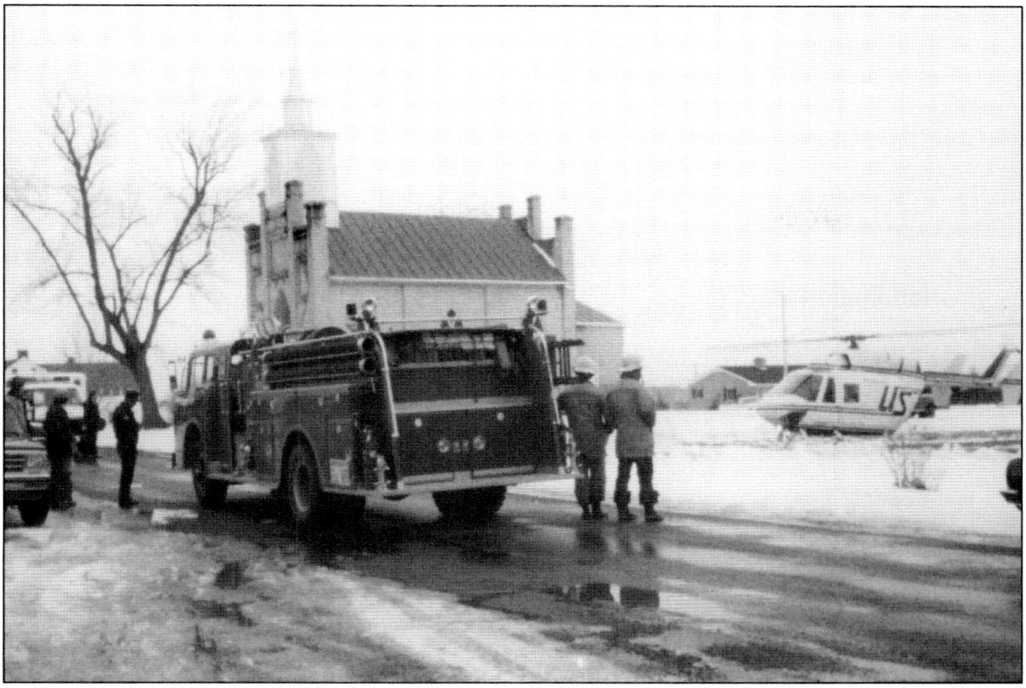

A snowy-day landing of a helicopter in the 1960s next to the historic St. Thomas Chapel prompted the response of the ever-capable Middletown Volunteer Fire Department. (Middletown Heritage Society.)

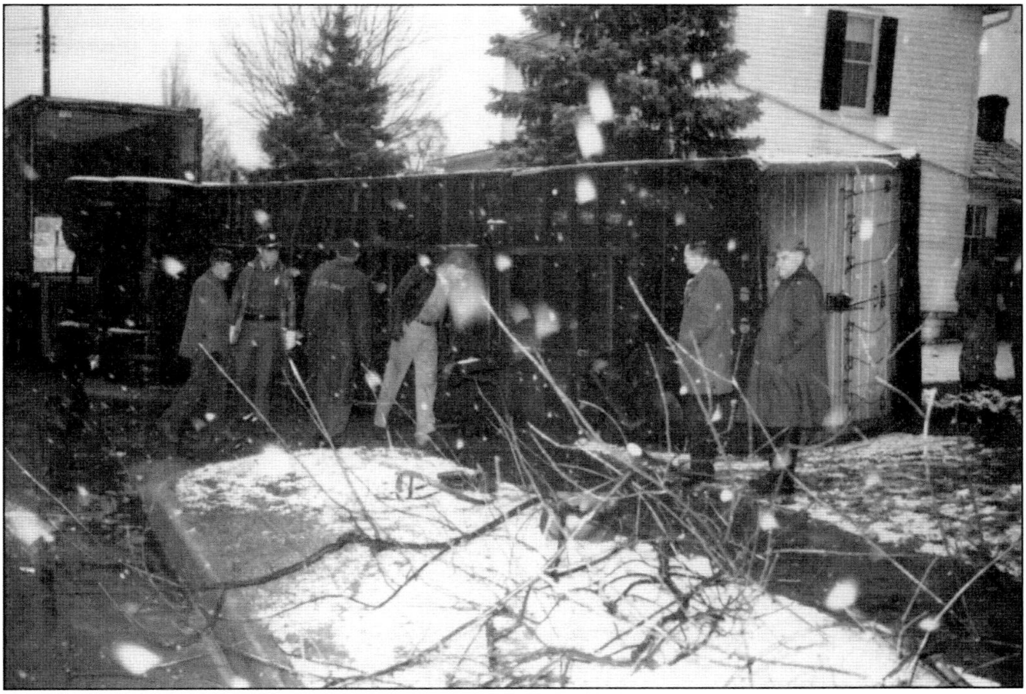

Yet another snowy incident is shown here, but this time on the Valley Turnpike (Route 11). Middletown Police and others discuss how to right the tractor-trailer that has flipped on its side. (Middletown Heritage Society.)

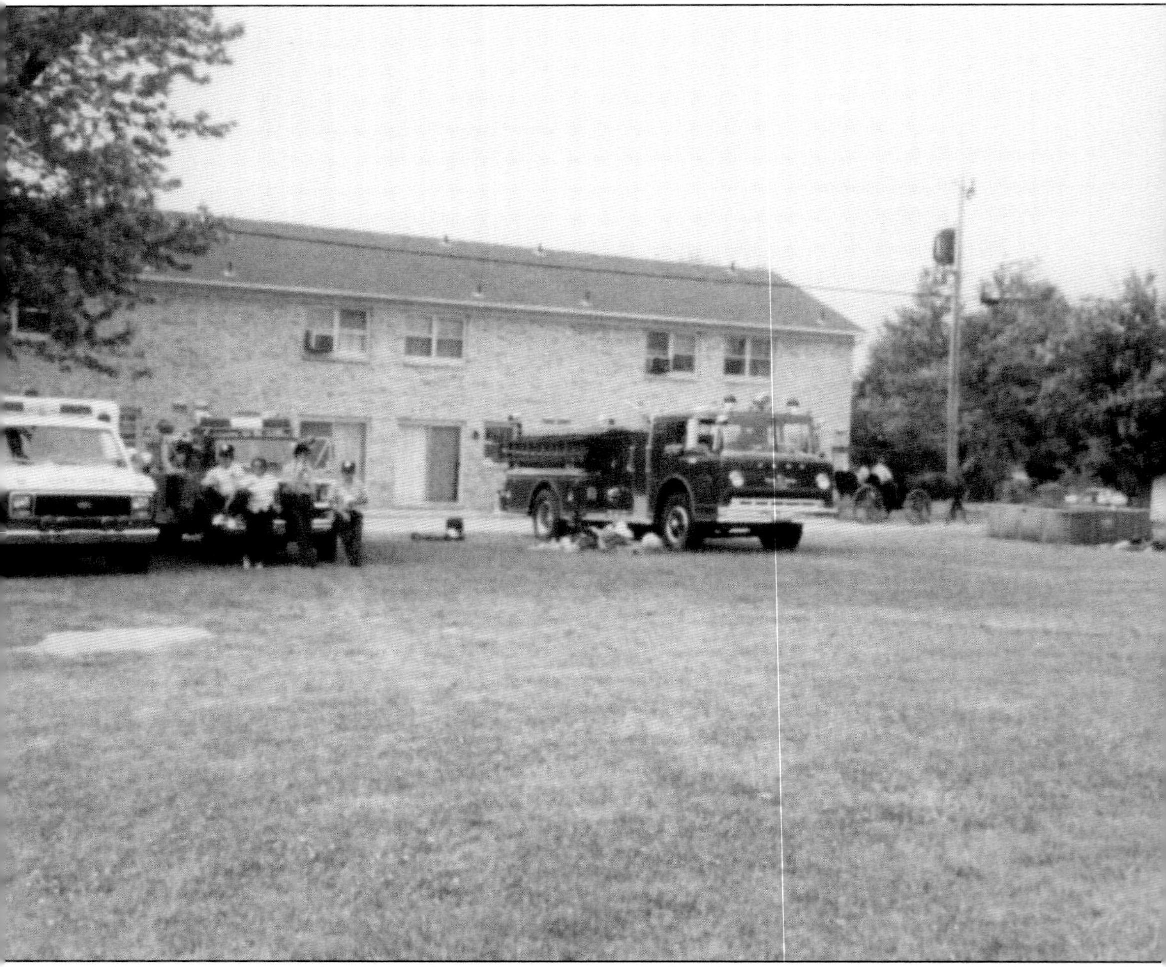

The Middletown Volunteer Fire Department is pictured here in 1985 while participating in the town's Fourth of July festivities. The fire department and subsequent Ladies Auxiliary organized the town's parade and other events for years. Note the horse and buggy traveling through town. (Middletown Heritage Society.)

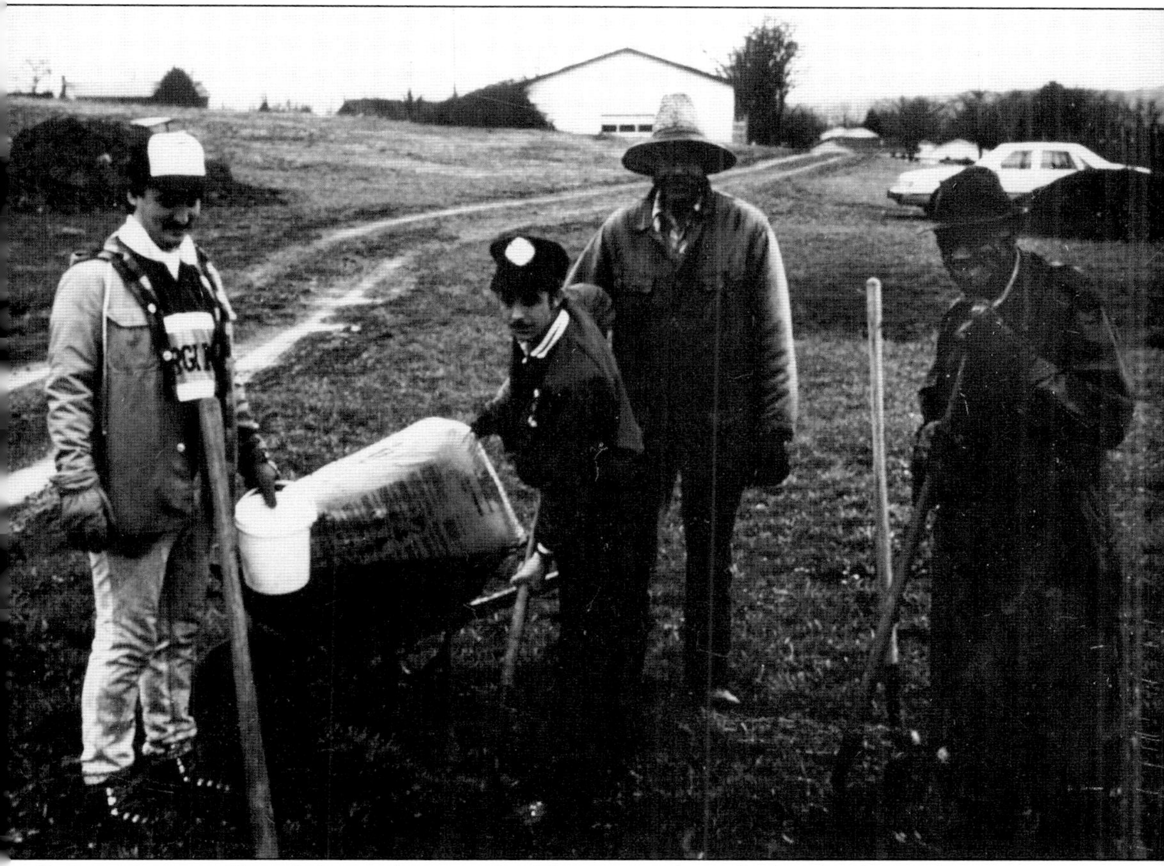

Robert Newman (far right) was a longtime Middletown resident who lived to be nearly 100 years old at his Senseney Avenue home. Here, Newman and others help to start a recycling program at the town park in the 1980s. (Middletown Heritage Society.)

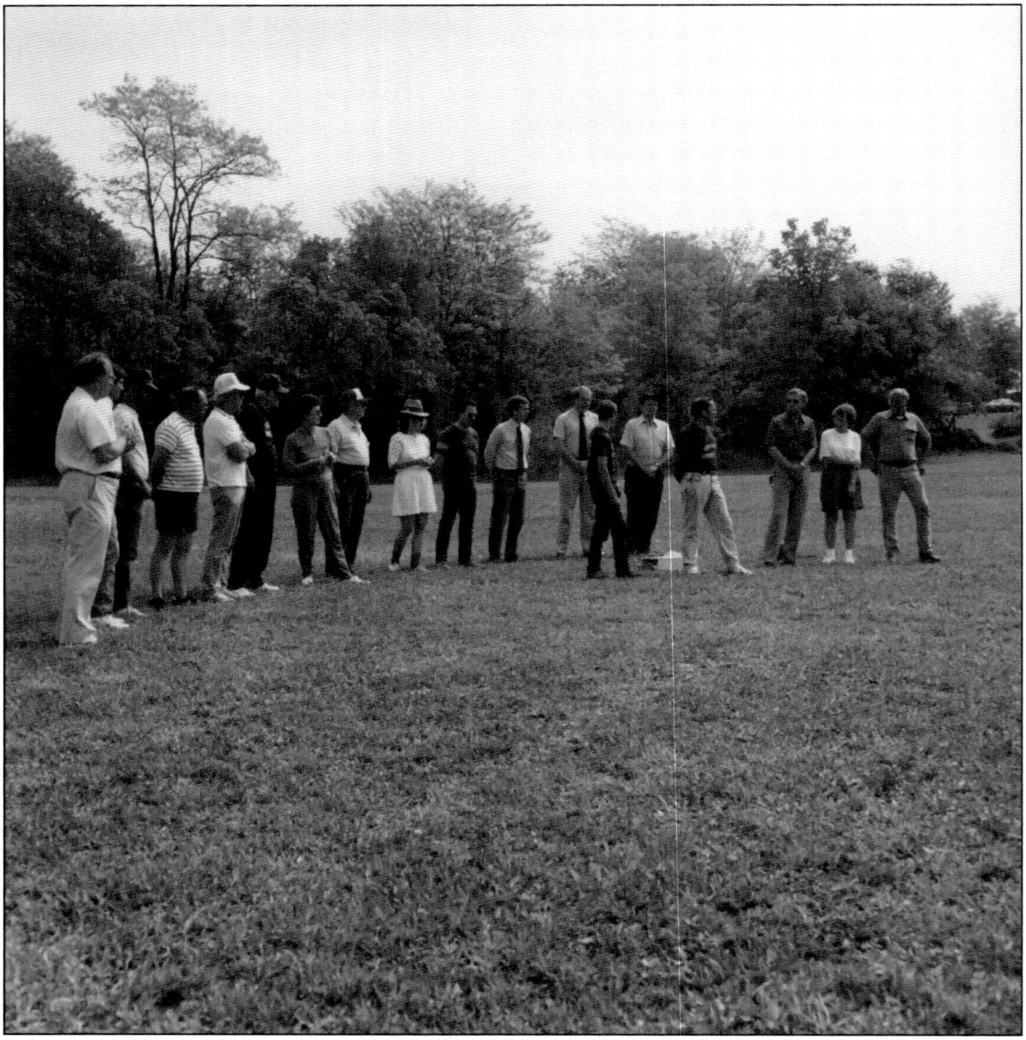

One of Ray Steele's many accomplishments as mayor from 1988 to 1992 was the establishment of the Middletown community park on nine acres of land off Senseney Avenue. In a ceremony on May 11, 1991, the contributions of council members and community leaders who had helped with the project were recognized. (Middletown Heritage Society.)

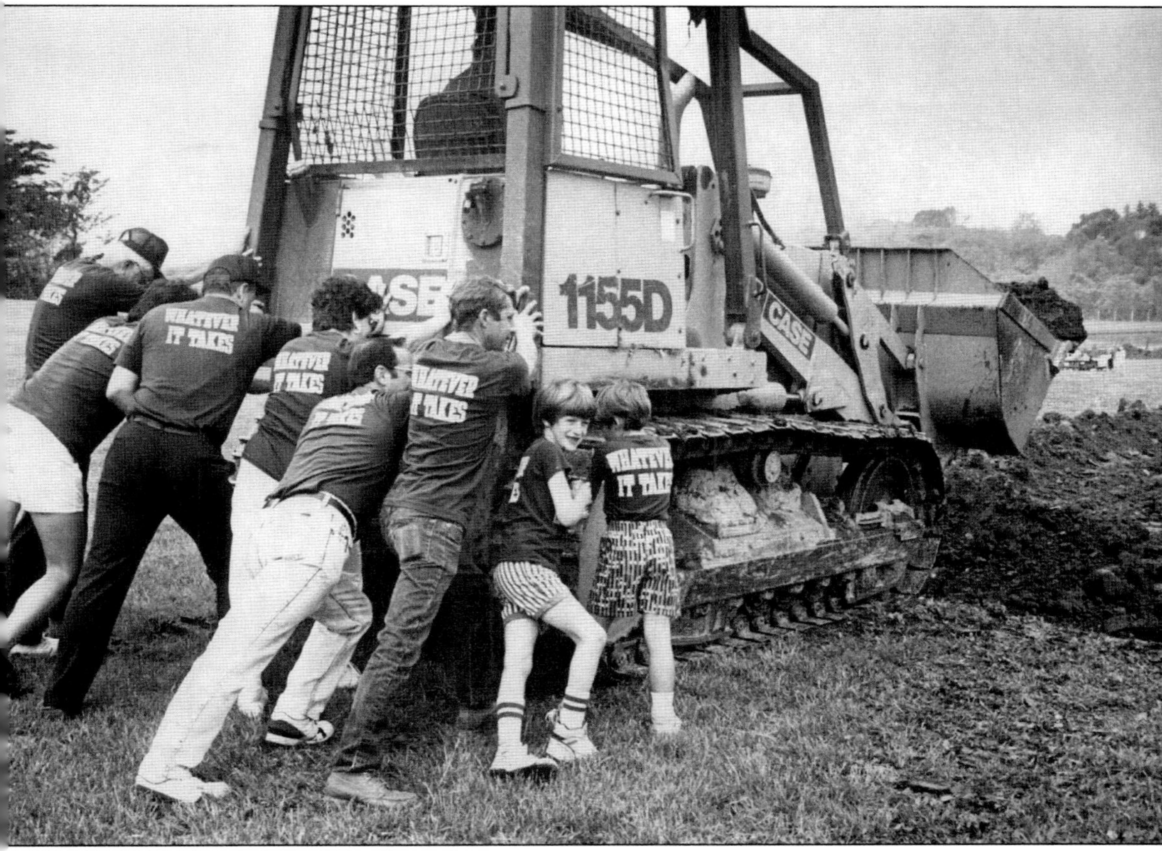

With the closure of Middletown High School and its playground, as well as the continued growth and development of town, came the need for a community park. Here, Gary Judy (the driver) "operates" construction equipment to break ground on the park. Mayor Ray Steele and the council's slogan for the project was "Whatever It Takes." (Middletown Heritage Society.)

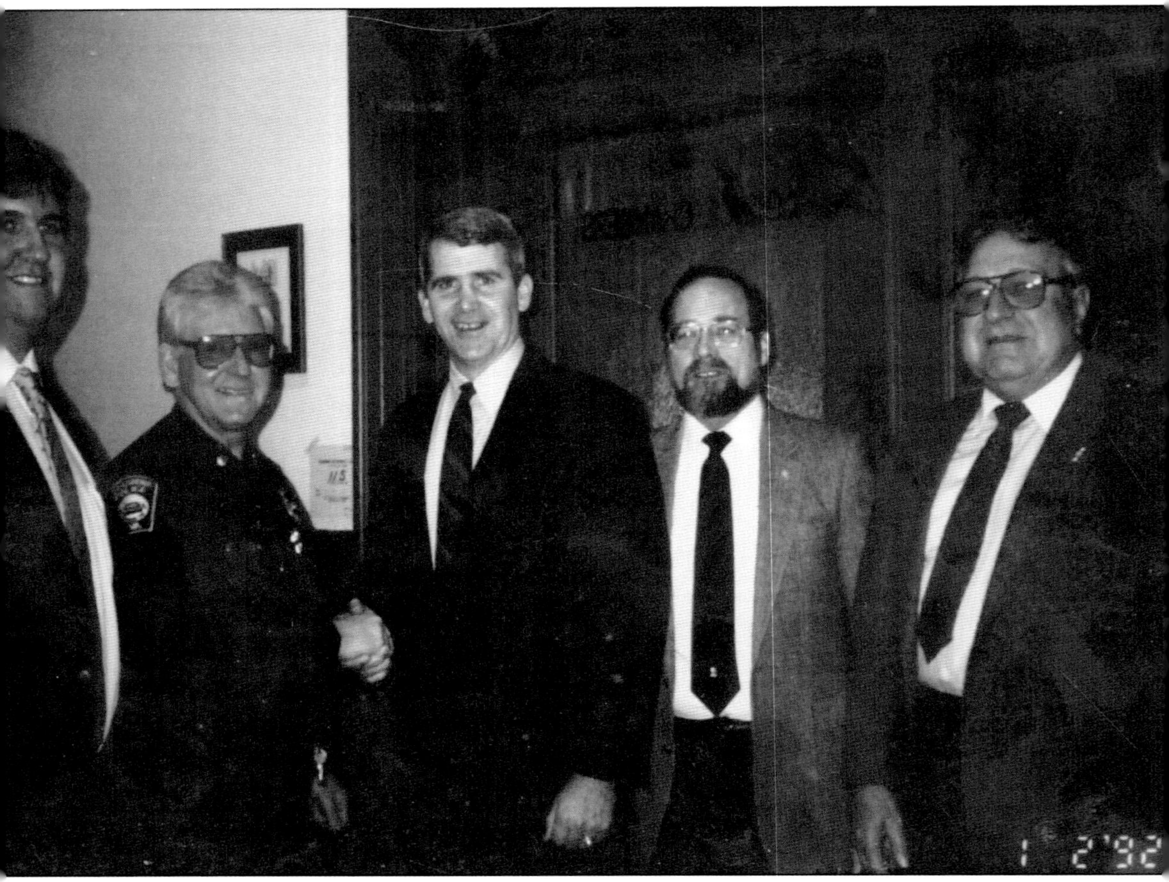

On January 3, 1992, Middletown mayor Ray Steele attended a meeting with Guardian Technologies. From left to right are Strasburg town manager Kevin Foltz, Strasburg police chief James E. Hall, Oliver North, Ray Steele, and Strasburg mayor James Racey. Oliver North gained nationwide fame for the Iran-Contra affair in the late 1980s and his bid for Senate in 1994. (Middletown Heritage Society.)

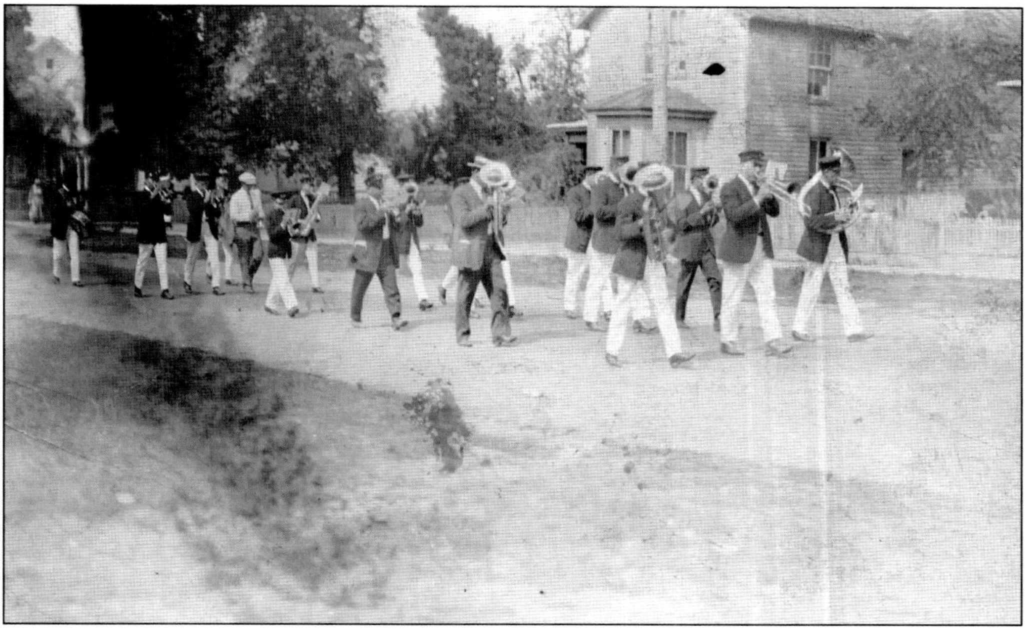

In this image from a postcard dated August 17, 1924, a Middletown band performs in the annual Fourth of July parade. On the reverse of the card is a message from a sender identified only as Pearl stating, "Please save this card for me." (Joyce D. Tucker.)

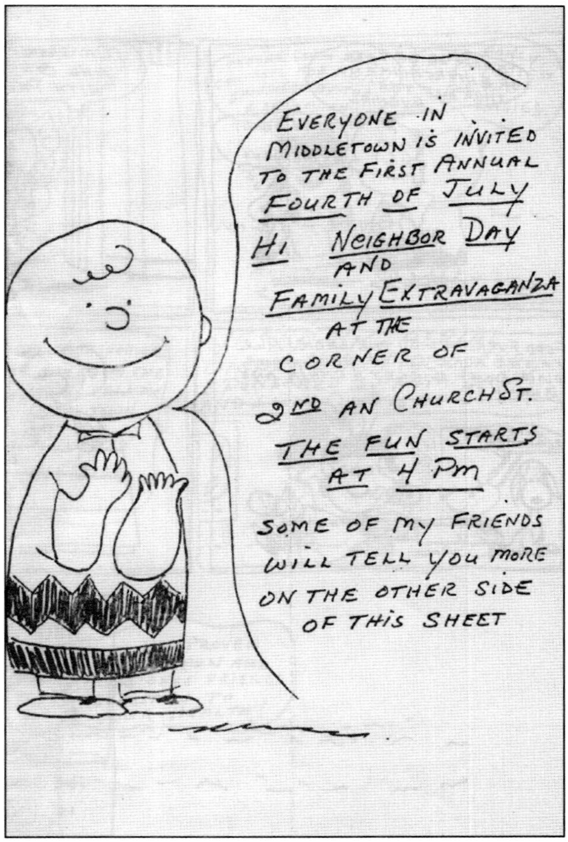

The town of Middletown has long been known for its Fourth of July festivities. Though a small town in population, its celebration is on par with much larger towns. An annual rite of passage for many, the parade on the Fourth is currently the only Independence Day parade in the area. Pictured is a flyer from an inaugural parade. (John Owings.)

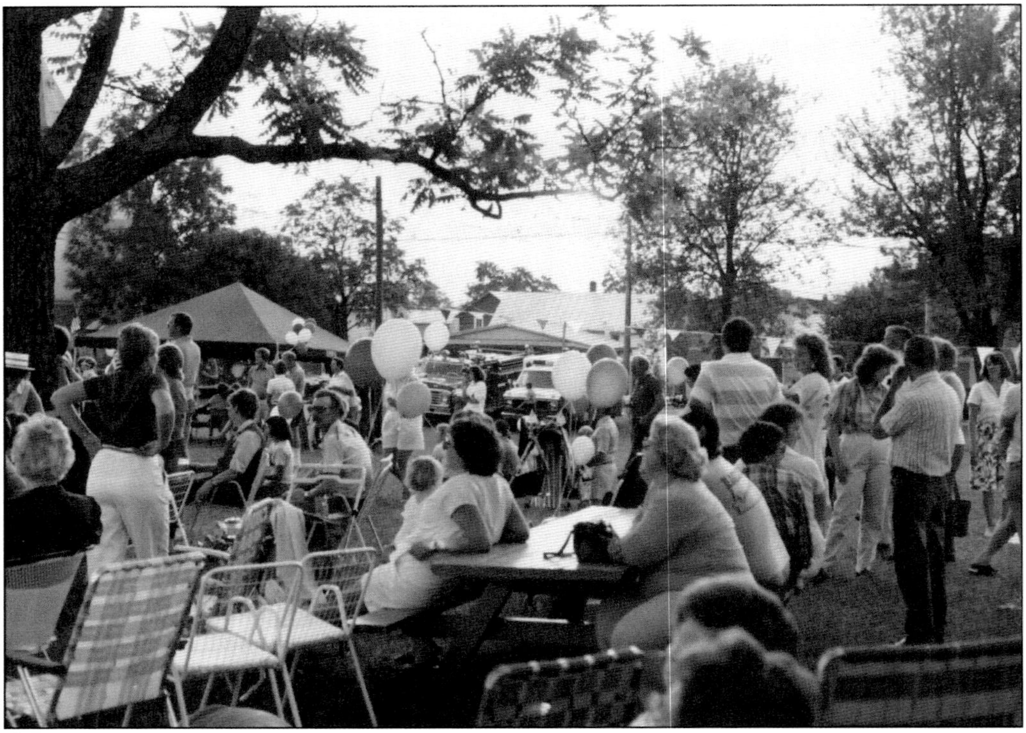

A Fourth of July festival was held at the town commons in 1985. The day was marked with a full schedule of events, including an annual softball tournament in the morning, food vendors, crafters, and games all day until the parade rolled out at 5:00 p.m. Afterward, participants were treated to live bands and entertainment before the fireworks display at dusk. In recent years, the festival has undergone a boom period, resulting in its move to the town park to accommodate the growing crowds. (Harold Gardenhour Jr.)

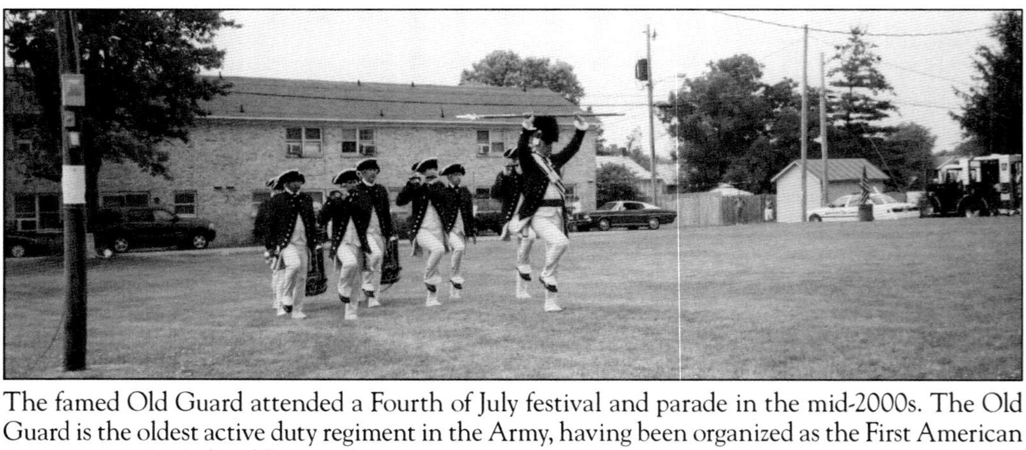

The famed Old Guard attended a Fourth of July festival and parade in the mid-2000s. The Old Guard is the oldest active duty regiment in the Army, having been organized as the First American Regiment in 1784. (Middletown Heritage Society.)

Five

MOVING FORWARD

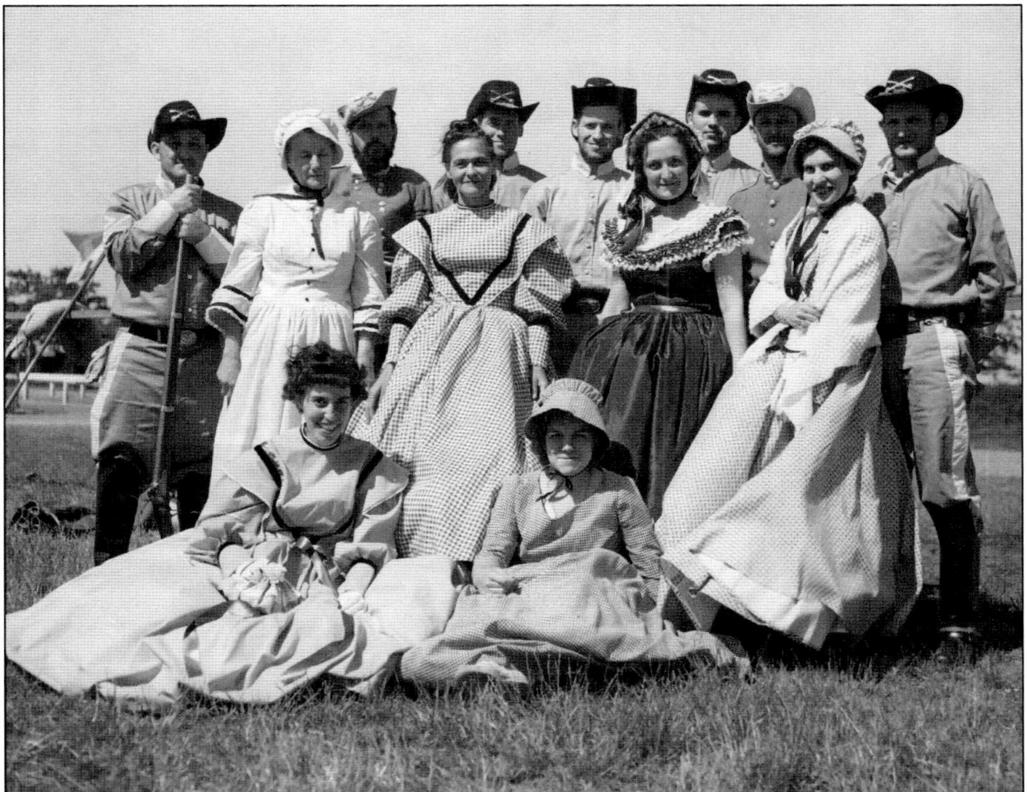

The Civil War has been permanently etched into the souls of Americans as perhaps no other event in US history has. A collective interest has grown with the stories of veterans who lived into the 1930s, then exploded during the 1960s with initial attempts at historical reenactments, including those of the target shooting experts of the North South Skirmish Association (NSSA), whose range of which is located at Fort Shenandoah, north of nearby Winchester, Virginia. The Cedar Creek Battlefield Foundation organized and sponsored this early reenactment in Middletown, which now draws thousands of spectators and reenactors annually. Funds raised from the event go to purchasing and preserving additional battlefield land in and around Middletown. (Middletown Heritage Society.)

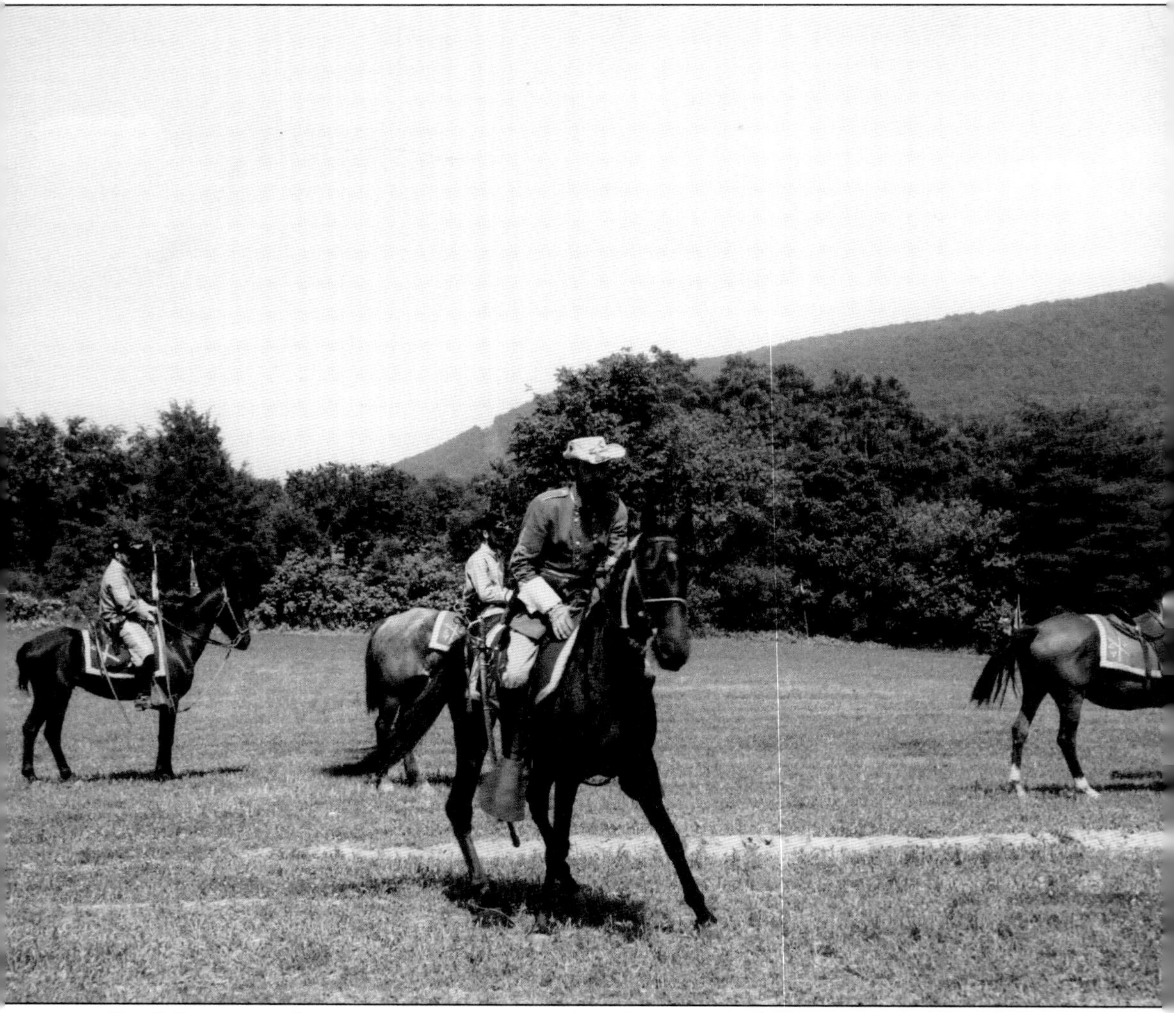

Confederate cavalry reenactors maneuver their horses at a drill in the 1970s. Further progress has been made in the hobby of reenactment, as evidenced by this group's improved attire. Visual presentations like the one shown here, as well as the annual Cedar Creek reenactment held on the third weekend in October, have heightened awareness of important sites and monuments in town. On October 19, 2014, the Cedar Creek Battlefield Foundation celebrated the sesquicentennial anniversary of the conflict. Today, Middletown holds fast to its history and heritage with a Middletown Historic District. (Middletown Heritage Society.)

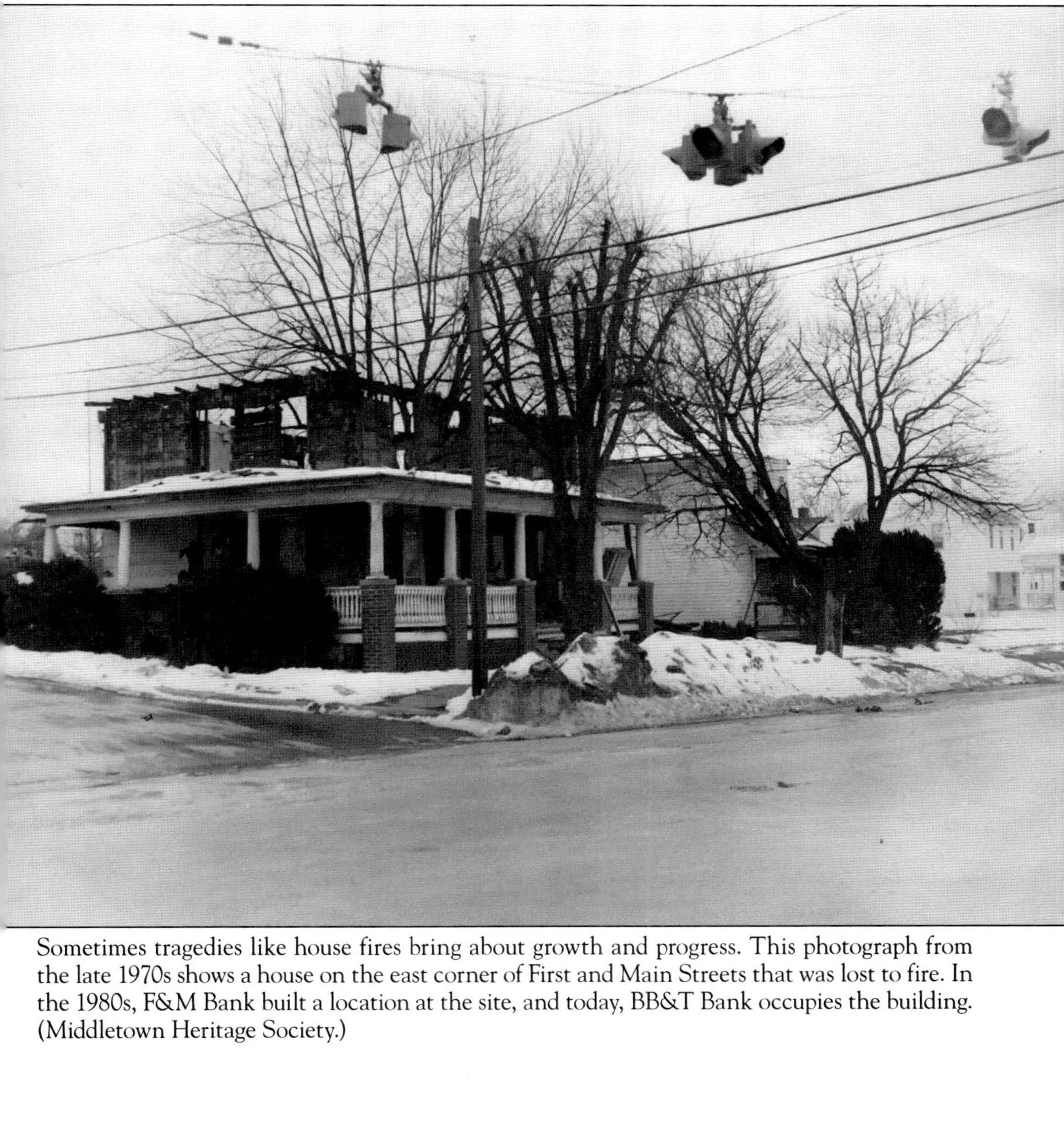

Sometimes tragedies like house fires bring about growth and progress. This photograph from the late 1970s shows a house on the east corner of First and Main Streets that was lost to fire. In the 1980s, F&M Bank built a location at the site, and today, BB&T Bank occupies the building. (Middletown Heritage Society.)

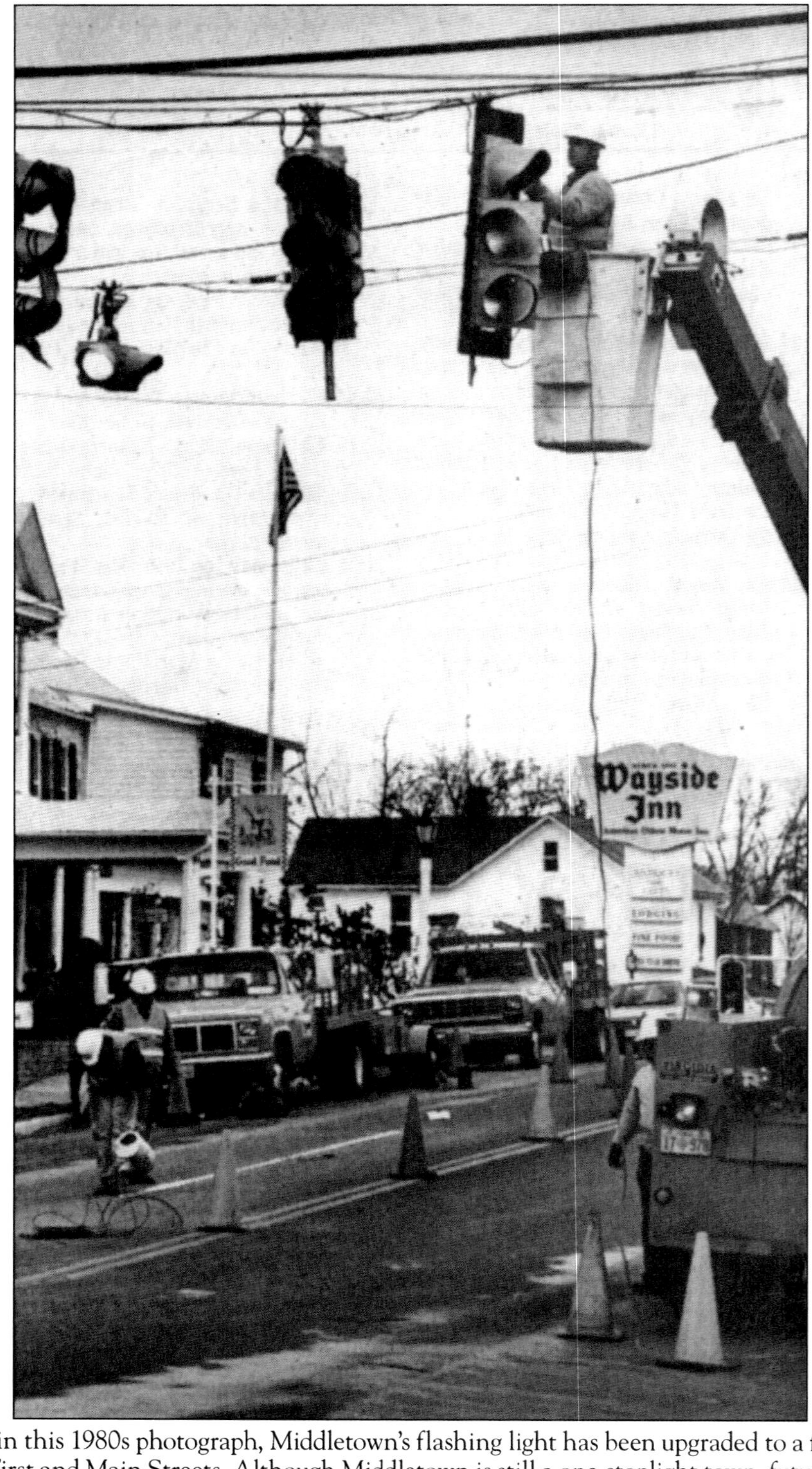

As seen in this 1980s photograph, Middletown's flashing light has been upgraded to a full signal light at First and Main Streets. Although Middletown is still a one-stoplight town, future growth along the interstate and expansion of Lord Fairfax Community College will result in the future need of additional traffic lights. (John Owings.)

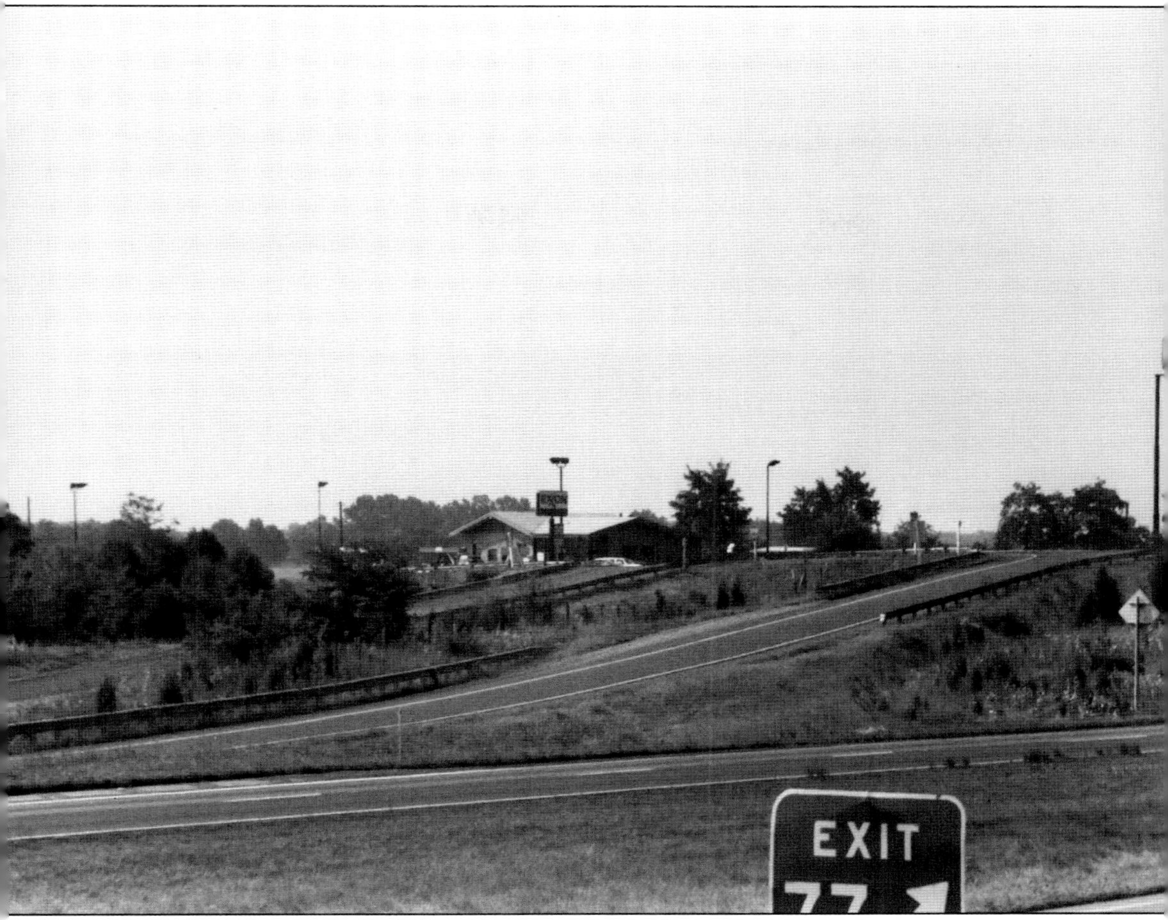

This is an older view of the Middletown exit from Interstate 81, showing the Exxon gas station. Interstate 81 parallels the old Valley Pike, known today simply as Route 11, and brings tourists to town and the nearby Belle Grove Plantation, Cedar Creek Battlefield, and Wayside Inn. Middletown is also at the confluence of Interstate 66, another major roadway that runs west to east, ending at Constitution Avenue in Washington, DC. This photograph from the early 1980s shows the exit number as 77; the current exit number is 302. (Middletown Heritage Society.)

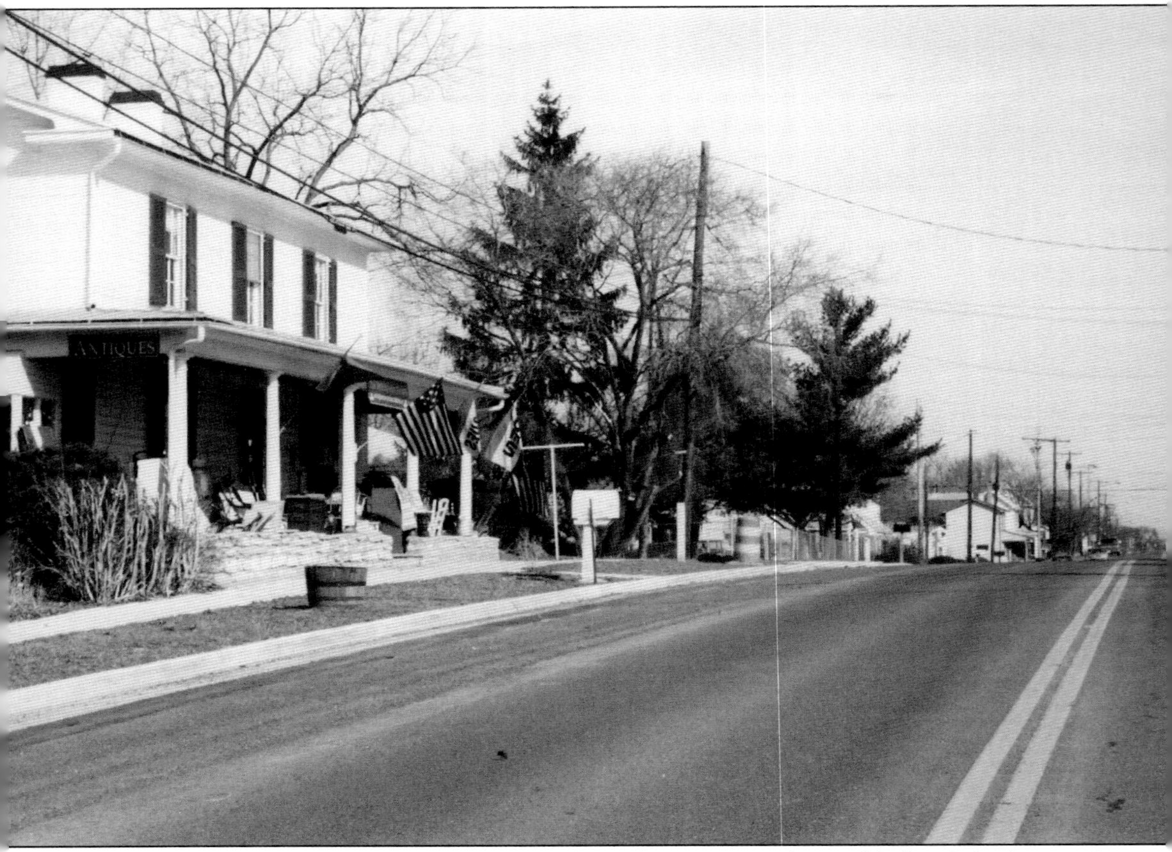

Built in 1856, the home of Isaac Rhodes has a log structure located behind the house that was used as a field aid station during the Battle of Cedar Creek. Like many historic homes in Middletown, the Rhodes house has been repurposed as a commercial location. It has been used as an antique shop, then a construction company, and now is home of Timeless Wines, owned by Mike Good. Middletown has many prime locations for small businesses in its historic homes on Main Street and looks forward to the opportunity of having more such shops in the future. (Helen Lee Fletcher.)

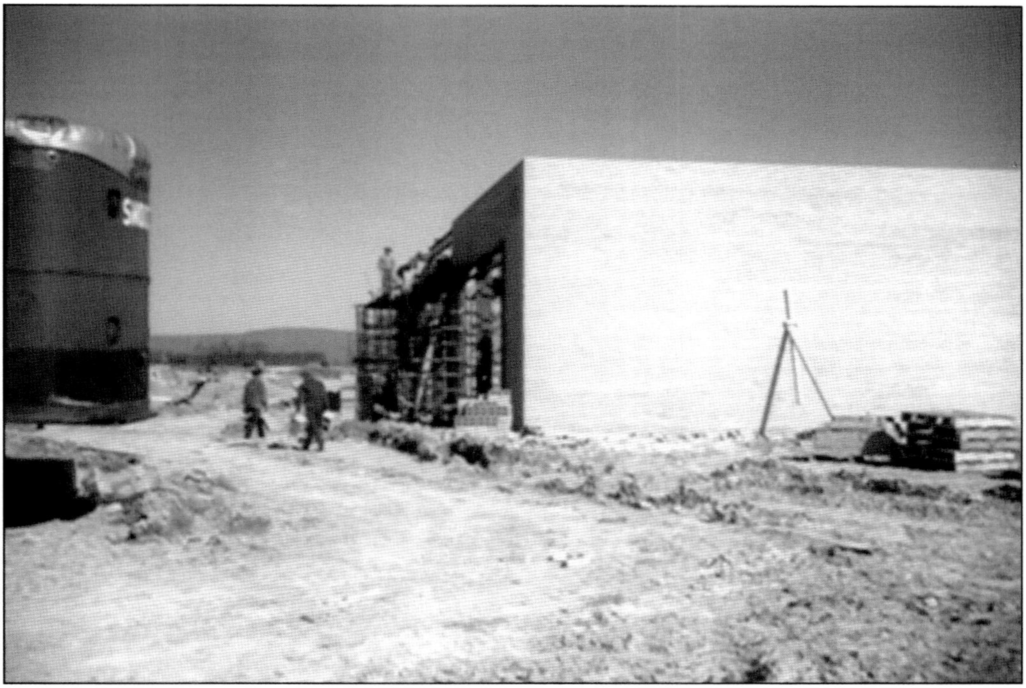

In 1964, the Virginia General Assembly passed legislation establishing two-year technical colleges. The Lord Fairfax Community College (LFCC) was named after Thomas Lord Fairfax VI, who moved to the Shenandoah Valley, near White Post in Clarke County, in 1752. Fairfax was the only resident peer living in North America who oversaw his vast amounts of land. The college is shown here during an early phase of construction. (Lord Fairfax Community College Archives.)

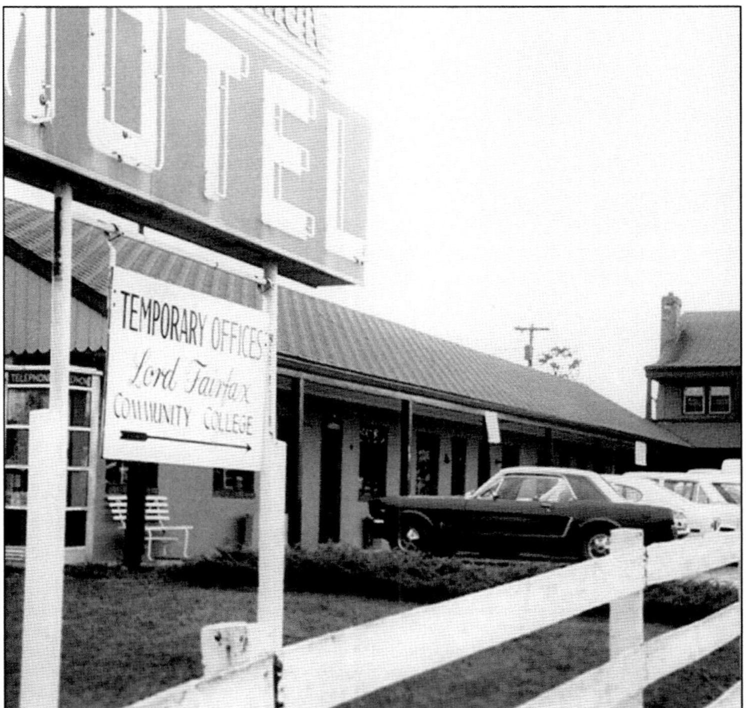

As seen in this 1969 image, the college had temporary offices set up at the Old Dominion Motel, located on Route 11 outside of town. There, the LFCC administration would remain until the completion of the permanent buildings in September 1970. (Lord Fairfax Community College Archives.)

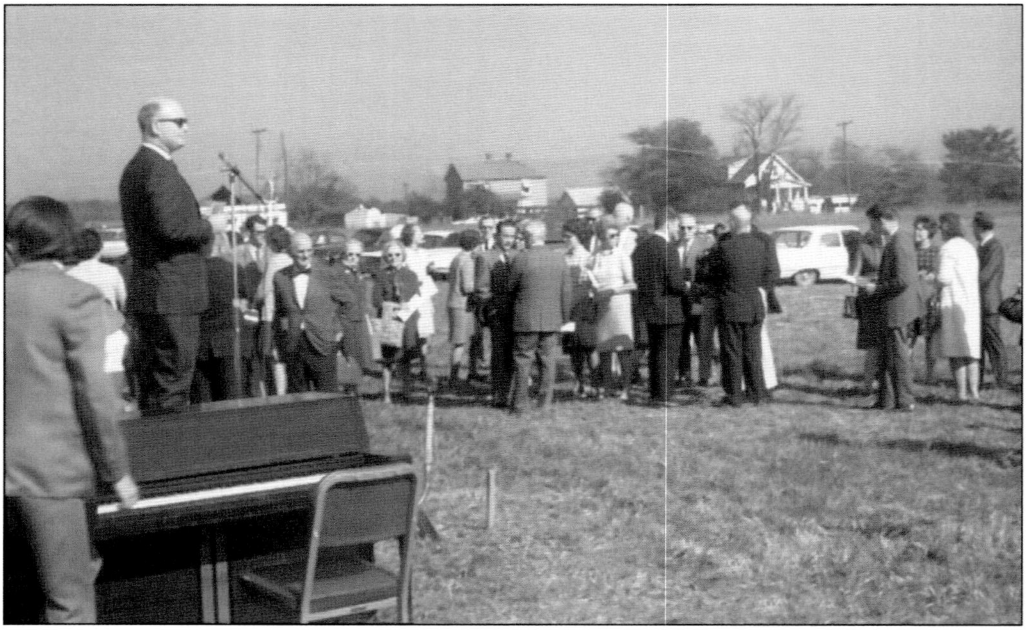

Built on 120 acres off the Valley Pike, the original college consisted of one large building with classrooms, laboratories, administrative offices, a bookstore, and student center. In its inaugural year of 1970, LFCC enrolled 577 students. Pictured is the ground-breaking ceremony. (Lord Fairfax Community College Archives.)

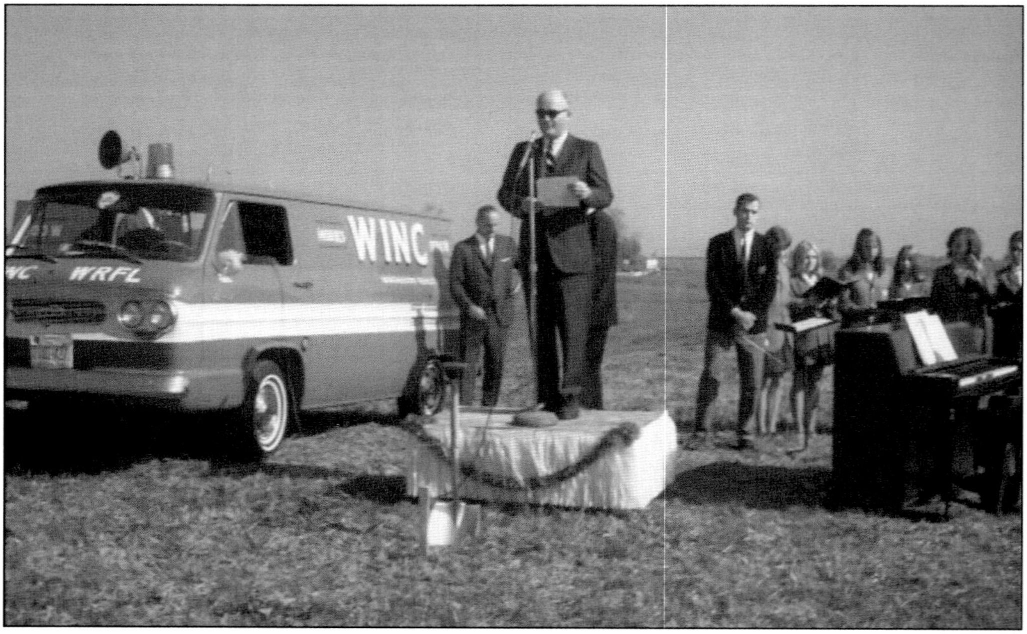

Dr. William H. McCoy was appointed as the first president of LFCC and served 18 years, until 1987. During his tenure, Dr. McCoy witnessed continued growth of the college, which started with only 23 full-time faculty members. In 1972, Dr. McCoy handed out diplomas to 92 students who had earned various degrees from the technical school. Later that year, on December 18, 1972, LFCC received accreditation from the Southern Association of Community and Junior Colleges. (Lord Fairfax Community College Archives.)

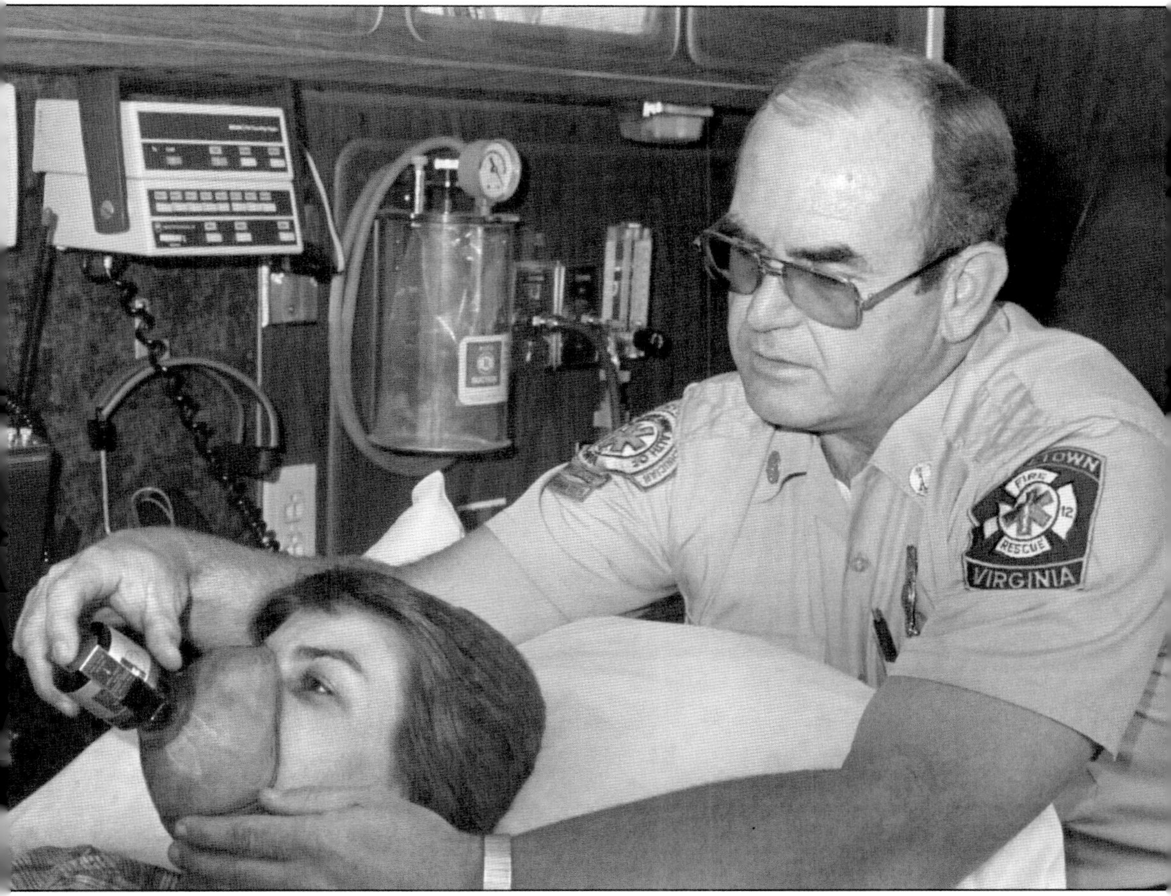

In 1982, former mayor of Middletown Neil A. Stallings assists a student during EMT class at LFCC. (Lord Fairfax Community College Archives.)

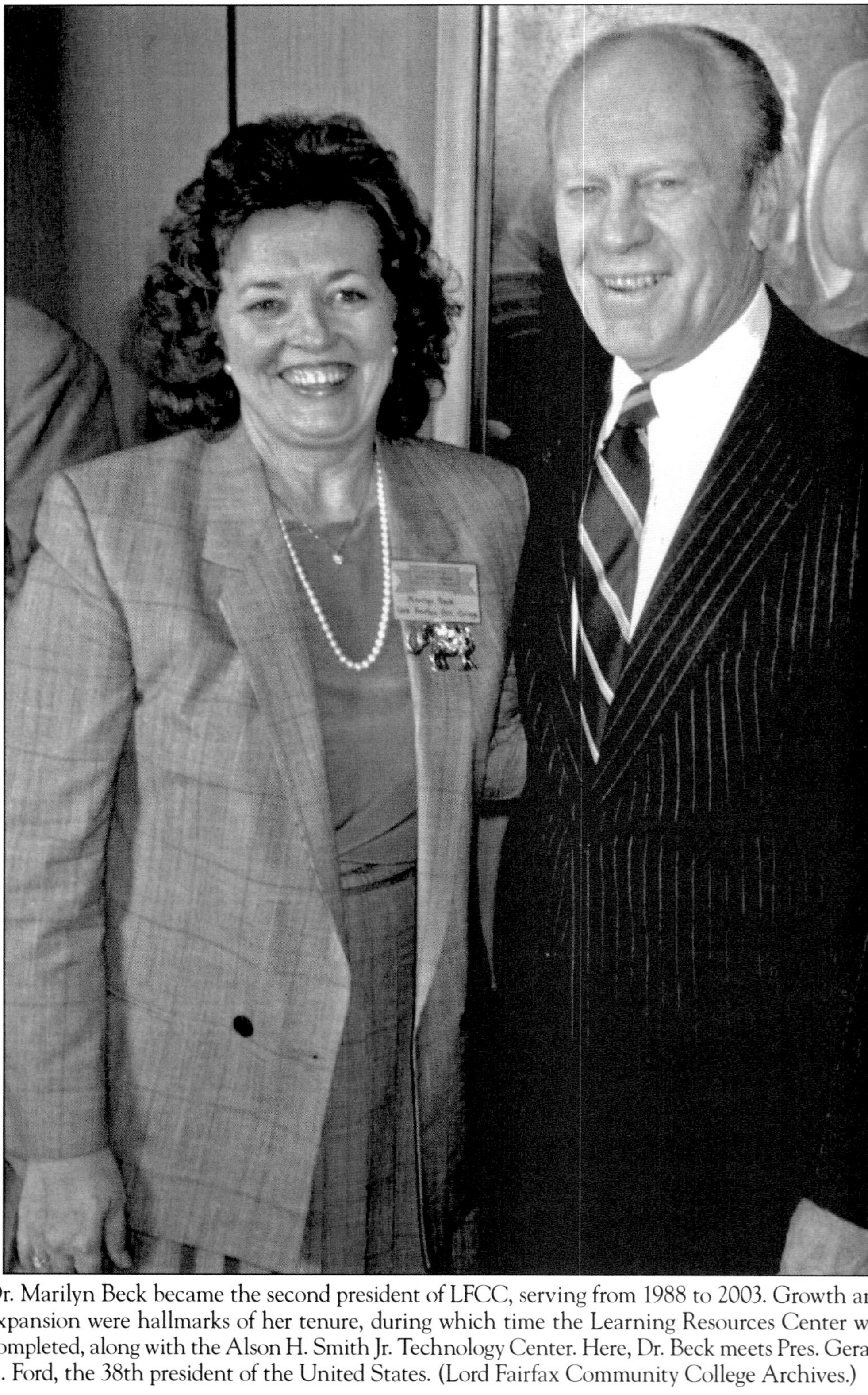

Dr. Marilyn Beck became the second president of LFCC, serving from 1988 to 2003. Growth and expansion were hallmarks of her tenure, during which time the Learning Resources Center was completed, along with the Alson H. Smith Jr. Technology Center. Here, Dr. Beck meets Pres. Gerald R. Ford, the 38th president of the United States. (Lord Fairfax Community College Archives.)

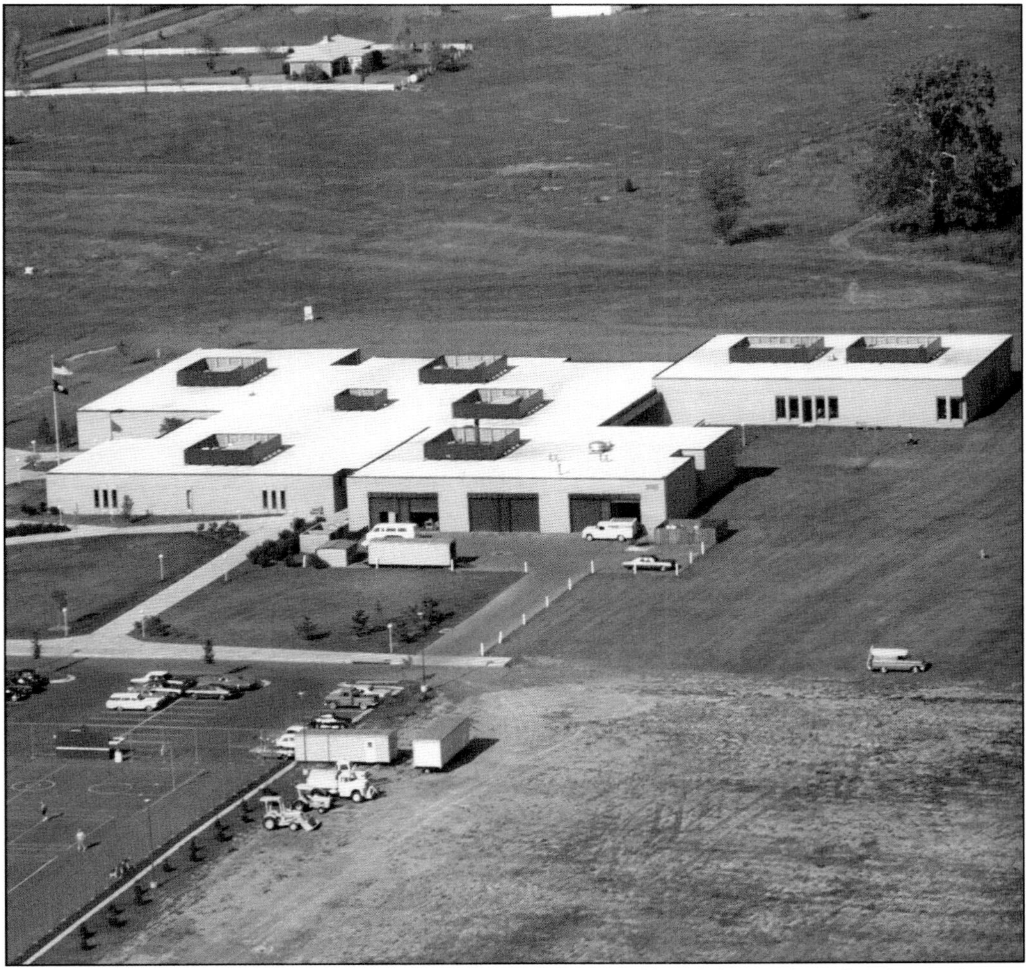

This aerial view shows the original campus, with Fairfax Hall and the Paul Wolk Library shown. Since 2008, LFCC has opened the science and health buildings, along with a student union building. Current president Dr. Cheryl Thompson-Stacy has overseen a boom in student enrollment, with over 7,600 students and more than 75 associate degree programs. Recently, it was ranked the third-fastest-growing college in Virginia. (Lord Fairfax Community College Archives.)